An Anthology of Nagauta

The University of Michigan Japanese Music Study Group performing in Rackham Auditorium, March 21, 1987

An Anthology of Nagauta

William P. Malm

Center for Japanese Studies
The University of Michigan
Ann Arbor, 2010

(w)
ML
1751
J3
M34
2010

Copyright © 2010 by The Regents of the University of Michigan

All rights reserved.

Published by the Center for Japanese Studies,
The University of Michigan
1007 E. Huron St.
Ann Arbor, MI 48104-1690

Michigan Monograph Series in Japanese Studies
Number 66

Center for Japanese Studies
The University of Michigan

Library of Congress Cataloging in Publication Data

Malm, William P.
    An anthology of Nagauta / William P. Malm.
        p. cm. — (Michigan monograph series in Japanese studies ; no. 66)
    Includes bibliographical references.
    ISBN 978-1-929280-56-8 (cloth : alk. paper) — ISBN 978-1-929280-57-5
(pbk. : alk. paper)
    1. Nagauta—History and criticism.   2. Nagauta—Texts.   I. Title.   II. Series.

ML1751.J3M34 2010
781.5'540952—dc22

                                                                              2009034792

This book was set in Palatino Macron.

Printed in the United States of America

Contents

Contents

Japanese Texts

Contents

CD CONTENTS

·⁀·

Preface

From 1964 until 1994 the University of Michigan Japanese Music Study Group performed annual concerts. The concerts included Edo *matsuri bayashi* festival music and occasional koto compositions, but the major genre was *nagauta*, a lyrical music originally written to accompany kabuki and classical dances. Students were involved in learning to sing in Japanese or play either the three-stringed shamisen plucked lute or one of the three drums of the noh drama as used in kabuki. The noh (*nōkan*) and folk flutes were taught. Other percussion instruments from the offstage *geza* music of kabuki were also taught as needed. The program was enriched by courses on Japanese music taught by a visiting professor, Kikkawa Eishi (1987); the resident teacher of shamisen and singing, Sugiura Hirokazu (1989); and Semba Kokun (1986), who also helped with percussion lessons. At each year's concert the audience was provided with a lecture on the pieces to be played and a translation of the text. The latter was essential because the music is word oriented.

This anthology is primarily based on the translations that were used during those thirty years of concerts and is printed in honor of the students who performed in them. The translators were usually students active during those decades. The names of many translators are now lost, but they are thanked anonymously for their contributions. Special thanks are added for translators who have since become noted in their fields, including David Hughes, George Gish, David Crandel, Barry Jackson, and Richard Winslow. Hopefully this anthology will make their early efforts more meaningful in the field of Japanese music studies. Dr. and Mrs. Jay Keister of the University of Colorado are specially thanked for their translation of *Musume Dōjōji*. Dr. and Mrs. Reinhard Zöllner of Erfurt University, Germany, kindly provided the translation of the *mondo* in *Okina Sanbasō* and of the piece *Kairaishi* while they were in residence at the University of Michigan. *Dōjōji* and *Kairaishi* were not played at Michigan.

Given the performance levels of the director and his students, not all pieces were performed complete. Still there was much to be learned and appreciated from any contact with such a rich musical tradition.

As a musician rather than a translator or Japanese literature specialist, the author is not qualified to deal with the deeper literary subtleties of the texts. Another important item missing in this study is choreography. The raison d'être of both the text and the music of most dance pieces is the movement, gestures, and costumes of the performer. Hopefully, some future researcher will produce a kabuki dance study as detailed as the noh study of Monica Bethe and Karen Brazell (1978). Some videotapes and digital video discs (DVDs) are listed in the bibliography. The locations of first performances and names of famous kabuki artists who danced these texts also can be found in some of the reference books listed in the bibliography, including Atsumi 1956; Asakawa 1955; and Leiter 1979. The commentaries in this anthology are limited mostly to the theme "What to Listen for in Nagauta Music."

One major problem in presenting materials from a non-Western, exotic genre is that most readers have no idea what the music sounds like. For this reason two compact discs (CDs) have been made of seven representative pieces from different periods, 1762 to 1967: CD 1 contains *Sagi Musume, Yoshiwara Suzume,* and *Azuma Hakkei;* CD 2 has *Tsuru Kame, Renjishi, Ame no Shiki,* and *Matsu no Midori.* The Crown Record Company and the Toonkai *nagauta* performers are thanked for their cooperation in making these important sounds available to Western listeners. Knowing that issues of CDs are unfortunately short-lived, some recordings available in 2004 are listed for most of the other pieces translated and discussed. The impressive HHK *nagauta no bigaku* series is presently available only in a three-volume CD set of thirty-six to fifty-four pieces. The Victor thirteen-volume *Taishi nihon no dento Ongaku* barely lasted a year. Volumes 17 through 20 are *nagauta.* Both collections are found in the music library of the University of Michigan. Production of the CDs that accompany this book was made possible through the generous support of the University of Michigan Office of the Associate Provost for Academic Affairs, Dr. Lester Monts. The Center for Japanese Studies of the University of Michigan is thanked for its decades of support of the program, and Bruce Willoughby is thanked for his careful editing of the publication. Jason Herlands kindly provided help with translations and corrections and copied the original song texts in Japanese. Finally, my thanks go to all the students who joined in the special experience of performing *nagauta* live.

Chapter 1

An Introduction to Shamisen Music History, Theory, and Practice

HISTORY

Details on the origins of the shamisen and its music are found in Malm 19
1959 and 2000. The music began as local songs (*jiuta*) performed by itinerant musicians on the street or by girls in party houses, particularly in the
Osaka/Kyoto area. The popularity of the music is evident in the publication
of song collections such as the 1664 *Shichiku Shoshinshū* and the 1685 *ōnusa*
volume of *Shichiku Taizen*.

The seventeenth-century *Kabuki sōshi emaki* scroll shows a blind shamisen
player in the street outside a kabuki theater. By the mid–eighteenth century,
shamisen performers are found inside, and the basic *nagauta* guild name
Kineya is seen on the list of musicians.

The second volume of the 1703 *Matsu no Ha* song collection has fifty
pieces called *jiuta nagauta*. The collection seems to be primarily composed of
Kyoto *jiuta* music, but the Kabuki tradition of *edo nagauta* was firmly established by the mid–seventeenth century.

GENRES

This anthology shows how the *nagauta* flourished as dance accompaniment
and then concert (*ozashiki*) music, but it is important to note that it was not
the only shamisen genre. Historically, shamisen music is divided into two
basic types: narrative (*katarimono*) and lyrical (*utamono* or *utaimono*). The
puppet-theater-derived *gidayū* genre is the best-known narrative music, and
nagauta remains the most commonly used lyrical form. However, over the
years many other genres appeared (see Malm 2000, 219). *Tokiwazu* and *kiyomoto* musicians are still a part of a kabuki ensemble. In the *nagauta* repertory,
gekibushi and its outgrowth, *ōzatsuma*, became important influences in the
attempts to add more narrative music to the lyric tradition.

ENSEMBLES

The basic element of a *nagauta* ensemble is the singer and the shamisen. Their number may vary from just one each to three or four each. An additional shamisen may be used, playing an octave higher. It is called an *uwajōshi* shamisen.

The *hayashi* ensemble of the noh drama is used in most *nagauta* performances as well. It consists of the *ō tsuzumi, ko tsuzumi,* and *taiko* drums plus the *nōkan* flute. The flute player also uses the *shinobue* or *yokobue* bamboo flute. The word *tsuzumi* is used in both the singular for the *ko tsuzumi* and the plural for the two drums together. The two are also called the *daisho,* "the "large and small." The *taiko* is normally played with the same size sticks (*bachi*) as those used in the noh, but smaller, thinner sticks are substituted when a folk or festival mood is desired.

Kabuki music can be studied in Malm 1959, 1978, and 2000. The offstage (*geza*) instruments can be included in a *nagauta* performance or recording. The large *ōdaiko* drum is always effective for moods or locations (see Malm 1978). The hand gong (*kane* or *atarigane*) may be used onstage for festival scenes. The wooden clappers (*ki* or *hyōshigi*) are heard in recordings intended for dance performances. Some of the music that accompanies the opening and closing of curtains may also be included. All of these elements are interesting, but the study and appreciation of *nagauta* is best done in the context of only the voice, shamisen, and *hayashi* music.

MUSIC THEORY

The major difference between Western and Asian music is harmony. The vertical combinations of different pitches fill Western traditional music with rich, thick, instant sounds called harmony or chords. They color the music in what could be called a polarity system. In simple terms, there is a melody on top, a bass line on the bottom, and in between the other pitches of the chords are filled in. The bass is particularly important because the common practice in the West uses a system of chord progressions. In the baroque, a so-called figured bass shows the bass line and the kind of chords built over it. In the twentieth century, "knowing the changes" was essential to the performance of popular music and jazz. These progressions create a tonal tension that pushes the listener forward to a point at which resolution occurs.

Most non-Western music has little or no interest in this powerful vertical tool. Instead, there is concentration on melody, tone system, and rhythm.

TONE SYSTEM

The basic tone system of shamisen music is the *yo* and *in* scales (fig. 1). The three basic tunings of the shamisen are *honchōshi, niagari,* and *sansagari* (fig. 2). In modern Japanese shamisen transcriptions written in Western notation, the pitch B is used as a bottom note. The pitch of an actual performance is set by the singer and is generally higher. However, if taken in the context of a C major scale, the note B best accommodates the whole and half steps of the *yo* and *in* scales.

With no chord support for tunes, modulation to a new pitch center requires only a few notes. Melodic tension and release must concentrate on what could be called upper and lower leading tones as shown in figure 3.

NOTATION

Shamisen and Vocal Lines

The popularity of kabuki and its music is evident in the large number of advertising prints (*banzuke*) and song texts. Figure 4 shows the 1864 print of the title page of the piece *Yoshiwara Suzume*. Figure 5 is from the song text inside

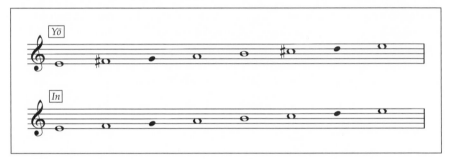

Figure 1.   *Yo* and *in* scales

Figure 2.   The *nagauta* shamisen tunings *honchōshi*, *niagari*, and *sansagari*

Figure 3.   Upper and lower leading-tone movements

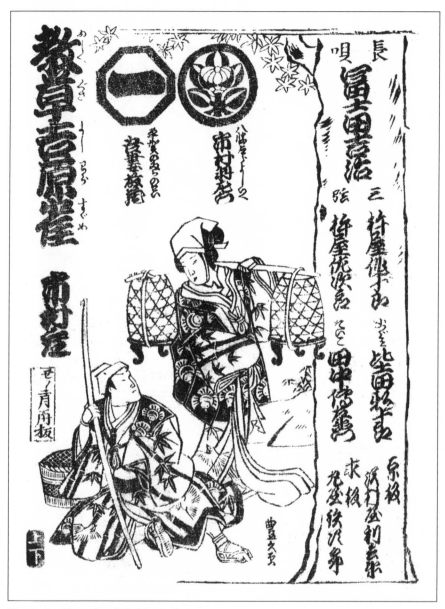

Figure 4.   *Banzuke* of *Yoshiwara Suzume*

of figure 4. It is part of a geisha song that is included in *Yoshiwara Suzume*. The translation of this section is found on page 41 at the word *jorō*. The only musical indications in this example are the *niagari* tuning (in the right-hand upper corner) and term interlude (*ai*) the fifth line at the section mark.

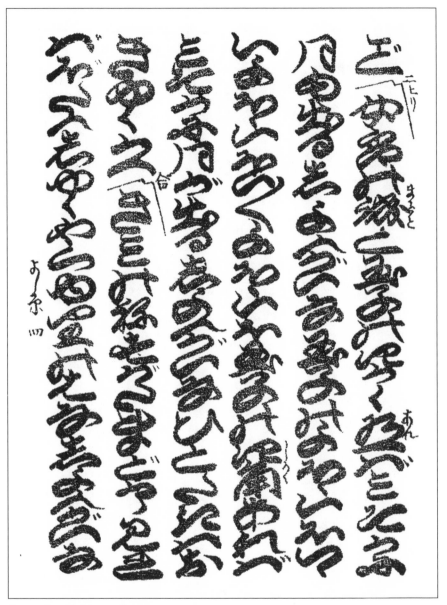

Figure 5. *Yoshiwara Suzume* song text

By the early twentieth century *nagauta* could be purchased in Western "violin" notation. However, the preference for eighteenth and nineteenth century traditional systems prevails to this day. Figure 6 is an example of the early *iroha* notation as used in a 1957 edition of the piece *Tsuru Kame*.

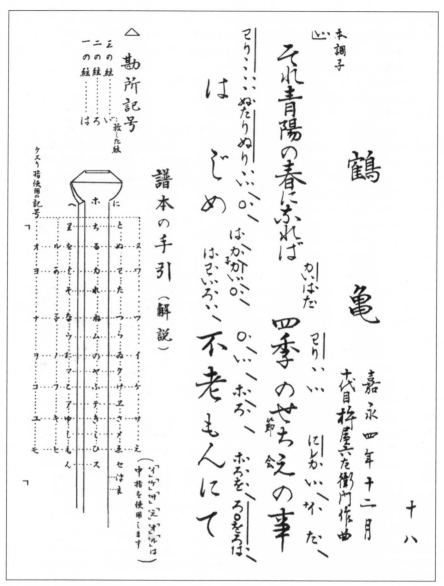

Figure 6.   *Iroha* notation for *Tsuru Kame*

The notation was edited by Kineya Sakichi. The term *iroha* is derived from the first syllables of a poem that Japanese children used to memorize the *kana* writing system. In music, they indicate the finger positions on the neck of the shamisen. With *i, ro,* and *ha* being used for the open three strings and other pitches being set in a sequence of vertical three syllable units as shown in the diagram attached to figure 6. The vertical lines indicate rhythm and are derived from the horizontal beams in Western eighth-note notation.

Another early Japanese mnemonic uses omomatopoeic sounds to indicate pitches or performance methods (up strokes, pizzicatos, etc.). It is often called *kuchijamisen* (mouth shamisen) and is still the most common method used to memorize or refer to the music. It can be seen parallel with the shamisen line in all three notations shown below.

Many other methods were created, but the three most common midtwentieth systems used today are the Bunka, Yoshizumi and Kineya. Bunka notation (*bunkafu*) was created by Kineya Mishiki and edited by Kineya Yashishi. *Yoshizumifu* was designed by Yoshizumi Kosaburō and edited by Kineya Sakichi. Some books call it *kosaburōfu* but performers prefer the term *yoshizmjifu*. The third system is known as the *aoyagifu* or simply *kineyafu* after the name of its editor, Kineya Aoayagi In the Bunka style (fig. 7), numbers are used to indicate finger positions on the three strings shown by the three lines. The music and text are written in the Western horizontal direction and include bar lines (2/4 time) and Western eighth-note beams. Above the shamisen line are *kuchijamisen* mnemonics (for the first three bars they are *tsute ton chin chiri chi*) Below the line is the vocal part. It is written using the same numbers that were originally finger position notation for the shamisen.

The Yoshizumi notation in figure 8 uses the same Western bar lines and rhythmic beams as Bunka but it is written vertically, in Japanese style. The numbers are derived from a French Chevé system in which the pitches of the major scale are 1–2–3–4–5–6–7. Note that 7 and 3 are the most important pitches (see E and B in fig. 1). The dots near numbers indicate the octave of the pitch. The Kineya style in figure 9 combines the three lines of Bunka with the vertical direction and numbers of Yozhizumi. The example begins with the word "miru yōde" (see Yoshiwara Suzume translation, p. 40) Note in the fourth and fifth lines that the declamatory (*serifu*) passages are marked by dotted lines.

Hayashi *Notation*

Drum or flute music was rarely taught by means of notation (see Malm 2000, 286). In kabuki, "use books" (*tsukechō*) would list in the song texts where and what to play and the style of music to use either off stage (*geza*) or on (*debayashi*). Figure 10 is a rare example (from the Mochitsuki guild) of *hayashi* notation for the two *tsuzumi* in the piece *Tsuru Kame*. It starts at the text "kimi ga yoi aogi kanadete" (p. 120) and the second is the noh pattern *mitsuji*. The last two columns show both the full pattern and a shorthand notation for kabuki-derived drumming, ending on the last beat with a pattern, called *age*. A Western score of *Tsuru Kame* may be seen in Malm 1969. Most drum music is learned only by *tsukechō* with lessons from the guild masters.

7

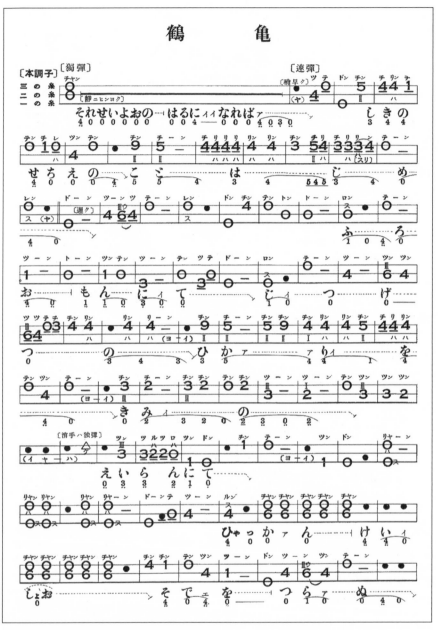

Figure 7. *Bunka* notation for *Tsuru Kame*

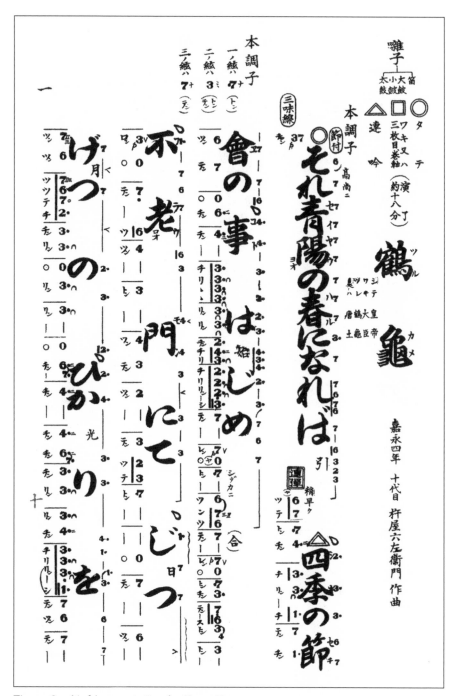

Figure 8.   *Yoshizum* notation for *Tsuru Kame*

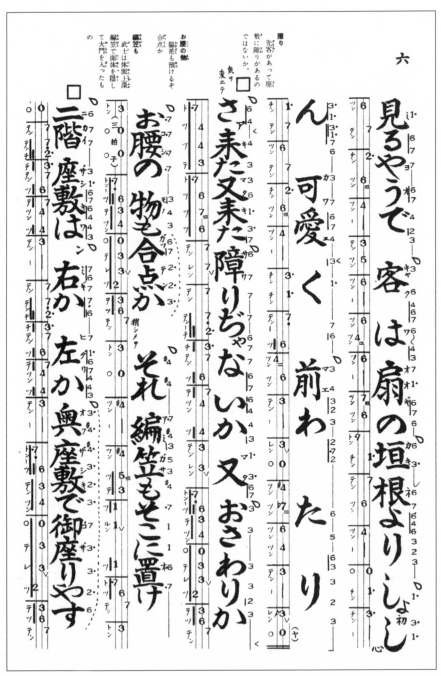

Figure 9. *Kineya* notation for *Yoshiwara Suzume*

Figure 10.   *Hayashi* notation for a *tsuzumi* passage in *Tsuru Kame*

COMPOSITION

The original kabuki production announcements (*banzuke*) and date lists (*nenpyō*) name all the musical performers as well as the scene and play in which the music was used. The actors and choreographers naturally are more important. With the increase in amateur *nagauta* performers, the publications of texts and later shamisen notations listed only the lead shamisen and author of the text when known. Pieces are thus listed in encyclopedias and *nagauta* studies with the lead shamisen or singer as the composer. Indeed, he was the controlling musician in the kabuki production of that piece, as well as in the concert or other dance music that was created outside the kabuki. He was the source of the melodic line. However, *nagauta*, as a complete sonic event, is created by what could be called "communal composition." To write the basic tune, the lead shamisen must first consult with the dancer, producer, poet, and lead singer. The head of the *hayashi* (*hayashegashira*) is then called in to create the percussion music. He also may tell the flute player where and what kind of music he should use in the composition. The wonder is that the result is an impressive whole. Like the neck of a well-made shamisen, one is not aware of the seams that hold the parts together.

Chapter 2

Form in Nagauta Music

ORIGINS

The early *nagauta* used the koto-based *kumiuta* form of alternate songs and interludes. In the late eighteenth century it was dance accompaniment and only later developed more independent instrumental forms. In some ways one could compare it with the growth of Western orchestral music during the same eighteenth and early nineteenth centuries in what is called in the West the common practice period. In the West, there were operas and dance suites that led to independent instrumental symphonic music. The minuet lasted the longest as part of the dance design, but the so-called sonata allegro form movements, with their themes, developments, and returns, became the predominant closed (i.e., ABA) form of Western music. In *nagauta*, the major formal structures were those of noh drama and kabuki dance, both of which are nonthematic and open forms (not ABA but ABCD, and so on).

TERMINOLOGY

Fundamental to most Japanese musical forms is the concept of *jo ha kyū* in which all large and small units can be thought of as having an introduction, an action, and a finale. The terms mean "introduction," "scattering," and "rushing toward the ending." They are not normally use in *nagauta* studies, but pieces derived from a noh drama use other, more specific, formal and musical noh terms. These are discussed in Malm 2000, 125 and their use in two *nagauta* pieces are outlined in Malm 1963, 37–40. They will be seen in the translations that follow.

The nomenclature of kabuki dance is equally frequent (see Brandon 2002). For actors, the sections are the entrance (*de*), narrative (*monogatari*), lament (*kudoki*), rhythmic finale (*odori ji*), and scattering (*chirashi*). Late-nineteenth-century scholars used the so-called kabuki dance form as their guide for music studies. It contains a beginning (*oki,*) the entrance music (*michiyuki*), the lyrical section (*kudoki*), the dance (*odori ji*), the finale (*chirashi*) and the cadence (*dangire*). The piece *Suehirogari* (p. 123) is a classic example of this form. One must keep in mind the fact that, like the Western sonata allegro form, there are many variations in the kabuki dance form, particularly as concert vis-à-vis dance accompaniment. Noh and kabuki dance form terms do not always appear in *nagauta* texts, but they have been inserted when necessary in the translations published here to help the reader follow the overall design of the composition.

CONVENTIONS

Music moves forward in time through conventional signals that indicate changes. As noted before, in the West chord progression is a major method. A so-called dominant chord creates a need for a tonic resolution. Chords can also imply mood or action, a minor chord for sadness and a trembling diminished chord for danger. Here are some of the common *nagauta* conventions along with their locations in the pieces that appear in this anthology.

Shamisen Conventions

Ōzatsuma te (patterns). These patterns were derived from an earlier shamisen genre of *satsuma* or later *gekibushi*. They accompanied a text similar to a recitative or declamations in the kabuki style (*serifu*). There are forty *ōzatsuma te*, each with a specific name. They are shown in Western notation in Malm 1963, 331–38. Figure 11A is a standard opening pattern for many pieces, including *Gorō Tokumune* (p. 107). Figure 11B shows an *ōzatsuma* dialogue in the *mondo* of *Tsuru Kame* (CD 2–1). An example of their use in kabuki declamation is found in *Kanjinchō* (p. 98).

Tataki. This pattern is used to accompany lyrical passages, particularly in the *kudoki* section of a piece. It maintains the forward motion of the music by stopping on unresolved upper leading tones. It is centered around E (fig. 12), but B and F-sharp are used as centers as well. Every composition seems to have examples of this convention. It is heard at the *kudoki* of *Sagi Musume* (CD 1–1).

Geisha house music. Patterns known by their mnemonics, such as *totsu tere totsu tere* or *ten tsuku ten tsuku*, always reflect the party music of the Yoshiwara (fig. 13). The jaunty drumbeat in figure 13B is also part of that convention. Note that the mnemonic includes upstrokes (*ku*) or pizzicatos (*re*). Famous tunes such as "Tsukuda" refer to areas across the river and the ferryboats that carried guests to the pleasure quarters there. Other tunes may place the scene in Kyoto or Osaka. Even the shamisen *ostinato* is slightly varied for such *kamikgata* locations. The piece *Yoshiwara Suzume* has several examples (CD 1–2).

Figure 11. *Ōzatsuma* patterns

Figure 12. The *tataki* pattern

15

Figure 13. *Yoshiwara* patterns

Dangire. This is the term for standard final cadences in most nagauta compositions (fig. 14). They are listed as *ōzatsuma* patterns, but their function is limited to finales. The most frequent version is heard at the end of *Tsuru Kame* (CD 2–1).

DRUM PATTERNS

Mitsuji. If a piece is derived from a noh drama or the text mood needs a more formal setting, the noh *hayashi* may appear (fig. 15). The most frequent *tsuzumi* example is *mitsuji* (three points). In *Gorō* it occurs on the words "Ide osore no" (p. 109) and is heard on the CD accompanying Malm 2000. The *ōzatsuma*-style shamisen is heard at the same moment. *Mitsuji* will be heard in any piece derived from noh. It is seen in figure 15 and can be heard in that passage from *Tsuru Kame* on CD 2–1.

Chiri kara. The term is the onomatopoeic mnemonic for an *ō* and *ko tsuzumi* of kabuki-style drumming played as shown in figure 16. The mnemonics for the example are "chiri kara chiri popo tsu ta tsu ta tsu pon." The *tsu* is the *ō tsuzumi* drum, and the *ta* and *po* or *pon* are different sounds on the *ko tsuzumi*. The pattern is heard in every piece, particularly those intended for kabuki dance. Many of the instrumental interludes in *Yoshiwara Suzume* (CD 1–2) are in the *chiri kara* style.

Figure 14. *Dangire* patterns

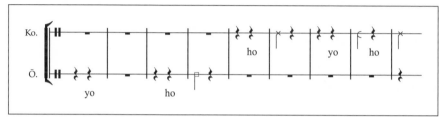

Figure 15. *Mitsuji*

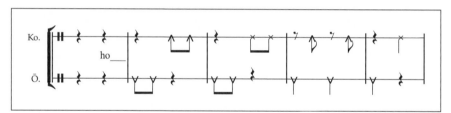

Figure 16. *Chiri kara* rythm

Wataribyōshi. This is a *taiko* and flute pattern commonly used behind text set in Yoshiwara or in flower-viewing scenes. Figure 17 contains the drum part and its mnemonics. It is heard in the *michiyuki* of *Ame no Shiki* (CD 2–3).

Kyōgen gakko. This refers a small drum (*gakko*) that hangs before the performer (*kyōgen*) in a street theatrical (fig. 18). The drum is actually used as a prop in *Sagi Musume* and *Echigojishi* dances. The pattern can be heard on the video *Suehirogari* (Malm 1996).

Bungo sagari ha. Another common *taiko* pattern used in Edo dance pieces, *bungo sagari ha* is also seen and heard in *Suehirogari* (Malm 1996; see fig. 19).

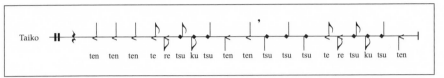

Figure 17.   *Wataribyōshi*

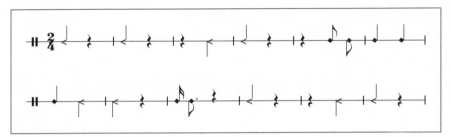

Figure 18.   *Kyōgen gakko*

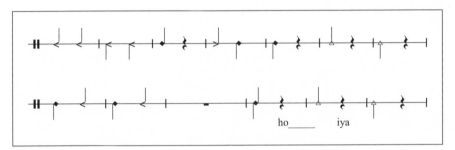

Figure 19.   *Bungo sagari ha*

Sandame. This is a kabuki version of a third (*san*) *dan* of noh drama *hayashi* dance music. It is heard in the *chirashi* of *Tsuru Kame* (CD 2–1) and in *Suehirogari* (Malm 1996). Western notation can be found in Malm 1963, 292–95, and the noh patterns used in it are listed in table 33 of that book. Another score can be found in Brandon, Shively, and Malm 1978, 162.

Nagauta music fans may not know the names of all these patterns or the many other such conventions in kabuki music. However, like Western music buffs, they respond to the moods or formal signals that traditional music creates.

Song Texts and Commentary

Format Guide

COMMENTARY TEXTS

Compositions are listed by title in the general order of the years in which they were composed. They are divided into five periods: eighteenth century, early nineteenth century, mid–nineteenth century, late nineteenth century, and twentieth century. The comments contain title translations, composers, text sources, recordings, and printed Japanese notation (in the Bunka, Yoshizumi, or Kineya style discussed in the previous chapter (p. 7). The recordings are CDs, audiocassettes, or video DVDs available in 2004.

TRANSLATIONS

All the texts are derived from recordings or notations of concert versions of each piece. Dance and kabuki performances may include materials not shown in the translations.

The Japanese text is in the left column in romanized script and includes long marks. Capitalization is only used for the names of persons and places. The left column also includes in small capitals the names of formal divisions in the text (Oki, Michiyuki, and so on). Shamisen tunings are noted in italics and parentheses. Recall that the actual pitch of a performance is set by the performers. The approximate length of a performance is shown above the right column. Long instrumental interludes are labeled Aikata in small capitals, and shorter ones are labeled *ai* in parentheses. If an interlude has a title, it is listed in the right column. In texts derived from noh drama, the singers are identified in parentheses and italics as *waki, shite,* or *ji.* Some attempts have been made to match Japanese and English key words. The Japanese texts are found on pp. 169–204.

Eighteenth-Century Compositions

Musume Dōjōji, 1753
The Young Women at Dōjōji Temple

Composer: Kineya Kasaburō (1875 version)
Text: Derived from the noh drama *Dōjōji*
Recording: Columbia cassette CAK 9060, NHK 3-13-1
Video: SHV DA 0199
Notation: Bunka, vol. 19; Yoshimura, vol. 4

Dōjōji is perhaps the longest-lived noh-based kabuki dance drama in Japan. The plot concerns a woman whose former lover had become Buddhist priest. Disguised as a *shirabyōshi* dancer, she enters the monastery, turns into a vengeful demon, and traps the priest in the temple bell. There have been so many variants of the plot that the term *Dōjōji things* (*Dōjōjimono*) has become part of kabuki nomenclature. In 1955 the author saw the story as part of productions at the Tokyo Nichigeki nude show. A saxophone led the music and the "priests" rubbed their rosaries between their breasts.

In 1957 a female koto musician, Hirai Sumiko, composed a *Kirishitan Dōjōji* for television. It won a prize in the Twelfth Arts Festival contest. In 1959 it was performed by the kabuki actor Nakamura Utaemon in a dance recital with choreography by Fujima Kanjurō. Utaemon also danced it in several kabuki programs. The text by Ishikawa Tangetsu changes the story from a vengeful dancer who destroys a Buddhist priest in a temple bell to the daughter of a defeated Christian convert who looks for her former lover as he studies to be a Christian priest. She turns into a demon after seeing a statue of the Virgin Mary as a symbol of his new love. The *nagauta* music includes quotes from Gregorian chant.

The September 2004 kabuki presented *Meoto Dōjōji* with basically the same music as a standard *Dōjōji*, but it is choreographed for two dancers. One is disguised as a man. The usual dramatic finale was turned into a comic dance using masks.

Since 1753 the kabuki productions of *Dōjōji* have been *kakeai*, that is, a mixture of musical genres, including *nagauta*, *tokiwazu*, and *gidayū* and other early genres. The 1829 *Kyakkō Dōjōji* is sometimes performed in that manner. The NHK recording uses *tokiwazu* and *nagauta*. As primarily a dance piece, different instrumental interludes have been inserted or changed to support the choreography of new actors. Excerpts from the piece are often seen in dance recitals. The 1860 concert piece *Kishū Dōjōji* dealt more with the original noh story and is an attempt at narrative *nagauta*. A partial translation of the kabuki version of *Musume Dōjōji* in found in Richie and Watanabe 1963. The *Musume Dōjōji* translation below is based on the concert version of the 1753 text as revised in 1875. It is often called *Kyōganoko Musume Dōjōji*. The videotaped performance by Tamasaburō has several changes not noted here and includes *gidayū* music. The translation is basically from the text found in Yoshizumi 1955, volume 4.

The story revolves around the dedication of a new bell at the Dōjōji temple at Kishu in Wakayama Prefecture, but, as noted, it soon wanders to a host of other images. In the original, a beautiful woman arrives at the temple and proceeds to perform many dances until her true vengeful spirit appears. She is angry about a priest who had rejected her love. She becomes a serpent and mounts the bell.

Although characteristics of the kabuki dance form are evident, the piece is considered to be in the older *kumiuta* style. This is a series of songs, often with unrelated texts, separated by instrumental interludes.

The first lines are sung in noh drama style (*utaigakari*) accompanied by *tsuzumi* drums. The opening text is derived from a different noh drama, *Miidera*, which deals with a madwoman who strikes a bell. The line is followed by an interlude played by the *tsuzumi* drums and noh flute. It is derived from a famous later scene in both the kabuki and noh versions in which the twist of the dancer's foot implies the vengeful evil spirit of the woman who then bursts into the fast *kyu no mai* dance. The twisting foot, however, is seen earlier in kabuki performances when the dancer looks toward the bell. In *nagauta* recordings the length of this section varies. It is followed by a quick shamisen entrance at "kane no urami." The next line is an example of the slow, lyrical *tataki* (see p. 15). In kabuki the actor is seen in costume with the *eboshi* hat of a *shirabyōshi* dancer (see Malm 2000, 55) as that is what she pretends to be. The five obstacles (*goshō*) for women in Buddhism are desire or jealousy, wrong action, breaking the law or dharma, wrong knowledge, and birth. The *aikata* in a new tuning may use offstage drums, and a bell (*rin*) sounds to imply the setting in a Buddhist temple. During this time, the dancer gives her hat to the stage assistants (*kōken*), who install a female comb for the more geisha-style dance at a faster tempo. The topic is an unhappy love. Perhaps it distantly implies the broken love between the woman and the priest in the original play.

In kabuki performances there is an instant costume change after "hasu hana monojae" that makes the dancer a younger girl. Shamisen and *tsuzumi* ostinatos plus a bamboo flute support a long dance that imitates a child bouncing a ball (*mari*). The topic and dancing change as verses are sung about the brothels of Yoshiwara and Naniwa (Osaka). At "koi no wakezato" the *taiko* and flute enter with the *bungo sagari ha* pattern (see p. 18). The ball-bouncing motions are seen briefly in the dance when the young girls in training (*kamuro*) are mentioned. Unfortunately, they must learn new games quickly if they are to become geishas.

In kabuki the actor exits for a costume change during the next *aikata* in another geisha tuning (*sansagari*). Then three verses of an eighteenth-century popular song accompany a new dance. The accompaniment is in the style of a *taiko ji*. The new dance is performed with a set of red hats. It is a common part of student recitals. A change of costume leads to yet another, longer dance with instrumental accompaniment only, particularly when played as a concert rather than a dance piece. In kabuki the "monks" dance with umbrellas to fill in the time. The music may be eliminated in concert versions.

The next dance about love uses typical *kudoki* lyricism with a slow tempo and the use of only solo singers and shamisen. The dancer has blackened teeth, a common beauty practice in earlier Japan. The text returns to the unhappy love of the brothel areas, often called the floating world. When she doesn't know what to do, a brief change from the *in* to the *yo* scale and a finger slide on the *ai* respond to the dance movements. A struggle with emotions (*futsuri*) is sung at the highest and thus the most intense pitch. Repressed jealousy indirectly links the text to the original story, but the major function of the words and music is to support subtle dance movements.

An *aikata*, using a faster tempo and full orchestration in a new tuning, gives the actor time to change costume offstage. The actor leaves the stage again as another long *aikata* with full orchestration occurs. This is called *kakko* because the dancer returns with a *kakko* drum tucked in her (his) obi. The percussion of the music uses only *tsuzumi* because the dancer pretends to play the stick drum often. The accompaniment is called *yamazukushi*, "listing the mountains," as all the famous mountains are described while the dancer makes the appropriate gestures. *Chiri-kara*-style *tsuzumi* dominates the accompaniment. Romantic puns on the words in the mountain names abound. Sudden brief modulations indicate falling flower petals. The *aikata* that follows shows off the shamisen's skills while the dancer is off for another costume change.

There are different versions of the final section, only one of which is translated here. The finales match from the word *omoeba* as, in the kabuki, the actor perches on the bell in a dragon-scaled costume as the *odaiko* rolls supernatural power over the *dangire* ending.

Oki (*sansagari* tuning)	Length 33'22"
hana no hoka ni wa matsu bakari	But for the blossoms there are only pine trees.
hana no hoka ni wa matsu bakari	But for the blossoms there are only pine trees.
kure shōmete kane ya hibikuran	At twilight the bell echoes across the land.

AIKATA

kane ni urami wa kazukazu gozaru

(*hayashi* interlude)

Her hatred of the bell is beyond measure.

shoya no kane o tsuku toki wa
shogyo mujo to hibikunari
goya no kane o tsuku toki wa
zessho meppo hibikunari
jinjo no hibiki wa

The strike of the evening bell declares
that all things are impermanent.
The strike of the early morning bell
says that all things born must vanish.
The sunrise bell tolls that rebirth is possible.

shōmetsu metsui iri ai wa
jaku metsu iraku to hibikunari
kiite odoroku hito mo nashi

The sunset bell echoes that we may
reach nirvana peacefully.
No one is surprised to hear these truths.

ware mo goshō no kumo harete

Five obstacles cloud a woman's enlightenment,

shin nyo no tsuki o nagame akasan.

but the moonlight of truth is within her view.

AIKATA (*niagari* tuning)

iwazu kataranu
waga kokoro
midareshi kami no
midaruru mo tsurenai wa
tada utsurigi na
dōdemo otoko wa
aku sho mono
sakura sakura to utawarete
iute tamoto no wake
futatsu tsutome sae
tada ukauka to
dōdemo onago wa
aku sho mono
miyako sodachi wa
hasu hana monojae

She will not speak.
Her heart remains silent.
Her confusion is like her tangled hair.
A man's cold heart
only moves from affair to affair.
Truly every man
has an evil nature.
In the song of the cherry blossoms
it is said that relationships die.
The duty of love is
simply careless.
Truly every woman
has an evil nature.
Women raised in the capital are like
flowers that repel water.

AIKATA

koi no wakezato
bushi mo dōgu o
fuse amigasa de
hari to ikiji no Yoshiwara

In the brothels of love
even samurai must hide their weapons
and their identities under their hats
in the competitive world of Yoshiwara.

25

AIKATA

hana no miyako wa	The flowers of the capital,
uta de yawaragu	softened by the poetry of song
shiki Shimabara ni	in the Shimabara pleasure quarters,
tsutome suru mi wa	giving their bodies.
dare to fushimi no sumisome	With whom will they spend the night?
bonno bodai no	Desire and enlightenment meet
Shumoku machiyori	like hammer and bell in the Shumoku district,
Naniwa yosuji ni	in the four corners of Naniwa,
kayoi kitsuji ni	as they pass through the intersections.
kamuro dachikara	Raised as attendants since childhood,
Muro no hayazaki	girls grow up quickly in the Muro district.
sore ga hon ni	Yes, it is true that many things
iroja hi fu mi yo	are learned step-by-step.
yotsuyu yuki no hi	Like dewdrops on a snowy day
shimo no sekiji mo	and frost in Shimonoseki,
tomoni kono mi o	she shares her body,
najimi kasa nete	lying down with someone familiar.
naka wa Maruyama	In Maruyama, intimacy grows
tada marukare to	between two people together,
omoi sometaga enjae	Falling in love was her fate.

AIKATA (*sansagari* tuning)
(first verse)

ume to san san sakura wa	The plum and cherry blossom,
izure ani yara	which one is the older brother,
ototoyara	which one is the younger brother
wakite iwarenuna	is impossible to tell
hana no iro e	from the flower's color.

(second verse)

ayame kakitsubata wa	The flag and iris,
izure ane yara	which one is the older sister,
imoto yara (*ai*)	which one is the younger sister
wakite iwarenuna	is impossible to tell
hana no iro e	by the flower's color.

AIKATA

nishi mo higashi mo	From the west and east
minna minikita	everyone came to see
hana no kao sayoe	this dancer's flowerlike face.
mireba koizo masue sayoe	If they see her,
kawa yurashi sa no	their love will grow
hana musume	for this flower maiden.

AIKATA
KUDOKI

koi no te narai tsui	The poetry of love
minaraite	she studies and learns.
dare ni mishō tote	For whom should she display
benikane tsukyozo	her rouged lips and blackened teeth?
minna nushi e no	For her lord she did everything
shinju date	to show her true devotion.
ōureshi ō ureshi	Oh how great was her happiness.
sue wa kōja ni na	In the end
sōnaru made wa	they would be together
tonto iwazuni	just as he promised her.
suma sozo en to	Until then she would say nothing.
seishi sae itsu wari ka	Was his letter of promise false?
uso ka makoto ka	Was it the truth or was it a lie?
dōmo nara nu hodo	Not knowing what to do,
ai ni kita	she came to meet him.
futsuri rinki semai zoto	She struggled to
tashinande mitemo	repress her jealousy
nasakenaya	and her wretched feelings,
onnago niwa nani ga naru	but there was nothing she could do.
(ai)	
tonogo tonogo	My lordship,
no ki ga shirenu	I did not know your heart.
ki ga shirenu	I do not understand.
akusho na akusho na	Evil, such evil,
ki ga shirenu	I do not understand.
urami urami te	With boundless hatred
kakochi naki	she breaks down in tears.
tsuyu o fuku mishi	Dewdrops weigh heavily
sakura bana	on this flower petal.

27

saraba	If lightly touched,
ochin fuzenari	it will fall.

AIKATA	"Kakko"
YAMAZUKUSHI	"Song of the Mountains"
omoshiro no shiki	Breathtaking in all four seasons
no nagameya	is the view
Sangoku ichi no	in all three countries;
Fuji no yama	Fuji is the greatest of all mountains.
yuki ka to mireba	Snow looks like
hana no fubuki ka	flower petals falling
Yoshino yama	on Mount Yoshino
chirikuru chirikuru	and scattering across
Arashiyama	stormy Mount Arashi.

AIKATA	
Asahiyama o	On Mount Asahi,
miwataseba	gazing out in the morning sun,
uta no Nakayama	hear the song of Mount Naka
Ishiyama no	and Mount Ishi
sue no matsuyama	on pine-covered mountaintops.
itsuka Oeyama iku no	Someday we will meet at Mount Oe.
no michi no tōkeredo	Although the way is distant,
koiji ni kayōfu	we travel the path of love
Asamayama	at Mount Asama.
hito yo no nasake	Longing for one night of love
Arimayama (*ai*)	on Mount Arima;
inase no koto no ha (*ai*)	will it be yes or no?
asuka Kisoyama	Waiting to see if tomorrow
Matsuchiyama	he would come or not,
waga mikami yama	she went to pray to her mountain god
inori kitayama	at Mount Kita
Inariyama (*ai*)	and Mount Inari;
en o musubi shi	hoping to be joined together
Imoseyama	as man and wife at Mount Imose.
futari ga naka no	As two they would prosper
Koganeyama	in the gold of Mount Kogane
hanasaku eiko no	where flowers flourish and die.

28

konoko no Obasuteyama	Life brought back from Mount Obasute.
mine no matsukaze	The sound of pine winds from the peak
Otowayama	of Mount Otowa.
iri ai no kane o	The tolling of the sunset bell
Tsukubayama	at Mount Tsukuba
tōeizan no	and Mount Toei.

AIKATA

tsuki no kaobase	The face of the moon rises
Mikasayama	over Mount Mikasa.
saru hodo ni saru hodo ni	As she dances,
teradera no kane	the temple bell tolls,
tsuki ochi tori nai te	the moon sets, the cock crows,
shimo yuki ten ni	a snowlike frost fills the sky
michishio	and the tide rises.
hodonaku kono yama	Soon this mountain
dera no kōson no gyoka	temple village, lit by torchlight,
urei ni taishite	becomes quiet.
hitobito nemureba	If the people are asleep
yoki himazo to	this is her chance
tachi ma o yōni	to appear to be dancing
nerai yōte	while taking aim at her target.
tsukan to seshi ga omoeba	Though seemingly going only to strike it,
kono kane urameshiya tote	this bell is the object of her profound hatred.
ryōzu ni te o kake	Perched on the crown of the bell,
tobu yo to mieshi ga	she appears to be flying,
hiki kazui te zo	but it begins to cover her
use nikeru	and she disappears inside.

Sagi Musume, 1762
"The White Heron Maiden"

Composer: Kineya Shōjirō, expanded in 1886 by Fujita Kichiji
Text: Hirokoshi Nisōji (b. 1721)
Recordings: Victor KCDK 1119; Columbia COCF 70123
Video: DVD of dance Shociku DA 0200
Notation: Bunka, 3352; Yoshizumi, vol. 4

BOOK CD: 1–1

Performers: voice, Nishigaki Yūzō, Miyata Tesuo; shamisen: Kikuoka Hiroka, Kineya Yasaburō; drums, Mochitsuke Taikouemon, Mochitsuki Taiko, Mochituki Sakichi, Tosha Rosetsu; flute, Fukuhara Hyakunosuke

This example of kabuki *nagauta* dance music was first performed in 1762 by an *onnagata* (female impersonator), Segawa Kikunojō (1741–73), and was restaged in 1886 by Ichikawa Danjūrō IX (1839–1903). It also is the oldest surviving example of a quick-change (*hengemono*) dance and is credited as being the first dance to use a revolving stage. It continues to be performed, most recently by Bandō Tamasaburō V. His performance can be seen on the Shochiku DVD listed above. A detailed description and pictures of the kabuki version of this piece may be found in Brandon 2002. The translation and commentary below are based on the concert version as heard on the book CD 1–1.

The dance revolves around the tale of a heron that became human and fell in love only to be rejected and sent to hell. Seven instant costume changes depict the tragedy from youth to death. It is a major challenge for both the dancer and the musicians as there are many tempi and a host of images and thoughts must be portrayed.

TEXT AND MUSIC

Oki. The *oki* section is marked as a *tsuzumi uta* (drum song). This was an ancient musical genre for female entertainers that was usually accompanied by a single *ko tsuzumi* drum (see *Shima no Senzai*, p. 153; and *Yoshiwara Suzume*, p. 36). The single stroke of the *tsuzumi* drums and a *kakegoe* (yo) are followed by a solo singer performing in long syllables in imitation of the ancient style. The opening text sets the mood and ends with a reference to a poem by the eighth-century Arihara Narihiro in which Mount Shinobu is mentioned. The shamisen enters at "waga kokoro," (seeds of quarrels), and a steady beat is established. The line implies the problem of unrequited love.

The *michiyuki* contains *tsuzumi* playing in the noh style plus a brief period of wavering low notes on the noh flute. The latter is a kabuki signal for ghosts or supernatural characters to appear. In some kabuki performances, the actor appears here (see Brandon 2002). Snow and the umbrella are essential parts of the staging and symbols in the text. The text clearly relates to the dance movements. One can imagine the gesture when a rubato cadence is used for the expression "road to love" (*koiji to ya*). The menacing flute is heard in the short interlude before the voice and shamisen enter, and it returns in the next interlude to keep the mysterious mood alive. The tempo picks up, but the dance calls for several rubato pauses. Further references to water and the heron's movements are accompanied by the thin sounds of only one voice and shamisen. The next *aikata* is one of several interludes that are set in dotted lines in the original notation and marked as "new." These may have been later additions to the dance or the concert version of the piece. The first one is played by a single shamisen, which follows the delicate bird movements in the dance. The tempo picks up as the bird moves through the water. The word *nurete* (wet) is sung low and slow but leads into a faster dance enlivened by the sound of *tsuzumi* playing in the *chiri kara* style as the tears have dried and a costume change has turned the bird into a young girl. The music moves quickly but slows down suddenly for the line "shinobu sono yo no hanashi" (recall when we talked).

At "eno musubu no," the *kudoki* section begins with a *tataki* pattern (see p. 15). It is followed by a new, fast-paced, shamisen duet, which prepares the audience for a fast costume change. There are sudden stops that might relate to the choreography though they do create the dramatic effect of silence in fast music. The bamboo flute now joins the ensemble as the topic and dance return to the sad love affair. At "suma no" the dancer mines collecting saltwater in two buckets she carries. The buckets are not used in the DVD performance. The interlude for the next costume change is a new shamisen duet with repeat marks. The voice then returns with more text about the heron and snow.

The *tsuzumi* return and accompany another *tsuzumi uta*. It can be sung again with a slow *tsuzumi* or shamisen ostinato. The long melismas on single syllables are found both here and in the first *tsuzumi uta* at the start of the piece imply that the *tsuzumi* here can accompany the singer throughout.

The following section can certainly be called an *odori ji*, with its umbrella dance, or a *taiko ji* with its use of *taiko* and bamboo flute throughout. They drop out at "sojae." A costume change interlude then begins with *tsuzumi chiri kara* and shamisen setting a faster tempo. In the original notation this interlude has repeat marks to extend the costume change as needed. The text shows that the umbrella is obviously being twirled.

The topic of the *chirashi* moves from sin to hell. A series of texts and new interludes begins with *tsuzumi* accompaniment. Note that at modern tempi the speed of the *chiri kara* patterns is probably faster than originally designed. After "kotogotoku," an interlude occurs that uses a unique tonality (C-sharp) and then becomes ever more intense. Onstage, there is an unusual costume change in which the first costume is quickly converted into another. The aggressive drums of Shura (at "shura no daiko") lead into an interlude with full *hayashi* accompaniment. It is marked as new. It may be part of the concert version of the composition. Only the *tsuzumi* and virtuoso shamisen are used. The noh flute shrikes a warning, and suddenly the shamisenists place their middle fingers under the top string to create a devilish sound. After a sudden silence, another virtuoso interlude is played. The "ghost" flute is heard near the end. Full *hayashi* enters briefly to set the *chirashi* mood, and the flute inserts some "ghost" music, but the shamisen and *tsuzumi* dominate the music until the *dangire*, where a standard full cadence occurs. It is easy to understand why this piece has remained popular in the repertory for so long.

OKI (*sansagari* tuning) Length 26'40"

(TSUZUMI UTA)

mōshu no kumo hareyarnu oboroyo no — On this hazy night clouded by attachment

koi ni mayoishi waga kokoro Shinobu yama — to this world, my heart, lost in love, endures the pain of longing on Mount Shinobu.

kuzetsu no tane no koikaze ga — Seeds of quarrels blow though the winds of love.

MICHIYUKI

fukedomo kasa ni yuki motte — Now snow piles on my umbrella as

tsumoru omoi wa awayuki to — thoughts of you collect in my heart.

kiete hakanaki koiji to ya — But these thoughts collect like the delicate snow that melts on the ephemeral road of love.

AIKATA

omoi kasanaru mune no yami (*ai*) — My heart is filled with longing.

semete aware to iugure no — Darkened in the sadness of dusk,

chira chira yuki ni nuresagi no — in drifting snow, the heron stands,

shonbori to kawayurashi — dampened and despondent yet lovely.

AIKATA

mayo kokoro no hoso nagare choro choro	The thin path of my bewildered heart is
mizu no hitosuji ni	like drops of water that dry and disappear
urami no hoka wa shirasagi no	even from the legs of a heron accustomed
mizu ni nare taru ashidori mo	to making her way through water.

AIKATA (costume change)

nurete shizuku to kiurumono	My sleeves remain wet even after my
ware wa namida ni	tears have dried.
kawaku ma mo sodeoshi aenu	I tried to forget the loving
tsukikage ni shinobu	moonlight nights recalling
sono yo no hanashi o sutete (*ai*)	when we spoke together.

KUDOKI

eno musubu no kamisan ni	How shameful is the happiness and
tori agerareshi	bounteous love bestowed on us by the
ureshisa mo amaru	god who bound our fates together
iroka no hazukashiya	as shy lovers.

AIKATA (costume change)

suma no urabede	It is even more difficult to dip into the
shiokumu yori mo	depths of someone's heart than to dip into
kimi no kokoro wa	the salt of the Suma Sea.
kumi nikui sarito wa	I know how true it is.
jitsu ni makoto to	Really how true it is.
omowanse (*ai*)	Folding formal cloths (*hakama*) is more
shinshu no hakama no	difficult than passing through his
hidatoru yori mo nushi no kokoro ga	heart.
torinikui sarito wa	
jitsu ni makoto to omowan se	Believe me, I know.
(*ai*) shiya hon nie	Really I can tell the truth.

AIKATA (costume change)

shirasagi no hakaze ni yuki no	The white heron's wings scatter the snow
chiri te	like swirling blossoms

33

hana no chirishiku
keshiki to mire do atara
nagame no yuki zo chirinan
yuki zo chirinan nikukaranu

one sees in a scene.
They blow away thought in flurries.
They even blow away snow.
How upsetting.

TSUZUMI UTA
koi ni kokoro mo
utsuroishi
hana no fubuki no chiri ka kari

A heart by love
worn down.
Thoughts loaded with a blizzard of
flowers.

harō mo oshiki sode nasa ya

This umbrella and these sleeves don't
want to brush them away.

TAIKO JI
kasa o ya kasa o kasunaraba

Umbrella, if I must open you as a
parasol,

ten ten ten hijirigasa (*ai*)
sashikakete
izasaraba
hanami ni gonse yoshinoyama

give me shade from the sun like the
flowers that fade,
change colors.
Then we shall see flowers at Mount
Yoshino.

(*ai*)
nihoi sakura no hannagasa

The sweet-smelling cherry blossoms
will

en to tsukihi no meguri kuru kuru

shade us from the sun and time,
turning,

kuru kuru megasa sore sore sore sojae
sore ga ukina no
hashi to naru

turning, like the twirling umbrella.
This was the beginning of the rumors
about us.

AIKATA
CHIRASHI
sōmo sowarezu amatsusae

Without really being husband and
wife,

jaken no yaiba ni sekitachite kono yo

you are taken by the cruel sword of
fate.

karasae Tsurugi no yama

Even in this world, I have met with
sorrow and grief of Hell's Mount
Tsurugi.

AIKATA
ichiju no uchi ni oroshi ya

Under the sheltering tree,

chigoku no arisama kotogotoku | even in just one curse Hell's fury can be felt. I am condemned to one of the hells.

AIKATA | (costume change)

tsumi o tadashite Emma no | It is as if the iron rod of Emma,
tetsujō masa ni ari ari to | Judge of Hell,
tōgatsu chikiushō shuro jijuku | condemns me to a hell of
Arui wa kyōkan daikōkan | perpetually renewed death, the realm of

shura no daiko wa hima mo naku | beasts, the hell of the human world, the hell of waiting, the hell of wailing. The aggressive drums of Shura beat increasingly.

AIKATA

okushotsu yō ni muragarite | The devils who torment the world are
tetsujō furiage kuro kane no (ai) | gathering everywhere. Raising their steel

kibakami narashi | rods and grinding their teeth,
botsutate botsutate (ai) | they drive the inhabitants of Hell day
nirokuji chō ga sono no aida | and night,
kururi kururi
oi meguri oi meguri | Around and around they chase them.
tsui ni kono mi wa hishi hishi hishi | Before you know it, one is tormented so that one's bones feel as it they are being crushed.

AIKATA
DANGIRE

awaremi tamae waga ukimi | Feel pity for this wretched being.
kataru mo | Even as I tell my story,
namida narikerashi | my tears flow.

‿ ⌣·

Yoshiwara Suzume, 1768
"The Sparrows of Yoshiwara"

Composers: Kineya Yajūrō, I and Fujita Kichiji
Text: Sakurada Jisuke I
Recordings: NHK 1-11-1; Columbia COCF 70098
Notation: Bunka 3326; Kineya 90; Yoshizumi 1955, vol. 7

BOOK CD: 1–2

Performers: singers, Nishigaki Yūzō, Miyata Tetsuo, Minagawa Ken; shamisen: Kineya Yasaburō, Kineya Rokudai, Kikuoka Hiroaki; drums: Miohizuki Taiko, Mochizuki Saemon, Mochizuki Sakichi; flute, Fukahara Hyakunosuke

This is one of the oldest kabuki dances still in the repertory; it has experienced many changes in choreography, arrangement, and text.

Text. The forty-fourth mikado (emperor) was a female named Genshōe (r. 715–24), perhaps mentioned since the piece is so much about a woman's life. The fourth year was 720. Figure 4 (p. 4) is an 1864 copy of the original printing of the text of this famous kabuki dance. The woman is carrying two birdcages as symbols of the girls of the Yoshiwara, who were certainly birds that needed release. The "bird floating asleep" is a metaphor for someone crying herself to sleep and is also used to describe a prostitute, who seldom has time to fix her bed.
   The *michiyuki* text in *niagari* tuning mixes the scene with names of birds. The terms *dotehachō* and *kuchihatchō* are standard references to the Yoshiwara border river embankment over which men pass, like seagulls (*kagome*), flying to brothels in groups by boat. The term *sukenzoneki* refers to customers who walk under the eaves of brothels with no intention of going in. Throughout the scene, wordplay with names of birds continues over party music.
   The scene changes to the girls looking at the men and then the first customer's (*shoshin*) entrance. The dialogue that follows is self-explanatory except for the reference to Amigasa hats. They have wide, low brims that help a customer hide his identity when visiting the Yoshiwara.

The *kudoki* text uses names of flowers to create a romantic mood. In the 1931 *Nagauta zenshu*, a poem is shown between the *kudoki* and *tsuzumi uta* sections, but it does not appear in the notation or recordings. It is about eastern clouds that pass one another. No source is listed.

The go-between (*nakōdo*) at the start of the *tsuzumi uta* is someone who arranges marriages. The incense is part of such a ritual. Here it is a wish rather than an action as the later text confirms.

Two verses of a humorous geisha popular song appear in the *niagari* tuning (at the line "jorō no makoto to"). "Shongai na" is a standard geisha slang phrase, and so it is declaimed in feminine style. When one thinks of the poor, overworked whores who frequently said this, perhaps "ain't that so" seems better that "isn't that right" or "it can't be helped." The phrase was originally a type of "rhythm words" (*hayashi kotoba*), which could be inserted by other singers between the phrases or verses of a song. Such inserts are frequently heard in folk songs and party music. Peony powder, referred to in the second verse, was a popular item of female makeup.

In the *sansagari* song that follows, the lament over the rooster call (*torigane*) of dawn is common in the romantic texts of many languages. In Edo literature it competes with the local Buddhist morning bell. Both mean that men must leave the brothel. The reference to twinkling stars implies that the morning after a drunk the stars are seen double. The woman Osan is the hateful wife of Jihei, a merchant who was in love with a prostitute. They are well-known characters in the Chikamatsu *bunraku* play "The Double Suicide at Amijima." The text remains ambiguous with a mixture of traditional references to letters, flowers, seasons, and hopes for love. The *monpi* is the monthly day of rest in the brothels.

There is always more to study in Japanese song texts. These few comments try to show how such dance pieces present the sweet and sour but colorful life of the Yoshiwara as it was portrayed in eighteenth-century kabuki music. Of course, an actual dance performance would do as well.

Music. The *maebiki* is a pattern called *tobi tataki*. The pseudo history that begins the piece is performed in free rhythm (parlando). The use of a single *tsuzumi* stroke before "kōshō" is a conventional coloring of text that deals with the imperial court. The use of the noh flute and the drum pattern *mitsuji* at "yōrō" does the same. Note that when the text moves to a festival topic (at "hachiman"), the drums change to the more "common" *chiri kara* style. The release of the animals is accompanied by quick beats on the shamisen and drums like a flight of birds. While such a detailed interpretation will not be applied to the entire piece, it is appropriate here at the beginning because it emphasizes the frequent word orientation that is common throughout *nagauta* music.

The scene now turns to Yoshiwara-style dance music beginning with a quote from *handayūbushi*, an early shamisen genre. The *niagari* and *sansagari* tunings are most frequently used in music from the floating world. Thus, the new Yoshiwara-related text is set in the *niagari* "geisha" mode. A faster party tempo and *chiri ikara* drum patterns enhance this vision. The boat numbers are called out (*serifu*) in brothel dialect, and the shamisen interlude begins with a gay ostinato that is well known in kabuki party scenes (see fig. 13A, p. 16). The return to *honchōshi* tuning begins with a fast shamisen interlude called *sanjū*, which is used before geisha house scenes. The next piece of music features the singer and shamisen only. The long, melismatic singing of "nareshi kuruwa no" may be derived from an eighteenth-century popular music genre called *ōzuebushi*. A direct translation of the words is "experiencing the brothel" and "no" is a possessive case sign. It literally leads one to the charming scents and activities of the Yoshiwara.

At "sa kitamaka," the tempo accelerates and the shamisen return to another brothel ostinato pattern. The words "Go farther back" are spoken in the style of the brothel madam. As noted above, these *serifu* in dialect occur throughout this section, as do brothel music patterns for the shamisen. The connecting phrase (called a *tsunagi*) that leads to the next section begins with a declaimed "shōshi." It could mean "pitiful" or "ridiculous" since a whore or a customer often says how nice it was after things are over. In the recording, the *serifu* implies that it is the girl speaking.

Another characteristic tuning for geisha music, *sansagari*, is used for the lyrical *kudoki* section. The *tataki* shamisen conventional accompaniment (see fig. 12) is heard at "hoka no kyakū." It is followed by a series of stops on upper leading tones that require resolution and another *tataki* pattern at "nadeshiko." The tempo increases with the girl's restless heart. A single *ko tsuzumi* stroke and drum call lead to a pseudo *tsuzumi uta*. This was a genre of female music accompanied by the *tsuzumi* (see *Shima no Senzai* in this volume). The first words, at "hitotake," are sung solo. The music then moves to another *tataki* passage with *ō* and *ko tsuzumi* accompaniment. At "sotchi no" one hears a *mitsuji* pattern that changes suddenly into fast *chiri kara* music. At "masanagoto" the shamisen play the geisha *totsu tere* ostinato pattern (see fig. 13A), which leads into a long virtuoso interlude in this recording. It was not part of the original piece, but there have been decades of changes in all kabuki compositions.

The piece returns to yet another geisha tuning (*niagari*). Several images appear in a party or folk style that no doubt generates some interesting choreography. The declamations are all geisha style. While she is saying how she hates the man ("hara ga tatsu") the shamisen quickly change to the other geisha tuning, *sansagari*. The tempo does slow down as the lovers part.

A new concert, vis-à-vis dance oriented, *aikata* occurs with only shamisen dialogues. Different versions of this interlude probably relate to the guilds used in a performance.

A conventional three-note shamisen introduction and the introduction of a bamboo flute are characteristic of the beginning of an *odori ji* section.

The *chirashi* is marked by the return of the *tsuzumi* drums, again first with a single stroke and a call, a *mitsuji* pattern, and then with a *chiri kara* in fast tempo. While the shamisen ending is conventional, a novelty in the CD performance is the return of the bamboo flute and a *tsuzumi* rolling pattern for the *dangire*.

Yoshiwara Suzume is an ideal example of conventional patterns combined with innovations introduced over the centuries.

MAEBIKI (*honchōshi* tuning)

OKI

oyoso ikeru o hanatsu koto
ninnō shijū yodai no mikado
kōshō tennō no gyou ka to yo
yōrō yonen no sue no aki
Usa Hachiman no takusen nite
shokoku niwa hajimaru
hōjō e

Length 27'11"

It is said to be that during the era of Emperor Kosho [fictional], the forty-fourth mikado, at the end of autumn in the fourth year of Yōrō, there was a Hachiman festival for the god Usa begun thoughout Japan in which all captured animals were released.

HANDAYU GAKARI

ukine no tori ni aranedo mo
ima mo koishiki hitori zumi
sayo no makura ni kata omoi
kawai kokoro to kumi mo sede
nanja yara nikurashi

Though not the bird floating asleep, I still live alone in longing on the pillow at night. Unknown, unrequited love. Ah this is terrible.

MICHIYUKI (*niagari* tuning) (*ai*)

sono te de fukami e hanmachidori
kayoi nare taru
dote hatchō kuchi hatchō ni noserarete
okino kamome no
nichō dachi, sanchō dachi

Like plovers (*hanmachidori*), you catch men's hearts through your seductive skills. You make men visit you frequently as they pass along the banks like seagulls. Flying together we are coming in two or three boats at a time.

AIKATA

sukenzomeki wa
mukudori no
mure tsūtsu kitsūtsūki kōshi saki

Men who tease are like starlings (*mukudori*) or like provincial woodpeckers (*kitsutsuki*) coming in crowds

(*ai*)

tataku kuina no

kuchi mamedori ni

kujakuzome kite mejiro oshi

mise sugaki no

ten-te-tsu-ton sassa oseose

ē ē

AIKATA (*honchōshi* tuning)

nareshi kurawa no

sode no ka ni

minu yō de miru yō de

kiyakū wa ōgi no kakine yori

shoshin kawayuku mae watari

sa kita mata kita

sa kita mata kita

sawari ja nai ka

mata osawari ka

okoshi no mono no gatten ka

sore Amigasa mo soko ni oke

"nikai zashiki wa migi ka

hidari ka

okuzashiki de gozariyasu

haya sakazuki motte kita

tokoe shizūka ni oide nasan shita

kae toiu ni zotto shita

shinzo kisama wa

wa nete mo samete mo wasurarenu

shinzo kisama wa nete mo samete mo
    wasuranu.

shōshi ki no doku mata kakesansu

nanina kakerumondae

KUDOKI (*sansagari* tuning)

sōshita kigiku to shiragiku no

onaji tsutome no sononaka ni (*ai*)

hoka no kyakūshu wa sute obune

---

like water rail (*kuina*) knocking

noisily on the brothel doors and easily
    trapped by the women.

Praising peacock (*kujaku*)

whores for their beauty, men

push each other around: push

in, push in.

(*sanjū* pattern)

The familiar scent of sleeves on

kimonos used in the brothels.

The girls spy as though averting their
    eyes, watching

customers through their fans.

Naive newcomers pass by with
    embarrassment.

"There's one. Here's another."

"There's one. Here's another."

"Aren't you busy?"

"Yeah, still occupied."

"Leave your weaponry."

"Why not put your Amigasa straw hat
    there too?"

"Which room on the second

floor should I go to?"

"It's the one farther back."

Sake cups are already there.

The girl silently slipped into

the room and startled the guest,

saying, "Please come in.

I truly won't forget you,

sleeping or awake."

"You poor thing, deceived again."

"Yep, it's really a deception."

Men float among girls like

yellow and white chrysanthemums.

Some customers are like

nagare mo ainu	abandoned little boats floating
momijiba no	apart like red maple leaves
medatsu fuyō no wake hedate	spreading the striking autumn
tada nadeshiko to kamikakete	primroses and swearing they are just carnations.
itsuka kuruwa o hanarete shion	"Someday, Aster (*shion*), you'll leave the brothel.
sōshita kokoro no oniyuri to	The more I think of your
omoeba	demon-lily heart (*sōshita*)
omou to kimo sekichiku ni naruwaina	my own feelings quickly shrink into a Chinese pink (*sekichiku*).
sue wa himeyuri	In the end we will be a princess lily (*himeyuri*)
otokoeshi	and a groom flower (*otokoeshi*), but my
sono tanoshimi mo uso momiji	excitement is as thin as a maple leaf (*momiji*)"
sarito wa tsurenai dōyoku to	"You really are cold and
kakine ni matō asagao no	merciless, like the morning
hanare gatanaki fuzei nari	glory (*asagao*) tangled in the fence. It seems hard for us to part."

TSUZUMI UTA

hitotaki kuyuru nakōdo no	"The go-between burns one stick of incense we sprinkled
sono tsugi kiko so enno hashi	and grafts our branches together.
sitchi no shiyo ga nikui yue	Because your ways are spiteful.
tonari zashiki no samisen ni	The shamisen playing in the
awasu warujare masanagoto	room next door unites our jokes and puns."

AIKATA (*niagari* tuning)

(1) jorō no makoto to	If such things as a prostitute's
tamago no	sincerity and a square egg ever
shikaku areba	exist, the moon would rise even
misoka ni tsuki mo deru	at the end of the month.
shongai na	Ain't that right?
tamago no yoi yoi, hoi, yoihoi hoi	Egg yoi yoi
yoihoi hoi yoihoi	
tamago ni shikaku	Square egg
areba misoga ni tsuki mo deru	The moon rising at the end of the month.

41

shongai na
hitotaki wa okyakukae (*ai*)
(2) kimi no nesugata mado kara mireba
botan shakuyaku yuri no hana
shongai na . . . .
shakuyaku yoihoi hoi yoihoi hoi yoihoi
shakuyaku botan botan shakuyaku yuri
no hana
shongai na
tsukezashi wa koichakae
e hara ga tatsu yara
(*sansagari* tuning)
nikui yara dōshō kōshō nikumu
torigane (*ai*)
akatsuki no myōjō ga
nishi e chirori higashi e chirori
chiori chiori to suru toki wa
uchi no shubi wa bushubi to natte.
oyaji wa jūmen kaka wa
gomen
jūmen gomen ni
nirami-tsukerare inō-yo (*ai*)
hodorō yo to
yutte (iute?) wa kogoshi ni tori-tsuite
naranu zo inashasenu
kono goro no shinashiburi
nikkui osana ga aru wai na

Ain't it so?
Incense from the guest room,
where your sleeping figure is seen.
Peony powder flowers, lily
flowers. Ain't it so?
powder yoihoi hoi
powder, peony, peony powder
from flowers.
Ain't it so?
Did you fill my cup with strong
tea? Oh how I hate you.

I hate the rooster telling us that
the morning has come.
The morning star reflects in my eyes.
It twinkles in the west,
twinkles in the east.
The plans for us fall apart.
Father backs away frowning.
Mother excuses herself with
puckered, disappointed looks.
Let's leave.
"Let's go back," you say
with a curt bow, but
I won't let you go.
I find you crude
You get as bad as Osan at home.

AIKATA
ODORI JI
fumi no tayori ni na
koyoi gonsu to sono uwasa
itsu no monpi mo nushian no
yabo na koto jaga hiyokumon

hanarenu naka ja to
shongae
somaru enishi no omoshiro y

Your letter said that you are
coming tonight.
Rumors imply that when my
day off comes, crude as you are, our
    seals will be crossed.
We'll never drift apart.
ain't it so?
How wonderful to be near this bond.

CHIRASHI

ge ni hana naraba hatsuzakura

tsukinaraba jusanya

izure otoranu surudoji no
anata e ii nuke konata no date
(*ai*)

If we are flowers, we are like the first
    cherry blossoms in early spring.

If we are the moon, we are like the
    summer moon (*jusanya*).

We are so playful together;

neither is inferior to the other.

You say this or that; you're good at
    evasive answers.

DANGIRE

izure marukare sorokashiku

But, after all, everything is all right,
    and so good-bye.

Takasago Tanzen, 1785
"The Takasago Bathhouse"

Composer: Kineya Shōichirō I
Text: Noh drama and Segawa Jokō I (1779–94)
Recordings: NHK II-7-1; Columbia COCF 70099
Notation: Bunka 3342; Kineya 27

An early example of kabuki dance music, *Takasago Tanzen* first appeared in the third act of the play *Otokoyama furisode genji*. *Takasago* is a well-known noh drama, and *tanzen* is the name of a famous bathhouse in the Yoshiwara district (see p. 135). Thus, the piece is a mixture of sounds and text from both traditions. New pieces, called *Shin Takasago*, were written in the late nineteenth century by Ikuta and Yamada koto musicians, and a *Shin Takasago nagauta* piece was written by Kineya Rokushirō in honor of the fiftieth performance of the Kenseikai school.

Text. Takasago, in present-day Hyōgo Prefecture, is famous in poetic allusions for its Onoe shrine, which contains a set of red and black pine trees that intertwine. They symbolize long love and are often called the Aioi (love) pines. The *jō* and *uba* are the two masks that are used in the original noh play. The lines about gazing at Sumiyoshi farther away are quotes from the Heian period *Ise monogatari,* which is about the amorous exploits of Ariwara no Narihira. Sumiyoshi, in southern Osaka, has a shrine with a famous poetic pine. The Sumiyoshi and Takasago pines are metaphorically considered husband and wife pine trees.

The "robes of love" before the interlude and *kudoki* represent the kind of love one holds as closely to oneself as one's own clothing.

The *yari* festooned poles or spears are frequently used in processions. Yanagi (Willow Branch) is the name of a major dance guild.

The first two lines of the *chirashi* are from the thirteenth-century poetry collection *Shoku-kokin wakashū*. The lines of the *utaigakari* are from an eleventh-century *Honchō monzui* collection of Chinese writings compiled by Fujiwara no Akihira.

Music. The atmosphere of the original drama is created by a prologue of noh flute, *tsuzumi* drumming using vocal calls (*kakegoe*), and noh patterns such as *mitsu ji* (see fig. 15, p. 17). This is followed by the traditional repeat of a first line of the noh drama *Takasago* sung in a *nagauta* version of noh drama *utai*. Compare this opening with the start of other noh-based compositions such as *Kanjinchō* (p. 98) and *Tsuru Kame* (p. 118). The drums turn to the *chiri kara* style as soon as the shamisen enter for the *maebiki*. At the *oki*, the *taiko* and noh flute enter to give it a more classical sound. The *tsuzumi* return with noh patterns at "hisashiki." Complete *hayashi* continues until "yo no tameshi." The shamisen and singer then perform in the style of an introductory *oki*. A bamboo flute is added to the interlude and continues into the *kudoki*. The *tsuzumi* returns in kabuki style for the interlude, which leads to a scene near the Tanzen bathhouse. Just the *ko tsuzumi* is added to the shamisen and vocal lines for the procession. The *taiko* and noh flute are added to the next interlude. *Kyōgen gakko* (see p. 18) and other kabuki-related patterns are used, as the location is very far from noh drama setting that began the piece. The change of tuning actually leads to a basic repeat of the *aikata* just played. The only change in the orchestration of the *odori ji* is the use of a bamboo flute. A brief parlando shamisen interlude precedes the *chirashi*. It follows the performance practice tradition of support from the *hayashi* in noh patterns except that the noh flute is not used. The opening line of the *utaigakari* is sung in noh style with a *ko tsuzumi* accompaniment. (The term utaigakaru means "in utai style.") A regular tempo and drums return, but the noh flute is not used until the *ai* before "iri kuru." Kabuki drum music helps intensify the approaching finale.

Three of our eighteenth-century compositions have a noh drama base, but *Yoshiwara Suzume* and *Takasago Tanzen* reveal a greater interest in the more "modern" styles of the Edo period.

UTAI SHIDAI — Length 20'17"

ima o hajime no tabigoromo — Now first putting on travel robes.
ima o hajime no tabigoromo — Now first putting on travel robes.
hi mo yuku sue zo hisashiki — The days ahead of me are many.

MAEBIKI (*niagari* tuning)
OKI

Takasago ya kono shitakage no — At Takasago, in the shade beneath
jō to uba — the trees, an old man pine and
matsu morotomo ni — old woman pine are together
ware mite mo — even as I gaze upon them.
hisashiku narinu (*ai*) — Farther away
Sumiyoshi no — Sumiyoshi grew.
kono urabune ni uchi norite — Gathered aboard this small boat,
tsuki morotomo ni ide shioya — the moon appears as the tide
kore wa medetaki — pulls us out. This is a grand and

45

yo no tameshi
oiki no sugata no hikikaete
imose warinaki myoto matsu
ha iro wa onaji fukamidori

miredomo omoi no tsukisenu wa
makoto narikeri koigoromo
ge ni koi wa kusemono

AIKATA
KUDOKI
tatoe banri wa hedatsu tomo
shitō kokoro wa
soriya iwansuna
asa na yū na ni
sora fuku kaze mo
ochiba goromo no
sode hikima tō
omō tonogo wa tsure na no
minishi
negura ni nokoru ada makura

AIKATA
sate mo migoto ni nā
futte furi komu hana yari wa
yuki ka aranu ka
chira chira chira to
shirotori ge
furesa furesa sode wa hira hira
(ai) daigasa tategasa koikaze ni
nabikanse (ai) zunto nobashite
shanto uketaru yanagigoshi (ai)
shinayari furiyari
nagashi me wa
kawaiyurashisa no
iro no shuku iri

old custom.
The old trees change shape.
The couple, the intimate husband
and wife pines with needles of the
same deep green.
No matter how much I look at
them, my feelings never diminish.
Truly these are the robes of love.

Even if ten thousand *ri* separate
us, I dare to express the longing
of my heart.
In the morning or at night,
the wind blows in the sky and
shrouds my sleeves in the robe of
fallen leaves.
Seeing that the master you long
for does not return your feelings,
your nest remains only memories of
our fleeting affair.

Now on to the spectacle!
Waving about the slower flowered
spears as though it is snowing,
swoosh swoosh,
sleeves flapping everywhere
parasols, umbrellas
bowing to the wind of love that
forcefully opens them
for the Yanagi dancing girls.
The retinue carries feathered
spears. The sensually adorable
courtesans give flirting glances as
they all enter the party house.

AIKATA (*sansangari* tuning)
ODORI JI

matsu no mesho wa	Places famous for their pines are
samazama ni	many.
are Mihō no matsu	The pine of Mihō
Hagoromo no	and Hagorormo's
matsu ni kaketaru	pine, upon which one thinks of the
Onoe no kane yo (*ai*)	bells of Onoe.
ai ni Aioi fūfumatsu (*ai*)	To meet the Aioi-spouse pine,
naka ni midori no	and in the middle is
itoshi rashisa no	the adorable green of the
himekomatsu	"princess" little pine.
nikai sangai goyō no matsu	Two or three five-needle pines.
ikuyo kasanen chiyoigusa	Many generations overlap,
shiorashiya (*ai*)	chrysanthemums so lovely.

CHIRASHI

nishi no umi	The western seas from between
Aoki ga hara no namima yori	the waves of the Aoki Plain.
araware ideshi kamimatsu ni	Out came a deity-pine on which
furitsumu yuki no Asakangata	the snow accumulates, Asaka Bay
tamamo karunaru kishikage no	on the shadowy banks where seaweed
	is gathered.

(*utai gakari*)

shōkon ni yotte koshi o sureba	Using the pine root rubbed
chitose no midori te ni miteri	against your back, one thousand
sasu kaina ni wa	years of green fill your hands.
akuna o harai osamuru	By the hand of the dancer
te niwa jufuku o idaki	evil is banished.
(*ai*)	Another wave of the hand
iri kuru iri kuru	embraces long life and good fortunes.
hana no kaomise klsen no	The flowers reveal their faces.
tamoto	Robes of the high and low
sode o tsuranete sassatu no	interlock their sleeves and flutter.

AIKATA
DANGIRE

koe zo tanoshimu isagiyōya	Voices so elegant and pure.

47

Early-Nineteenth-Century Compositions

1803, 1824	Kairaishi
circa 1820	Matsu no Midori
1820	Oimatsu
1820	Shakkyō
1832	Kokaji
1826, 1854	Fuji Musume
1828	Tomoyakko

Kairaishi, 1803, 1824
"The Street Puppeteer"

Composition: Kineya Saburōtsuke
Text: Sakurada Dai
Recording: NHK 2-9-2
Notation: Bunka, vol. 17

This kabuki dance first appeared with *gekibushi* accompaniment and later *katobushi*. The production of the 1803 version was a *kakeaki*, using *tomimoto* or *kiyomoto* and *nagauta*. Only the *nagauta* music survives, now in an 1824 version. The existing recording is for voice and two shamisen only, and no source has been found for a guide to possible *hayashi* music. While it has not been performed by the Michigan Nagauta Music Study Group, the translation of this interesting early piece is included thanks to Dr. Reinhard Zöllner of the University of Erfurt, Germany. The words were studied in 2004 when he taught a course on Edo period texts at the University of Michigan.

Text. Chinese and Korean street entertainers are found in fourteenth-century accounts, and their arts flourished in the Edo period as well. Thus, the words nishi no umi (western sea) could refer either to an overseas origin of the puppeteers or to the Osaka area. The Ebiso shrine in Nishinomiya was the home of many traveling one-person puppet shows, so they were called Ebisomai (Ebiso dance). The performer hung a miniature stage or flat box before him. Hand puppets were pushed onto the stage from the back and dolls were danced on the flat board. These itinerant street musicians were popular in the late seventeenth century until the more sophisticated bunraku puppets appeared. They remain as kabuki dance versions of Edo period artisans. Other such characters in kabuki are monkey trainers, blind masseur, lion dancers, and manzai comedy teams. Each has its particular music. In this way, the kabuki remains an exotic place for Edo period culture.

As staged in the kabuki, *Kairaishi* may use three actors to perform different parts. Playing rhythmic patterns on the box (*hakotsuzumi*) or some other item, such as a little wooden block, was a common practice among market hawkers (see *Ame no Shiki*, p. 161), storytellers, and singers. (*Kodan* narrators still play such patterns to mark passages in Tokyo theaters.)

Music. A second (*uwajōshi*) shamisen adds color to the *maebiki* and continues throughout the piece.

Oki. The shamisen play a walking rhythm as we learn of life on the open road. The music from "heigemae" on to the end of the *oki* maintains the dialogue style of the original *gekibushi* composition. Declaimed speech (*serifu*) and *ōzatsuma* shamisen dominate the scene (see p. 14). Sung lines are found at "jochū no koe" when a girl calls out and when the puppeteer replies. The music moves toward a cadence. This mixture of declamation and song is typical of pieces that grew out of the narrative *gekibushi* tradition, as well as pieces based on noh (see *Shakkyō*, p. 60).

The text of the *niagari* music for the first puppet is derived from an old popular tune, *Okura odori no uta* (Song of the Okura dance), as is, no doubt, the choreography of the kabuki dancer. The sad text and the music are in the *kudoki* style. The *tataki* pattern (see fig. 12) is heard at "itsuka." It marks a *kudoki* section in *nagauta* form, as does the sad lyrics of the text. "Mountain cat" is a term for a prostitute.

The change in tuning and tempo for the second puppet topic is like an *odori ji.* The opening line is from text found in the first printed shamisen music, the *Matsu no Ha* (1703). As the text wanders off to a description of the puppeteer's family, there are great opportunities for more than one kabuki dancer to mime the portraits. Three actors were mentioned earlier. At "sanin," an *ōzatsuma* declamation is used, but the useless firstborn is described over a sad *tataki* pattern. The next two sons seem to do better musically. The child rides on his shoulders to a bouncy shamisen ostinato. The spinning sound, "maware maware," is matched by the shamisen accompaniment.

The *chirashi* is in the *sansagari* tuning and uses a text derived from the the lighthearted *kyōgen* play tradition that was part of the full performances in noh drama theaters.

At the *honchōshi* opening the singer chants, in noh drama style, the names of two legendary weavers. The words are important because the puppeteer wants to be paid for the show he has given. Note that both the names have the syllable *kure* in them, as this means "to give." In performance, *kureha* sounds like *kureba*, "to pay." The word *mitsugimono* (tribute) is declaimed in *serfu* to make the point clear at the end that more than just the puppets should go back into the box.

MAEBIKI (*honchōshi* tuning)   Length 11'34"

OKI

ukiyo no waza ya, nishi no umi,	In pursuit of the way of the
shio no hiruko no sato hiroku	floating world, one of the many
kuniguni shugyō no kairaishi	puppet players from the home of

tsure ni hanarete yuki no shita
tsubaki ni narabu aoyagi no
shizuku mo karuki harusame ni
gakuya o kamuri tōru ni zo,

Ebisu [Settsu Province] on the
western sea's ebbing tide, who
practice all over the country,
separated from his company,
    wearing his cap amid the light
    spring rain, was passing through
    Kamakura while the blossoms of
    the camellia and green willow
    were dripping like rain.

heigamae e naru mado no uchi
yobikakerarete yukashikumo,
tachidomareba uruwashiki,
jochū no koe nite
Kairaishi, ikkyoku mawase! to
nozomareshi,
kotoba no shita yori toriaezu,
koe ashikeredo.
hakotsuzumi, hyōshi tori-dori
ningyō o amata idashite sore-
zore to utaikeru koso okashireke.

When someone called him from a
lattice window, he stopped
because he was curious. A
maiden's voice requested:
Puppet player, let your puppets
dance to a piece!
As you wish, for the time being,
although my voice is terrible.
Beating the box rhythmically, like
a drum, he took out a lot of
puppets and sang with each in turn.
    It is amusing.

KUDOKI (*niagari* tuning)
Ogura no nobe no hitomoto
susuki itsuka ho ni dete obana to
naraba, tsuyu ga netaman
koigusa no tsumori-tsumorite
ashibiki no yamaneko no o no
naga-naga to hitori kamo nen
sabishisa ni.

In the fields of Ogura, when a
single grain of pampas grass
grew an ear and became a spike,
the dew fell in love with it, and
its lovesickness piled up as high
as a mountain cat's tail, as a
prostitute [mountain cat] is
    desolate in the long nights when
    she sleeps alone.

ODORI JI (*honchōshi* tuning)
Yunbe mukaeshi hanayomesama
wa "kama mo yoku kire chigusa
mo nabiku." Kokoro yosaso na
kamisama ja, (*ai*) ora ga nyōbō o
homura ja nai ga, mono mo yoku
nui, hata mo ori soro,

As for the bride you received
yesterday night, "when the sickle
is sharp, all the plants bend to it."
She seems to be a good-hearted
wife. I don't intend to praise my
wife, but she knows well how to

51

AIKATA
aya ya nishiki ya kinran donsu

sew and weave, even weaving
twill damask and brocade, gold
brocade and satin damask, once
in a while.

MONOGATARI
ori-ori koto no mutsugoto
sannin mochishi kodakara no
sōryō musuko wa ōyō nite, chichi
no mae demo futokorode, mono
o yūtemo henji sezu, niban
musuko wa sei takaku, sanban
musuko wa itazura nite, warusa-
zakari no mutsu nanatsu naka de
itoshiki chi no amari,

And while exchanging whispered
intimacies, we got three children.
The heir apparent is so liberal
he never bothers doing anything,
even for his father, and never
answers when told something.
Our second son is tall. Our third
son is in the midst of his
mischievous, evil-bearing six, seven
years and abounds with energy.

Kata ni uchinosete miyako no
meisho maware-maware!
Kazaguruma (*ai*) hariko katsuko
ya furitsuzumi (*ai*) ne ni motte
asobesa.

Give me a ride on your shoulders
and a tour of the famous spots of
the capital! A spinning pin-
wheel and a paper drum and a
rattle drum in my hands, let's play!

CHIRASHI (*sansagari* tuning)
hana ga mitakuba Yoshino e
gozare, ima wa Yoshino no
hanazakari, yoisa-yoisa,
hanazakari, hanagasa kitsure
shana-shana to.

If you want to see the cherry
blossoms, go to Yoshino. Just
now Yoshino is flourishing, yoisa-
yoisa, wear a flower hat,
shana-shana.

(*honchōshi* tuning)
Kono hashita wa suizutsu o
tamoto ni makite karatama ya,
tsui akirakeki amatsusora,
sakura-gumori ni kyō no hi mo,
sakura-gumori ni kyō no hi mo,

This servant rolls a water bottle
into her sleeve and a Chinese
jewel. The sky is clear at last on
this day once more clouded with
cherry blossoms. When the sun sets
on this day once more clouded
with cherry blossoms.

UTAIGAKARI
Kureha Ayaha no tori-dori ni,
Kureha Ayaha no tori-dori no

What a blessed age it was when
the weavers, Kureha and Ayaha,

mitsugimono sonauru miyo koso medetakere to	collected tribute in appreciation.

DANGIRE

hako no uchi nizo osamekeru.	He puts things back into the box.

·ᴗ ᴗ·

Matsu no Midori, circa 1820
"The Green Pine Tree"

Composer: Kineya Rokusaburō IV
Text: Unknown
Recording: Columbia COCF 70107, 70110; NHK 1-1-1
Notation: Bunka 3302; Kineya 1; Yoshizumi 1955, vol. 2

BOOK CD: 2–4

Performers: singer, Nishigaki Yūzō; shamisen, Kineya Yasaburō, Kikuoka Hiroaki

One of the best-known *nagauta*, this piece is a part of neither the kabuki nor the classical dance world (*buyō*). Its fame comes from the fact that every kabuki actor has to learn to play and sing it when in training. It remains a fine piece for beginners. It was originally written in honor of the daughter of the composer, who had just acquired a professional shamisen name in the Kineya school.

Because of the shortness of the piece, the words and music are discussed together.

The *maebiki* is said to represent the wind in the pines. The word *nao* in the second phrase was supposed to have been sung in the style of an older *sonohachi* shamisen genre. The text is filled with references to the Yoshiwara floating world where geishas also receive ranks as they mature. The "figure-eight walk" is a famous geisha movement. It is still seen in kabuki scenes such as the entrance of Agemaki in the play *Sukeroku*. The *geta* shoes are so high that the geisha has to hold onto shoulder of a male servant and drag one foot around the other in order to walk. If *hayashi* is used in a performance, the *taiko* plays the Yoshiwara-related pattern *wataribyōshi* (see fig. 17). Some performances have used the noh drama *tsuzumi* pattern for the opening section to give the music a sense of formality. Another arrangement is to add just the bamboo flute to the entire piece. Only one singer and shamisen are heard on the book CD. This best illustrates the lyrical beauty of *nagauta*, especially since the singer, Nishigaki Yūzō, and the first shamisen, Kikuoka Hiroko, were the author's teachers.

(*honchōshi* tuning)

kotoshi yori	Length 7'50"
chitabi mukauru	This year
harugoto ni	greets its thousandth spring,
nao mo fukame ni	and each year
matsu no midori ka	still deeper is the green of the pine.
kamuro no na aru	"Green" an apprentice geisha's name
futaba no iro ni	the color of young pine needles
taifu no kaze no fukikayō (*ai*)	through which blows the air
matsu no kuraru no	of the rank of "pine",
soto-hachimonji	with her "figure-eight" walk
hade o misetaru kedashi-zuma	gorgeously exposing her attractive underskirt.
yō nita matsu no neagari mo	Its silhouette calls to mind a pine's surface roots
hitotsu kakohi no (*ai*)	escaping through the single layer of
magaki ni moruru (*ai*)	the surrounding pale [fence].
sato wa nebiki no besseikai (*ai*)	The [Yoshiwara] quarter is an
yoyo no makoto to ura omote	uprooted world unto itself.
	Its truths are the opposite of the other world's.
kurabe goshinaru tsutsuru,	Comparing heights
furiwakegami mo itsuishika ni	by the well side—
oi to naru made suehiro o	a young girl's hairdo, too, will someday, as she grows older, spread out like a fan newly opened.
hiraki sometaru nakoso shuku-seme	Let us celebrate the newly opened name.

Oimatsu, 1820
"The Old Pine Tree"

Composer: Kineya Rokuzaemon IX
Text: Unknown
Recording: Columbia COCF 70102, NHK 1-1-3
Notation: Bunka 3306; Kineya 12; Yoshizumi, vol. 2

Text. Oimatsu shares with *Shakkyō* the role of being the first concert, vis-à-vis dance, to accompany *nagauta* compositions. The title and first text are derived from an earlier noh drama. The same title appears in other shamisen genres, but the text and style differ as the *nagauta* piece was written for a concert in honor of the composer's eighty-year-old mother. In Japan, the pine tree is a symbol of age and eternal freshness. Like the text of *Takasago Tanzen* (p. 44), images about old trees and longevity from classical poetry and noh drama texts dominate much of the piece. The reference to the Akama inkstone reflects that style. Stone from Akama is used to make inkstones, but the previous text about scenery viewing links the word to the scenery at the Akama Barrier.

Music. If *hayashi* are used in a performance, the *shidai* is prefaced by the sound of the *tsuzumi* and a long "yo" from the drummers in noh drama style. These set the mood of the opening. The first lines are then chanted in noh *utai* fashion. They are quoted from the original noh drama opening. The *michiyuki* adds *hayashi* to support the noh atmosphere.

The *hayashi* remain in that style until "tsungaru ru." The *nōkan* returns at "iroka ni" to enhamce the mood of dream-filled sleep. The *tsuzumi* return in noh style at "mazu" until the word "wind" (*kazu*). Here the shamisen and *ko tsuzumi* "blow" the wind with repeated notes. The drums then turn to kabuki style patterns until the change of tuning.

The *kudoki* uses only shamisen and bamboo flute accompaniment. The *tataki* pattern (see fig. 12, p. 15) is heard at the words "tada tawaji." The change of scene to courtly dance leads to an *aikata*. The *hayashi* under the shamisen melody are actually derived from two sections (*dan*) of a noh drama dance called *Kagura mai*. The term *kagura* is used for sacred Shinto music. This mixture to two idioms is found in many noh-derived *nagauta* (for example *Kanjincho* and *Tsuru Kame*).

The change of tuning and topic in the *odori ji* are curious in a composition dedicated to an aging mother and were criticized in reviews. For example, the flirting, secret meeting, and the green color of the pine tree "matsu no iro" that could stand for young lovers.

The *hayashi* provides typical conventions for an *odori ji* section. The *taiko* and noh flute play the *wataribyoshi* pattern (see p. 18). They are followed by *tsuzumi chiri kara* rhythms and the bamboo flute. The same call and response patterns that follow between the *taiko* and *tsuzumi* can be heard in the *odori ji* of *Gorō Tokimune*, p. 107. The change of the text to the classical crane and tortoise image beings the *tsuzumi* back to noh drama style (compare to *Tsuru Kame*, p. 118). The wind in the pines is depicted by a long dialogue between the main shamisen and a second, independent *uwajoshi* part. The *chirashi* has a typical full orchestration with the noh flute marking the end of the *dangire*.

OKIUTA SHIDAI (*honchōshi* tuning)	Length 18'56"
ge ni osamareru yomo no kuni	Truly peace is found in all directions of the country.
ge ni osamareru yomo no kuni	Truly peace is found in all directions of the country.
seki no to sasade kayohan	The road barrier gates are open.
kore wa oiki no kamimatsu no	This is the ancient sacred pine, having
chiyo ni yachiyo ni sazare ishi no	lasted for 1,008 years until
I wao to narite koke no musu made	pebbles became rocks overgrown with moss.

MICHIYUKI

matsu no hairo mo toki mekite	The color of the pine needles befits the
tokaeri fukaki midori no uchi	seasons and deepens over the centuries.
nemureru yume no hayasamete	Waking up too soon from dream-filled
iroka ni fukeshi hana mo sugi	sleep, the color and fragrance of flowers
tsuki ni usofuki mi wa tsunagaruru (*ai*)	have blown past and entangle with the moon.
itotake no en hikarete	Pulled by the sound of strings and winds
utsura utsura to chōsei no	gently, gently one feels as if one were
izumi o kumeru kokochi seri	dipping a drink from the spring of long life.
mazu shadan no kata o mite areba	The eye that surveys the shrine with awe

kita ni gagataru seizan ni

sees to the north a steep blue mountain

irodoru kumo no tanabikite

covered with crags and colored clouds

kaze ni hirari hirameki wataru konata niwa (*ai*)

blown by the wind,

suichō kōkei no yosōi mukashi o warurezu

fluttering over you the green and red ornaments recalling past days.

migi ni kodera no kyūseki ari (*ai*)

To the right one sees the remains of the

shinshō sekibon no hibiki

old temple. Morning and evenings the

tayuru kotonaki nagame sae

tolling of the bell never ceases.

akamasuzuri no fude zusami

Let the brush flow freely on the Akama

koko ni tsukusa o shirushi keri

inkstone, placing here the official mark.

KUDOKI (*niagari* tuning)

matsu to iu monji wa kawaredo matsu

The character for "pine" (*matsu*) can be

koto no ha no (*ai*)

changed to the word "to wait."

sono kai arite tsumitoshi ni (*ai*)

Celebrating long life

kotobuki iwau tokiwagi no

with continual fresh music

shirabe zo tsuzuku Takasago no naru

in Takasago,

hotori ni Sumiyoshi no

there grows at Sumiyoshi,

matsu no oiki mo

an old pine tree that tells tales of youth

wakaki o kataru hazukashisa

shyly of everlasting fidelity.

tada kawaraji to fukamidori

The wonderful age of two pines growing

ureshiki yoyo ni aioi no

together with limitless memories of ages

ikuse no omoi kagiri shirarezu

past.

yorokobi mo kotowari zokashi

How happy is our life forever and ever.

itsu made mo

The pure, measured, sacred,

kiyo isame no kami kagura

bugaku o sonaru kono ie ni

and courtly dance musics sound in this house [temple].

koe mo michitatsu arigataya

Voices fill the air with thanks.

AIKATA

ODORI JI (*sansagari* tuning)

(*kagura* dance)

matsu no tayū no uchikake wa	The outer robe of the courtesan named
tsurū no moyō ni, fuji iro mo	Matsu ["pine"] has an ivy pattern in purple color.
itoshi kawai mo minamina otoko wa	"It is adorable," says every man.
itsuwari jamono (*ai*)	"It's all lies," she replies
tsunete misete mo sonomama yosoe	as she flirts with one man and then is off to see another.
aruyo hisoki ni tsuki ai no	Some nights they meet secretly, calling
kumo no magaki no kake kotoba (*ai*)	out across a wicker fence on a cloudy
e, e nikurashii kogakure ni	night. He says, "How pitiful" from his hiding place behind a tree.
harete au hi o matsu no iro	Meeting on a sunny day, green as the pine tree
yutaka ni asobu, tsuru kame no	playing to their hearts' content, the crane
yowai o sazukuru konokimi no	and tortoise bring long life to our
yukusue mamore to waga shintaku no	emperor and protect him in the divine order.
tsuge o shirasuru matsu no kaze	The wind in the pines is the voice of the gods.

CHIRASHI

fūkijizai no hanei mo	Wealth and status, glory and success.

DANGIRE

hisashiki yado haru koso	May this eternal house always prosper.
medetakere	

·⁔ ⌣⁓

Shakkyō, 1820

"The Stone Bridge"

Composer: Kineya Saburōsuke IV
Text: Noh drama
Recordings: NHK 1-2-12; Columbia COCF 70103
Notation: Bunka 3350; Yoshizumi, vol. 4

This is considered to be one of the first *nagauta* concert pieces (*ozashiki*) vis-à-vis dance accompaniment music. It is often called *gekibushi shakkyō* because dialogue sections are accompanied by *ōsatuma* patterns (see p. 15), derived in this case from another shamisen music genre called *gekibushi*. The 1878 *Shin Shakkyō* (New Shakkyō) by Kineya Shōjirō is an expansion of the characters in his 1872 *Renjishi* from two lions to three!

A comparison of the noh and 1820 *nagauta* versions of *Shakkyō* can be found in Malm 1986. Another possible comparison is between the *Shakkyō* translation and Kineya Katsusaburō's *Renjishi* (1861), also translated in this anthology (p. 141).

Since the text is claimed to be derived directly from noh, the formal divisions of the noh play (*nanori*, *issei*, and so on) along with kabuki dance terms (*aikata*) are used. The division of lines among the noh drama performers (*shite*, *waki*, and *ji*) are also shown, although they vary with the performance of the *nagauta* composition. Recall that this is a concert not a theater piece.

In some performances, a noh flute plays a prelude to set the mood. The entire *nanori oki* section is sung unaccompanied in noh singing style (*utaigakari*). The *issei* is performed by shamisen and voice without percussion. The interlude that follows brings in the noh-style drumming and flute. This would be the *michiyuki* entrance music in either *nagauta* or noh. As it would in the *sageuta* in the original noh drama or at the end of the *michiyuki* in *nagauta*, the *hayashi* drops out. The *ageuta* text is set as a lyrical *kudoki*. On the word *matsu* (pine), the voice and shamisen wave in the wind. They also extend the syllable *higeshiki* (precipitous) as the woodsman moves along the narrow path.

The *mondō* dialogue is supported by *ōzatsuma* patterns, the singer imitating a noh drama dialogue. The comment "staying only half a day as a guest" comes from the noh drama *Kantan* in which a monk sleeps on a magic pillow while waiting for food at an inn. He dreams of twenty-five years of power and glory but is awakened by a call to eat. The experience leads him to enlightenment. The story appears in several koto and shamisen genres.

The *kuri* begins with standard *ōzatsuma* patterns (see p. 15 and *Gorō*, p. 107). It then returns to normal melodic style with *tsuzumi* and noh flute as mood support. When the *sashi* begins at "sono hoka," the drums turn to kabuki-style *chiri kara* as the text becomes more dramatic and deals with the dangerous path over the high canyon. The shamisen plays dotted rhythm, uses the "dangerous" B-flat pitch, and even slides when the slippery path (*ashi mo tamarazu*) is mentioned. Later it slides down a chromatic scale to evoke the deep abyss (*senjō tomo*). The shamisen and drums play a short, two-note call-and-response to represent an echo in the canyon. Such an echo drum pattern (*kodama*) is a standard in kabuki mountain scenes. As we speed through the history of bridges, the texture becomes thicker and the tempo faster. In the interlude after "nareba," the *uwajōshi* shamisen plays a fast, high, repeating note to intensify the drama of the scene.

All this leads to the most unusual *hayashi* interludes in the genre. They are discussed in detail in Malm 1986. Time seems to move with the tension of a rubber band that suddenly snaps. Then all sound is reduced to a single *ko tsuzumi* sound, silence, and a *taiko* response. It is probably the most challenging passage to play in the whole drum repertory. This is followed by a dramatic, full *hayashi* section. After a *taiko* cadence, two shamisen lines join in to accompany the lion, which in dance performances is in a grand costume with a flowing white mane.

The *chirashi* is filled with noh drum patterns, a busy shamisen part, and words pouring past. One can picture the lion's fierce pose (*mie*) when the *dangire* cadence closes a powerful piece.

In thirty-four years, the Michigan Japanese Music Study Group played this piece only once. It was not the busy music that challenged us but the moments of silence.

UTAIGAKARI, NANORI

OKI (*honchōshi* tuning) — Length 26'8"

waki

kore wa Oe no Sadamoto shukke shi	I am the dharma master Jakushō, who
Jakushō Hōshi nite sōrō	left home as Oeōe no Sadamoto
ware nittō toten no nozomi sōraite	with the hope of entering China and
hatō o koe	crossing to India. I have passed over the
kore wa haya	billowy waves, and have now
Shakkyō nite sōrō	arrived at the Stone Bridge.
mukai wa Monju no jōdo Seiryōsan	Mount Qingliang of Manjusri's Pure
nite sōrō hodo ni	Land is on the other side.
kono atari ni yasurai	I think that I shall cross over
hashi o watarabaya to omoi sōrō	this bridge after I rest here awhile.

Early-Nineteenth-Century Compositions

ISSEI
shite

matsukaze no	A pine wind blows against my firewood,
hana o takigi ni fukisoete	frosting it with cherry blossoms, on the
yuki o mo hakobu yamaji kana	mountain path, where I even carry snow.

AIKATA (*michiyuki*)
ISSEI

shōka bokuteki no ko	Sounds of a woodcutter's song and a herd boy's flute.
ningen banji samazama ni	The karma of humans is to pass
yo o watariyuki waza nagara	through a world where there is every kind of lifestyle and destiny.

SAGEUTA

| amari ni yama o tōku kite | Having come quite far through the mountains, |
| kumo mata ato o tachidate | where clouds have formed, veiling, my footprints. |

AGEUTA

iritsuru kata mo	I do not know the way I have come.
shiranami no tani no kawaoto	I hear the rushing water in the valley
ame tonomi	only as rain.
kikoete matsu no kaze mo nashi	Even the sound of the wind in the pines cannot be heard.
ge ni ayamatte	Truly I had been lost.
hanjitsu no kaku tarishi mo	Though a guest for only half a day,
ima mi no ue ni shiraretsutsu	now I am enlightened.
tsumagi seoute	Carrying brushwood on my back and
ono katage,	shouldering an ax,
iwane hageshiki	I go along a precipitous place
sobatsutai	where the crags below are severe.
ozoasa o wakete ayumi kuru	Parting bamboo grasses, I have arrived.

MONDŌ
waki

| ika ni sore naru yamabito | Hello, mountain dweller. |

kore wa shakkyō nite sōrō yo	Is this the Stone Bridge?
shite	
san zōrō kore wa shakkyō nite sōrō	It is so. This is indeed the Stone Bridge.
yo, mukai wa Monju no jōdo nite,	On the other side is the Pure Land Manjusri.
Seiryōsan to zo mōsu nari	It is called Mount Qingliang.
yokuyoku on ogami sorae	You would do well to pay your respects.
waga mi no ue o butsuryo ni makase	Even renowned high and venerable
hashi o watarabaya to omio sōrō	priests thinking of crossing the
shibaraku sōrō sono kami naru	bridge have spent days and months
nao etamaishi kōsō	here performing acts of austerity,
kisō to kikoeshi hito mo koto nite	penance, and relinquishing the body.
tsukihi o okuri tamai	
nangyō kugyō shashin no gyō nitte	Only then did they cross the bridge.
koso hashi, o mo watari tamaishi ga	But, as they say, even if a lion eats a
shishi wa kochū o haman tote mo	small insect, he first prepares himself to do so.
mazu ikioi o nasu to koso kike	If you were to have dharma powers, you
waga hōriki no areba tote,	probably would think it easy to cross, but
tayasuku omoi wataran koto,	what a precarious act it would be.
ara ayōshi no on koto ya	
iware o kikeba arigata ya	Now that I've heard the story, this
waki	
naonao kono hashi no iware	bridge is really extraordinary.
kusashiku on monogatari shōrae ya	Tell me more particulars about the history of the bridge.
shite	
katatte kikase mōsubeshi	I shall tell you the story.

KURI

ji

sore, tenchi kaikyaku no kono kata	The bridge has been here since the first
uro o kudashite kokudo o wataru	parting of heaven and earth. Coming
kore sunawachi ame no ukihashi	down through the rain and dew, it
tomo ieri	crosses the country and so is also called the floating bridge of heaven.

63

SASHI

shite

sono hoka kokudo sekai ni oite	Elsewhere in the country and the world
hashi no nadokoro samazama ni shite	there are all sorts of famous bridge sites.

ji

suiha no nan o nogarete wa, banmin	It may indeed be due to the goodness of
tomeri yo o wataru mo	bridges that many people are able to
sunawachi hashi no toku to ka ya	escape from drowning in water and waves and pass safely across the bountiful world.

KUSE

shikaru ni kono shakkyō wa iwao	However, because this stone bridge is one
gagataru genseki ni onore to	that hangs by itself on the crags and rocks,
kakaru hashi nareba	jagged and towering high,
shakkyō to koso nazuketare ge ni	it has been named Stone Bridge.
kono hashi no arisama wa,	The conditions of the bridge are truly
sono omote wazuka ni shite,	severe.
shaku yori wa semau	Its surface is small, narrower than a foot.
wataseru nagasa sanjō amari	It spans a distance of more than thirty feet.
koke wa namerite	The moss upon it is slippery so that
ashi mo tamarazu (*ai*)	one's feet cannot rest firmly, and
tani no sokubaku fukai koto sū	the abyss of the canyon seems to be
senjō tomo oboetari	more than ten thousand feet deep.

shite

haruka ni mine o miagureba (*ai*)	When the peaks are viewed from a distance

ji

kumo yori otsuru aradaki ni (*ai*)	the mist is murky and dark.
kiri mōrō to kurau shite	All around, the wild waterfalls are
shita wa nairi mo shiranami no,	descending from the clouds.
oto wa arashi ni hibiki aite	The sound of white waves reverberate in the tempest.

kokū o wataru ga gotoku nari,	It seems to be hell down below.
hashi no keshiki o miwataseba,	It is like crossing an empty space.
kumo ni sobiyuru yosōi wa,	On looking over the scene of the bridge,
tatowaba sekiyō no ame no nochi	its array, which soars into the clouds,
niji o naseru sono katachi mata	is like the form rainbows take after a rain
yumi o hikeru gotoku nite	at even tide, or the shape of a drawn bow.
jinpen butsuriki no arazu shite	Without the permutations of a god or the
susunde hito ya wataru beki	powers of a buddha, who will advance and
mukai wa Monju no jōdo nite	cross over? On the other side is the Pure Land of Manjusri,
tsune ni seiga no hana furite	flowers continue to fall, accompanied by mouth organ songs.
shōkin kugo yūhi no	Panpipes (shō), zithers (kin), and harps (kugo) are heard
kumo ni kikoyu beki	from beyond the clouds around the
mokuzen no kidoku arata nari	evening sun. It is an auspicious miracle before our eyes.
shibaraku matase tame ya	Wait awhile. Perhaps even the time for a
yōgō no jisetsu mo ima iku hodo ni	heavenly apparition (of Manjusri)
yo mo sugiji	will be coming fairly soon.
RAIJO RANJO AIKATA KURI AIKATA CHIRASHI (KIRI)	(hayashi interlude) (lion dance [shishi mai])
ji	
shishi toraden no bugaku no migin	The season for the lion and Toraden music and dance.
shishi toraden no bugaku no migin	The season for the lion and Toraden music and dance.
botan no hanabusa nioi michi michi	Peony blooms full, full, with fragrance.
taikin rikin no shishigashira	The lion's head with great muscular
ute ya hayase ya	strength—
botanbō, botanbō	Peony perfume, peony perfume.
kōkin no zui arawarete	The stamina of golden yellow coming
hana ni tawamure	forth, [the lion] frolicking in the

eda ni fushi

ge ni mo ue naki shishi ō no ikioi

nabikanu kusaki mo

naki toki nare ya

banzei senshū to mai osame

bansei senshū to mai osame

DANGIRE

shishi no za ni koso naorikere

flowers, lies down and rolls in the branches.

The authority of the Lion King is truly unsurpassed.

Indeed, it is a time when all the plants and trees bow to it.

For a myriad harvests and a thousand autumns, he perfects his dance,

For a myriad harvests and a thousand autumns, he perfects his dance,

and he seats himself on the Lion Throne.

Kokaji, 1832
"Kokaji"

Composer: Kineya Katsugorō (I or II)
Text: Geki Shinsen
Recording: NHK I-15-1
Notation: Bunka 3307; Yoshizumi, vol. 1

Based on a noh drama *Kokaji*, this story is about a swordsmith from Sanjō named Kokaji. In making a sword for the Emperor Ichijō, he succeeds through the spirit of the Shinto god Inari. It is unknown whether the composer was the first- or second-generation Katsugorō. There is a *Kokaji* in the *itchūbushi* shamisen genre and two more in *nagauta*, *Imayo kokaji* (1852) and *Shin kokaji* (1864). The 1852 composition was used for a new kabuki production in 1939. The original text is certainly germane to the Japanese military interests of that time. Today the piece appears in dance concerts, often using two or three dancers. Such a performance practice in amateur recitals is practical for both choreographic and financial reasons as the cost costumes and dressers, plus a full ensemble onstage, is high. The text of *Kokaji* may vary depending on the school of dance using it. Both the music and the dance are conventional, and the text is obvious in its content. *Kokaji* provides a clear example of the conventions in Japanese dance music.

Oki. The opening solo song, called a *tsuzumi uta* (see p. 30), is accompanied by occasional drum and drum-call sounds. The shamisen enters after "kogitsune," and the *tsuzumi* briefly play noh patterns.

Michiyuki. The full ensemble enters, all playing the rhythms of what must be those of the dance movements. This is clearly helpful to beginning dancers. An ostinato shamisen and *chiri kara tsuzumi* patterns support the first phrase, "In China," up to an *ōzatsuma* cadence. The tale is in the tonal area of narrative (i.e., F-sharp) with a steady beat in the shamisen and *tsuzumi*. The word *blacksmith* (*kana takumi*) is declaimed (*serifu*). The same support of rhythm remains throughout the section and continues in the long *aikata* that follows along with an *uwajōshi* ostinato shamisen. It would be hard for a young dancer to get lost.

After *sore moro*, the *hayashi* enters in noh drama patterns and includes the noh flute. It continues in that style until "kana to ko ni." The next *aikata* (called *kuru*) is faster and uses shamisen and *tsuzumi* in kabuki style. Stops and other changes in rhythm relate to the movements in the dance.

A *taiko* enters with its "ten ten," which usually signals the beginning of a *chirashi* section that uses full *hayashi* in noh style and contains much text. A *dangire* follows for the final pose.

OKI (*honchōshi* tuning)   Length 12'27"

TSUZUMU UTA

Inariyama, mitsu no	On Mount Inari the three torches
tomoshibi	burn brightly; the ways of the
akiraka ni, kokoro o migaku,	blacksmith refine the heart.
kaji no michi	The name of the sword called
Kogitsune-maru to, sue no yo	Kogitsune-maru will remain
ni	esteemed throughout the
nokosu sono na zo, ichijiruki	ages to come.

MICHIYUKI

Sore morokoshi ni	In China, as it is told . . .
tsutau kiku, ryūsen taia wa	Lung-cuan and Tai-a
iza shirazu, (*ai*) waga hi no moto	knew nothing of the
no	blacksmiths of
kana takumi	our land of the rising sun,
ama kuni ama noza	striking with the power of the
jinzoku ga	fox deity. With the clashing of
kokkachin gono tsuru nimo	swords, the foe was cut to
masariwa surutomo otorajito	bits. The word of such
kami no chikara no aizuchi o	inspiring feats.
utsuya chōchō shite korori (*ai*)	when forging a sword or beating out
	linen garments
yoso ni kikusae isamashiki	on a cold night, the sound of

AIKATA

utsu to yū, sore wa yosamu	striking the block, carries into
no asagoromo. (*ai*)	the distance. The thought
ochi no kinuta mo oto soete,	of "striking" reminds one of
ya utsutsu no, utsu no yama (*ai*)	the mountain of Utsu.
hina mo miyako mo aki	In the countryside, as well as
fukete	in the capital, in the late
furu ya chigure no hatsu mo	autumn, the early red maples
migi	falling in the rain, leave a
congaruru iro kana to ko ni	blaze of color on the anvil.

AIKATA
CHIRASHI
hikagen yukagen, himitsu no
daiji,
yakiba watashi wa, inyō wagō,
tsuyu nimo nurete, utsu
momiji,
somete iro masu, kanairo wa
shimoyo no tsuki to
sumi masaru,
tegara no hodo zo, tagui naki
(ai)
seiko rin rin (ai)
uruwashiki, wakate no
wazamono, kiremono to (ai)

DANGIRE
yomo ni sono nawa
hibikikeri

The temperatures of the water
and the fire are guarded
secrets; to forge a tempered
blade is to unite opposing
forces; even when the dew
dampens the pale red maples,
it turns them into the color of
red iron, and the moon on a
frosty night becomes clear;
such rare feats are beyond compare.
A delicate, awe-inspiring
elegance of the sharp-edged
young blade.

Its name has been heard in all
directions.

Fuji Musume 1826, 1854
"The Wisteria Maiden"

Music: Kineya Rokusaburo IV
Text: Katsui Gompachi
Recordings: Columbia CD COCF-70104; NHK 2-190-2
Video: DVD of dance, SHV DA 0204
Notation: Bunka 3347; Kineya 77

Originally one of a series of dances to be done in order by one actor, *Fuji Musume* has survived as a perennial solo kabuki and classical dance piece. The text of the kabuki version and comments on the complexities of the text and the dance movements are found in Brandon 2002 169. Given the lyricism of the dance, it is sometimes performed as a *kakeai*, that is, using both *nagauta* and *kiyomoto* music. The *itako odori* section was added by the actor Onoe Kikugoro VI (1800–1886) and is often heard in dance recitals. It also can be replaced by yet another folk-based "Wisteria Dance" (*Fuji Ondo*). This translation only includes the original insertion.

Text. The term *Otsue* (Otsu pictures) is sometimes included in the title of the dance for two reasons. First, the village of Otsu, near Lake Biwa, was in the original name of the kabuki production. Second, the region was famous for its pictures, which were sold as souvenirs and seen in well-known woodblock prints such as *Eight Famous Views of Omi.* One wonders how knowledgeable kabuki audiences were about all the double meanings that the writers and performers must have enjoyed. Perhaps copies of the pictures were used as part of the original scenery to explain the different characters the actor represented (a maiden, blind man, footman, boatman, and calligraphy god). Today only the sad maiden scene remains, but the text maintains an ambiguity that a musicologist is not qualified to explain. A few examples must suffice. The opening line locates the listener in the Osaka area often called Naniwa. The word also could mean "sad flower" or refer to a local narrative tradition (*naniwa bushi*) that is still performed there today. The names of places seen in the prints are laced throughout the text. The mountains are obvious. Karasaki village is less clear. It was pictured in the woodblock prints and has the famous pine tree mentioned earlier. The village name becomes a pivot word, for *utsusemi no kara* is the cicada shell and *kara* also is the first syllable of Karasaki. The opening phrase of the *odori ji* relates to an Arima song tradition that is found in the earliest shamisen text collection (*Matsu no Ha*, 1703), although this text is not used. The term *kouta kakari* (*kouta* style) is found in some printings of the text, as is the term *tsuzumi uta*. That drum was used frequently in geisha houses.

Music. The form and orchestration of *Fuji Musume* are excellent examples of the conventions of the kabuki dance form. A kabuki precurtain (*makimae*) piece called *shiagari* is heard before the actual piece begins. The *oki* uses only shamisen and a singer. The short *tsuzumi uta* begins with one stroke on the *tsuzumi* drums and a drum call, "yoo." This is a standard opening for music in the noh drama style in *nagauta*. The singer chants the first line solo in that style. The first poetic figure is "serious," but its second line, "hana o," is performed by the singer and shamisen in a style that led to text and topics for a dance set in eighteenth-century Edo. The entrance music of the *michiyuki* adds the *taiko* and noh flute playing *wataribyōshi* patterns (fig. 17) enchanced by the *kane* (hand gong). When the singer reenters, the percussion changes to yet another standard pattern, *bungo sagari ha* (fig. 19) Carrying a wisteria branch implies a leaf-viewing promenade, so the soft sound of a festival gong is added. This string of standard signals supports the mood of the music. At the Yoshiwara slang term "shongai nai," the percussion drops out and the first screen images appear. The shamisen *tataki* patterns (fig. 12) mark the start of the lyrical, sad *kudoki* section.

The inserted dance (*itako*) consists of four verses plus a refrain as in folk music. The text may differ for different schools of dance. The basic orchestration is for voice and shamisen alone. However, it may be changed for each verse. In the Columbia recording, the first verse adds a bamboo flute, the second uses only *tsuzumi* drums, the third uses the flute, and the fourth uses the flute, *tsuzumi,* and hand gong.

A faster shamisen interlude (*ai*) provides time for another costume change. The *odori ji* orchestration follows the typical progression of two exchanges between the *taiko* and flute sections and those of the *tsuzumi* drums and then a combination of all by the last phrase (see *Gorō*, p. 107). A *chirashi* section barely exists, with only one line of text, followed by the equally short *dangire*. They are also unusual in that only the shamisen and singer appear. In either dance or kabuki performances, there usually is a percussion postlude after the curtain closes.

Oĸɪ (*sansagari* tuning)	Length 27'40"
tsuno kuni no Naniwa no haru wa	Spring dreams from the singers of
yume nareya	Tsuno,
haya hatatose no tsukihana o	viewing decades of moon and flowers in
tagameshi fude no irodori mo	color drawings. Prints completely
kakitsuku sarenu kazu kazu ni,	piled like mountains of excellent

71

yama mo nishiki no ori o ete
kokyō e kazaru sode tamoto.

brocade. Returning home with a print
in the bag of one's sleeve.

TSUZUMI UTA

waka murasaki ni togaeri no
hana o arawasu matsu no fuji nami.

The waves of wisteria twisted around
the pine branch are like the pine
flowers that bloom only once every
hundred years.

MICHIYUKI

hitome seki kasa nurigasa shanto
furikatagetaru hito eda wa

A painted lacquer hat carefully
conceals the young woman's face from
prying eyes.

murasaki fukaki suido no mizu ni
somete ureshiki, yukari no iro no
itoshi to kaite, fuji no hana
ee, shongai na
suso mo hora hora
shidokenaku

Dyed the purple shade of deep Edo
channels, a branch of wisteria flowers
drapes over her shoulder.
Saying "It can't be helped,"
her skirt flaps open,
and she does not trouble to fix it.

AIKATA

kagamiyama hito no, shiga yori
kono mi no shiga o kaerimiru me no
shio naki umi ni, musume sugata no
hazukashiya

Rather than reflecting on the faults
of the people of Mirror Mountain,
one should reflect on one's own faults
entangled like the seaweed of Lake
Biwa. Oh, how disgraceful the
maiden's disarray.

KUDOKI

otokogokoro no nikui no wa,
hoka no onago ni kami kakete
awazu to mii nokanegoto mo
katai chikai no Ishiyama ni
mi wa utsusemi no karasaki ya
matsuyo o yoso ni,

The hateful thing about a man is that,
although he vows not to meet
with other women and the
marriage is as firm and certain as
Mount Rock, he is, after all, untrue.
I feel as empty as the discarded shell
of a cicada.

Hira no yuki tokete ōse no
ata netamashii yō mono seta n
i washi ya, noserarete

The nights I spent waiting for you,
you spent elsewhere. How jealous I am
when the snows of Hira melt and
you are able to meet her.

fumimo katata no katadayori

How cleverly you have used me. I send
you letters but there is no response.

kokoro yabase no kakochigoto	My heart's complaints leap to my tongue.

ITAKO ODORI (*honchōshi* tuning)

Itako dejima no makomo no naka de	In the port of Itako there are among
ayame saku towa,	the water oats the blooming of
shiorashiya	sweet iris. Oh, how beautiful.
sa yon, ya sa yon ya sa	Row on, row on.
Uji no shibafune hayase wo wataru	The brushwood boat from Fuji (Uji) passing through the swift current.
watasha kimi yue, noborifune	I, for you, would ride the boat
sa yoi ya sa yoi ya sa	upstream. Row on, row on.
hana wa iro iro gojshiki ni ukedo	The flowers' colors come in five types.
nushi ni mikaeru hana wa nai	One can't prefer one from above another.
sa yoi ya sa yoi yasa (*ai*)	Row on.
shina mo yoya hana ni ukarete ichi odori	Liking them all, a dancer floats among the flowers.
sa yoi ya sa yoi ya sa (*ai*)	Row on, row on.
(Other version)	
(hana o hitomo to wasurete kitaga	(Intoxicated by the flowers,
ato de sakuyara chiraku yara)	people dance beautifully).

ODORI JI (*kouta kakari*)

matsu o ueyo nara	If you plant a pine, plant it at
Arima no sato e uesanse	the village of Arima.
itsumademo kawaranu chigiri, kaidori	We will travel together with the hems
tsuma de yoretsu moretsu	of our kimonos tucked up out of
mada ne ga taranu.	the muddy road,
yoi emakura no mada ne ga taranu	our eternal pledge unchanging.
fuji ni makarete ne to gozaru	As we cling to each other,
aa, nanto shō ka	I feel our time together is too short.
dosōi yokai na	On the soft pillow, still, it is not
washi go komakura otemakura	enough. Ah, what can we do, what can be done? My hands serve as a pillow.

CHIRASHI, DANGIRE

sora mo kasumi no yuderi ni	The geese return home despondently
nagori o oshimu kaeru karigane.	across the hazy sky in the evening rays.

．．－'

Tomoyakko, 1828
"The Worthy Footman"

Composer: Kineya Saburōtsuke IV
Text: Segawa Jokō
Recordings: Columbia COOF 70120; Toshiba TOCF 4008
Notation: Bunka 3334

The piece is one part of a famous *hengemono* in which the actor changes character and costume seven times. It became popular as part of dance recitals. Statues of a little footman posing with his lantern (*chōchin*) are found in souvenir and dance accessory shops.

Text. The pantomime nature of the dance is evident for most of the words. The *odori ji* and *kudoki* sections are full of riddles, puns, and comments on the erotic pleasures of the master's night at the brothels. As the piece became part of many young girls' dance recitals, the text had to be cleaned up or entire sections deleted. Words and phrases that are still heard in recordings are left in the text for the reader to puzzle over and perhaps enjoy. The *roppō* dance is a famous kabuki event in which the actor hops on one foot. The Naniwa Shishō was one the stage names of Nakamura Utaimon III (d. 1838) who was from Osaka (Naniwa) and was famous for his Yakko performances. The text of the *kudoki* section is filled with double meanings. The riddle of *ha* and *na* in the published music score are *ho* and *re* in other books. Neither is really explained. The first syllables can be thought of as hana ("flower") while *hore* deals with love. Taking off a women 8 kimono plus an underkimono of only 3 layers and sash would certainly leave a brothel customer happy and lying down among the pile of clothes. The scandal of who slept with whom in the Yoshiwara "floating world" would probably be forgotten after 75 days.

The various versions of the text may relate to the particular school of dance or choreography involved. In the drunken scene, one can imagine the dancer making gestures for each of the possible hangover cures. The choreography leads to a posture (*mie*) when the theater name is sung (Narikoma). The dancer holds the staff with a tassel on the end (*keyari*) that appeared at the beginning of the piece. This prop can be seen in many pictures of big processions. The *mie* with the large lantern describes the gestures of the dancer before the final pose. The text is not great poetry, but it makes understanding the choreography easier.

Music. In dance performances there is no *oki* because the loud drum roll (the *geza* pattern *oroshi*) is played as the dancer rushes onstage holding the *keyari* like a spear. It will be used vertically later in the dance and is seen in other dances (see *Takasago*, p. 44). The opening line is declaimed in *serifu*, and a full *hayashi* accompanies what could be called the *michiyuki*, although the dancer is already onstage.

Other declamations by the singer (in lieu of the actor/dancer) are done in *serifu* throughout the text. As in most dance pieces, the *tsuzumi* match *chiri kara* patterns to the shamisen rhythms. The *taiko* and flute use many standard Yoshiwara conventions such as *sarashi*, *kyogen gakko*, and *bungo sagari ha*. At the change of tempo at "wakiyore" one hears the first half of the *taiko* and flute pattern *wataribyōshi* (fig. 17) repeated many times up to the next cadence at "kake tsukeru." The entire drum part is a good example of how the percussionists fill requests for background music in a dance piece. It is like the harpsichord player in baroque orchestra music. One seldom hears his or her part, but the music is barren without it.

The *odori ji* continues to demonstrate standard percussion behind the shamisen and singer. After three *taiko* beats, the *taiko* and bamboo flute accompany first, followed by *chiri kara tsuzumi* at the interlude before "kyasha ni." The *taiko* sounds only for cadences during the *tsuzumi* section, perhaps as a guide to the dancer. At "ato," the *tsuzumi* and *taiko* enter into their standard call-and-response and support the music until the cadence at "idetachi." Like most *kudoki* sections, percussion is not used. The emphasis in the shamisen line on upper leading tones keeps the lyrical line moving forward.

The more active *aikata* brings the *tsuzumi* back in *chiri kara* style and moves to a very fast tempo in the concert version.

The orchestration remains the same with the new tuning. Again one can note how close the shamisen and drums are in rhythmic support of the dance movements. The *taiko* and flute return at "korya, korya" with the pattern *kyogen gakko* (see p. 18).

The next *aikata* shamisen and *tsuzumi* lines are again closely aligned with the dance movements, particularly when specific rhythms (*ashibyōshi*) are beat with the feet on the floor by the dancer. In kabuki theaters, dances are staged over a special hollow flooring that adds to the sound.

OKI (*niagari* tuning)	Length 15'47"
shite koi na yatcha shite koi	Hurry up! quickly now!
konya no otomo chitto okurete	I left a bit late for tonight's
dekaketa ga ashi no hayai ni	duties, but, because my feet are
ga ga ore tanbo wa	quick through the rice paddies, I
chika michi mihagurumai zo	follow a shortcut, careful not to
gatten da	lose my way. You can be sure of that.
futte kesharu na	I take care not to put out the

daijōchin ni	lantern on which is painted my
gojōmon tsuki	master's coat of arms.
dekkari to	Respectfully, I set it down.
fukureta kon no	This starchy blue outfit that I
dainashi wa	wear with pride shows me to be a
date ni kinashita	true footman.
yakko ra sa (*ai*)	
buke no katagi ya	Neither a martial spirit nor the
hōkō konjō yare sate	bearing of an apprentice
itsuka nao dasha shonai (*ai*)	do I display in the slightest.
hibi ya akagire	Never minding chapped skin or
	frostbite on
kakato ya sune ne	my feet and legs, even in snow as deep
	as on
Fuji no yuki hodo	Mount Fuji at any hour of the day I am
aru to te mo	ready to serve. A faithful, honest man
nan doki kagiranu (*ai*) otsukai wa	am I.
kakasanu shodoki (*ai*)	
shōdō mono yo	
waki yore (*ai*)	Step aside
tanomzo (*ai*) waki yore	I ask you step aside
isogi kuruwa he (*ai*)	Speeding to the brothel district
ichiban mokusan	To the first house
iki o kitte zo	I gasp for breath
kaketsukeru (*ai*)	As I run along

ODORI JI

onra no dannna wa	You know my master
kuruwa ichiban kakure nainai	In the district's obvious hiding
tanzen-gonomi (*ai*)	he spots
kyasha ni meshiru (*ai*)	the Tansen girl who wears the
kiahimaki-baori	hemmed up jacket (haori)
kirikiri to shanto	fast and effective
shanto kiri to	
takamono dachi no	my sashi and hakama
hakama tsuki	pants are both tied up for action
ato no geroo ga *ozōri*	Later a servant will remove my
	sandals
soresa koresa (*ai*)	here and there

76

kokimi yoi yoi	Oh it feels good, good
roppō-buri ga (*ai*)	I do the roppo dance
naniwa shishō no	In the style of Naniwa Shishō
sono furozoku ni	Is it the custom to do so?
nita ka nita za nimashitari	Did I do it?
sate sate na	Sure I did
kankatsu karei na idetachi	Making a gaudy, elegant figure

KUDOKI

Ohamoji nagara haru kata e	For those who aren't embarrassed
ha no ji to na no ji no nazokakete	I'll solve a riddle of the letters "ha" and "na".
hodokase no yae hito e	(two versions) 1. Unravelling 3 layers of obi,
tokete ureshiki shitabushi ni	2. unravelling 8 layers and an underkimono
a a mama yo adanaga dokato to	How happy I am
hito no uwasamo	A man lying down
shichijuuugo nichi	Though they seldom last more than 75 days,
tento tamaranu (*ai*)	how vicious are the rumors about people
tsuyu no kewai no hatsu zakura	Make up is as damp of first cherry blossoms

AIKATA (*honchōshi* tuning)

misome misomete	As if seeing for the first time, I
me ga sameta	awaken from an evening of
sameta yūbe no kenzake ni	drinking games.
tsui tsui tsui tsui	Time and again I lost and was
sasareta sakazuki wa	forced to drink a new cup with
ryu chei pama de su	each defeat. Six, seven, eight,
kai to itte haratta	nine, more and more I drank.
hatta kenpiki	Moxacautery,
chiri chiri chirike	acupuncture,
inome yaito ga	or magic potions
kukkiri to	will surely cure me.
neji kiri karageta	My skirts tucked up,
chidori ashi	I reel on unsteady feet,
tekkubi tenohire shikka to	but with my hand firm I keep
anigetta ishizuki	grip on my staff.

korya korya, korya korya	Here, here, here, here,
narikoma yakko to yonya sa	a veritable Narikoma ya am I.

ASHI BYŌSHI NO AIKATA   foot rhythm music

CHIRASHI (*niagari* tuning)

omoshiroya	How interesting.
ukarebyōshi ni nori ga kite	A lively rhythm has captured me
hyokkuri danna ni	suddenly; the fear of being
suterareta	discharged by his master
urutae manago de	brings a look of worry to his
chōchin o	eyes. He lights his lantern,
tsuketari keshitari	and when it flickers out lights it
tomoshitari	again, thus continuing on his
ageya ga kado o ikisugiru	way past this house in the pleasure
	quarters.

Mid-Nineteenth-Century Compositions

Azuma Hakkei, 1829
"Eight Famous Views of Azuma"

Composer: Kineya Rokusaburō IV
Text: Unknown (Kineya Rokusaburō IV?)
Recording: Toshiba 70106
Notation: Bunka 3315; Kineya 33

BOOK CD: 1–3

Performers: singers Nishigaki Yūzō, Miyata Tetsuo; shamisen Kikuoka Hiroaki, Kineya Yasaburō

A common topic in Japanese paintings, scrolls, or folding screens is the eight views of something, usually in the four seasons. *Azuma Hakkei* depicts eight famous places in Tokyo during the Edo period: Nihonbashi, Mount Fuji, Gotenyama, Suruga, Miyatogawa, Sumidagawa, Emonzaka, and Ukishima. The scenes start on an early spring morning and end on a winter evening.

Text. The opening line sets the first location in a wordplay manner for *hi* and *hon*, the first syllables of *Nihon*, the indigenous word for Japan. Separately they could mean "sun" and "origin," which also implies the morning.

Although Surugadai is a hill in the Kanda area of Tokyo, the other meaning in the text is Suruga Province in which on Miho beach an angel dances for a fisherman in order to get back her robe. This is the legend of the noh play *Hagaromo* (The Angel's Robe).

The "shinobu" that begins the *nakauta* is said to have been derived from poem 724 of the *Kokinshū*.

Music. *Azuma Hakkei* is one the favorite early compositions in purely concert (*ozashiki*) *nagauta*. Free of choreography, the shamisen is able to expand its interludes into genuinely new music. The composition is usually performed by singers and shamisen alone. Instead of the traditional kabuki dance form, the piece is influenced by the *kumiuta* tradition, which consists of alternate songs and instrumental interludes. Thus, the translation is marked by the terminology of that tradition: song (*uta*) and interlude (*tegoto*). The opening *maebiki* and first song are meant to reflect the mood of Edo near the first famous scenic place, Nihonbashi. Throughout the piece there is a second shamisen (*uwajoshi*) line enriching the sound with octave support, duets, call-and-response patterns, and ostinatos. During the ostinatos, the horizontal orientation of Japanese lines, vis-à-vis the vertical orientation of the West (see p. 2), becomes evident when the two lines come in and go out with bi-tonal sounds. This is usually a shock to Western listeners, who expect lines to match in tonality or "fill in" the same chord. Remember that Japanese music has no great interest in chords.

When "kouta" is mentioned, the shamisen play double stops in imitation of geisha party music and changes to a "geisha" tuning. The "tsukuda" interlude is an impressive shamisen duet that uses additional conventional sounds for the music of brothels over the river from the Yoshiwara. As played today, the two instruments are sometimes in different scales! The term *tsukuda* refers to rice paddies such as those seen about the brothel areas, but music of that name is associated with riding a boat across the river to other party houses. The next major interlude uses the other geisha music tuning *sansagari*, but it is titled "kinuta no aikata." This refers to the sounds of cleaning clothes by pounding the cloth over a special wooden block (*kinuta*). The image is found in ancient poetry and noh dramas. Such a specific action does not seem to be germane to the subject at hand, but the title provides an excellent opportunity for the shamisen to perform a complex interlude over an ostinato or with calls-and-responses. In the next song, the sounds of a geisha music pattern (*sugagaki*) is played when the geisha scene is described. The third *tegoto* (*gaku*) is used in many pieces to represent courtly music (see *Tsuru Kame*, p. 118). The music does use the *kangen* courtly pattern once, but mostly it contains interesting shamisen duets.

The final song is in typical *chirashi* accelerated syllabic style, which leads to a satisfying *dangire*.

The innovations of *Azuma Hakkei* inspired later *nagauta* composers to move in new, more instrumental directions. The next best-known example is *Aki no Irogusa* (p. 110).

MAEBIKI (*honchōshi* tuning)	Length 19'33"
MAEUTA (OKI)	
ge ni yutakanaru hi no moto no	The mist at the foot of Nihonbashi Bridge.
hashi no tamoto no hatsugasumi	As if dyed by Edomurasaki grass,
Edomurasaki no akebonozome ya	Bountiful Japan has turned pink.
minakami shiroki yuki no Fuji	Mount Fuji is capped with white snow.
kumo no sodenaru hana no nami	Abundant flowers at the edge of the clouds.
memeto utsukushii goshozakura	Beautiful Gosho cherry blossoms, appealing to the eye.
gotenyamanasu hitomure no	At Gotenyama, crowds of people.
kaori ni eishi sono no cho	Butterflies, drunk on the fragrance of the flowers

hana no kanzashi o kaimami ni

in the garden, peeping at a
    lady with a [*kanzashi*] hairpin,

aosu no obune utau kouta no
koe takanawa ni

singing merrily on the boat
with a reed screen.

TEGOTO (*niagari* tuning)
haruka kanata no hototogisu
hatsune kaketaka hagoromo no
matsu wa tennyo no tawamure o
miho ni tatoete Suruga no na aru
dai no yosei no iya takaku
miorosu kishi no ikadamori
i o seoutaru amidagasa

Nightingales far away singing
the first song of spring.
The pine tree on which an angel
hung her heavenly dress
and danced in Miho in Suruga.
Looking at the raft man far
below the cliff of Surugadai wearing
    an Amida straw hat reflecting
    the sun.

nori no katae no Miyatogawa
nagarewatari ni iroiro no
hana no nishiki no Asakusa ya
mitera o yoso ni ukaereo wa
izuchi e soreshi yadaijin

The Miyato River, which runs
near a temple, goes flows through
Asakusa carrying various flowers.
Instead of going to the temple,
where has the happy young man
    gone? He is getting drunk at a
    sake shop.

monpi ni ataru tsujiura no
matsuba kanzashi futasuji no
michi no ishibumi tsuyu
fumiwakete
fukumu yatate
no Sumidagawa
me ni tsuku
aki no nanakusa ni
hyoshi kayowasu kamiginuta
shinobu mojizuri midaruru kari no
tamazusa ni (*ai*) tayori o kikan

On the day of the festival, I stroll
through the streets, divided like a
matsuba hairpin.
Treading on dewdrops
on my way
to the Sumida River,
my eye catches
the seven autumn grasses.
The sound of pounding cloth comes
to my ears.

TEGOTO (KINUTA NO AIKATA)
NAKAUTA
fujime o kiri no watashi ni
saosasu
fune mo itsu
koetayara Emonzaka.

(cloth-pounding interlude)

The letter the messenger brought
excites my heart. Opening the letter,
shall I learn the news?
When did the boat pass Emonzaka?

misesugagaki ni hikiyoserarete

tsui itsuzuke no

asa no yuki tsumori tsumorite

nasake no fukami

koi no sekisho mo

shinobu ga oka no

hachisu ni yoreru itotake no

shirabe yukashiki Ukijima no

katanasu moto ni komoriseba

ATOUTA

gakunone tomo ni toe yori mo

kaze ga furasuru hanamomiji

te ni te awasete kisen no chikai

Benzaiten no mikage moru

ike no hotori no tōtoku mo

meguriteya min yattsu no

nadakoro

Attracted to the *misesugagaki*,

the music geisha girls are playing,

I forgot myself and stayed too long.

Just like the morning snow,

my love deepened,

but must not endure.

I heard very pleasant koto music

when I stayed overnight with the geisha

at an inn near Ukishima island.

With the music, the wind from

Mount Toe blew the maple leaves like flowers.

Both the rich and the poor give offer prayers

to Benzaiten, the goddess of music.

I will visit the eight famous sights

near the venerable lake.

Hōrai, circa 1840
"Hōrai"

Composer: Kineya Rokusaburō IV
Text: Unknown
Recordings: Malm 1986; Columbia COCF 70108
Notation: Bunka 3312

Nagauta have been composed in honor of a new guild ranking (*Matsu no Midori*, see p. 54), new clothing (*Shizu Hata Obi*), new tea (*Hana no Tomo*), and a new brand of sake (*Nokiba no Matsu*). *Hōrai* was written in honor of the opening of a new geisha house. The exact date or place is not known, but the results are clearly related to the event. Hōrai is the name of a mythical mountain somewhere in the ocean between China and Japan. The term is seen in other geisha-related *nagauta* (see p. 136). Both the text and the music plus interpretation are discussed in some detail in Malm 1986. Only a few comments will be made here.

Text. To appreciate the text one must remember that the function of the piece was to dedicate a new geisha house. While Mount Hōrai was said to be filled with angels in beautiful clothes, the kimonos described here are those of the "princesses" who make their living in this house. Note also that the many references to flowers throughout the text relate to the "flowers" of the geisha world. References to salt ovens are found in classical poetry, but here the text continues to be sensual and full of double meanings. *E nantoshō* and *shongae* are geisha terms common in many Yoshiwara pieces (see *Yoshiwara Suzume*, p. 36). The word *patto* here describes birds startled by waves on the rocks. It was used to mean a "plop" of snow off a roof in *Shiki no Yamamba* and bird droppings in *Azuma Hakkei*. The bellflower also shows up in many love stories, not to mention the more obvious pillows, beds, and wet clothing the morning after lovemaking. The crane, a symbol of good fortune, is yet another frequent topic in *nagauta*. The analogy to koto playing is appropriate for the better class of houses of entertainment and love. Close your eyes and think of being in such a place for the *Hōrai* debut performance seated among music lovers, steady customers of the house, and young women in full geisha dress. Then the beauty of the music will be more than the just the sound.

Music. One characteristic of *nagauta* composition is its Buddhist imper-manence. The core of the composition is the text and the shamisen and vocal lines. I have emphasized elsewhere that the orchestration changes with the nature of the performance and the guilds of the performers. The earlier study of this piece (Malm 1986) compared four different performances. One used only the bamboo flute and one *tsuzumi.* The next added light bell sounds (*orugoru*). Another used the bamboo and noh flutes and *tsuzumi,* and the fourth used all four *hayashi* instruments. A fifth, on a 2002 NHK recording, uses bamboo flute and *hayashi.* Using the maxim that form follows function, one can surmise that the bells and full *hayashi* are probably meant for dance accompaniment and the others for concert use. My study also showed that the drum parts for each performance were not the same. Such examples help to explain why the Western full-score approach to composition is nei-ther useful nor accurate in *nagauta* research. The comments below are on the fifth example, the recording not studied in the 1986 publication.

Given the topic, one presumes that geisha musical genres such as *hauta* influenced the shamisen style. The slow tempo and little slides to or from shamisen pitches reflect a feminine, sensual origin. This is less evident in the NHK recording. Besides the bamboo flute support of the melody, *tsuzumi* play quiet noh drama patterns and the texture is further softened by means of light bell sounds. With the entrance of a second singer at "hagoto no," one might think that a *michiyuki* has begun. The ensemble drops to just shamisen and one singer after "soyokaze ya." When the geisha's standard remark "Oh, what shall I do?" is sung, the shamisen phrase briefly moves from an *in* to a *yō* scale, see fig. 1, p 3. It is like the little gesture a girl might make when voicing such a complaint. The *kudoki* follows tradition by beginning with a *tataki* pattern. Up-and-down shamisen octaves startle the birds.

The stanza form of the *odori ji* is typical of geisha house songs (see *Yoshiwara Suzume*). Each verse begins with a shamisen ostinato and melis-matic first word. The tonality begins in the more "folksy" pentatonic *yo* scale and moves to the "sadder" *in* for the second phrase about the wretched ex-istence, only to go back to the *yo* scale at the wet sleeve and geisha remark "shongae." The "gae" is stretched out, evoking the coy gesture or three-part head movement seen in all geisha-related classical dances.

The *chirashi* changes tempo and adds *tsuzumi* in *chiri kara* style. They drop out at "tataki," leaving room for the shamisen to pluck koto style in imitation of the crane's feet. The flute and drum return for the *dangire.* As the geishas say, "What more can I do?"

OKI (*ni agari* tuning)	Length 10'50"
uraraka na hi no iro somite	Steeped in brilliant sunlight, the
ko no ma ni mo	flowers between the leaves of the
hagoto no hana no ayanishiki	trees intermingle like the damask

kasaneshi nui no date moyō

and brocade designs of a flashy kimono.

kitsutsu narenishi
yamahime wa hito no nagame
no mayoigusa
musubikanetaru soradoke wa
isso uwaki na soyokaze ya

Bedecked in such finery, the
mountain princesses beguile men
with their appearance.
Their liaisons dissolve and are
gone like a capricious breeze.

KUDOKI
uramite kemuru shiogama wa
mune ni taku hi no kiekanuru
ē nan to shō
adashi adanami
yosete wa kaesu iwamakura

Looking back at the smoking salt oven,
underlying fire burning in its breast.
Oh, what shall I do?
The fickle, flirting waves are
welcomed, then sent off, by the rocky
pillow of the shore.

ukina wa patto tatsu tori no
negura o shitau koi no yama

Scandal springs up suddenly, like
a startled bird, on the mountain where
love yearns for a roost.

ODORI JI (*honchōshi* tuning) (*ai*)
hagi no shiratsuyu
oki-fushi tsuraki
iro to ka no shigerite fukaki
toko no uchi
honcho [??] no wakare ni
sode nurasu, shongae
maneku susuki wa
itazuramono yo
ominaeshi aju na ki naru
hana no iro
samenu kikyō no
kawayurashi, shongae
utsutsu na ya

The white dew on the bush
clover—the luxuriant bed, rich
in color and perfume—what a
wretched existence! At
morning's parting, a wetted
sleeve. Shongae.
The beckoning plume grass is
but a mischievous rogue.
The lady-flower so piquant,
the bellflower so charming—
her color does not fade.
Shongae.
It's a daydream.

CHIRASHI
nagamtsukisenu tonozukuri
ge ni Hōrai no miageureba
tataki shirabe no
matsu-ge-e ni??
koto hiku yō na
tsuru no ashidori

It is as in a vision—one never
tires of looking at Hōrai palace.
Truly, looking up, one hears
among the pine boughs a high melody;
a crane whose feet grasp the
branches as if plucking a koto.

86

‿ ‿

Okina Sanbasō, 1830, 1856
Okina and Sanbasō

Composer: Kineya Rokuzaemon X
Text: Anonymous
Recording: NHK 12-36-3
Notation: Bunka, vol. 21; Yoshizumi, vol. 7

Some forms the Okina and Sanbasō dances are performed at the first of the year, when a season opens, or at the dedication of a new location for every theatrical genre in Japan. It also is use in hundreds of other Shinto events. *Okina Sanbasō* seems to be the most ancient, indigenous dance in Japan. Okina and Sanbasō (or Sanbasōsō) may be performed separately. The masks are different from all other Asian mainland examples, and the dance contains ancient earth-pounding movements. The music, though sophisticated, has a "primitive" sound, with repetitive, short *tsuzumi* patterns, that is found in no other piece. The opening flute part is thought to be distantly related to unknown flute mnemonics. It is still sung at the opening of the piece, and the repeating drum pattern occurs throughout the piece. Given the fundamental importance of the piece, there have been many versions of it over the centuries. The first known kabuki version is dated 1678, and the earliest *nagauta* piece still performed is the *Hinazuru Sanbasō* of 1755. The kabuki version of the 1812 *Shitadashi* (sticking out the tongue) *Sanbasō* uses both *kiyomoto* and *nagauta* music and is translated in Brandon 2002 (2:50–61). There is also *Ayatsuri Sanbasō* in which the actors are manipulated as if they were *bunraku* puppets. The puppets themselves perform it at bunraku openings with *gidayū* accompaniment. Noh theater companies perform their versions annually as does the bunraku.

    Okina Sanbasō is of special interest musically because it contains a complete version of both Okina and Sanbasō in one piece. It is one of the longest pieces in *nagauta* but has little to do with the traditional *nagauta* form. The influence of noh is evident in the terminology. The actual title of the first half of the piece is *Okina Senzai* with Okina as the primary actor (*shite*) and Senzai as the interlocutor (*waki*). In kabuki performances, this person carries the box that holds the mask. He does not actually appear in the text of the *nagauta* piece as the exchange of lines occurs only between Okina and a chorus. The latter is not listed using the noh term *ji* but rather as *tsure* (companion). This word is customarily used for an additional actor or group of actors in a noh play.

Noh flute and *ko tsuzumi* drum dominate the accompaniment, playing repetitive short patterns unique to this play. These are heard as *hayashi* alone and continue when the opening mnemonic texts begins. In the context of *nagauta* conventions, it creates a powerful image of something exotic and "special" before the dancer appears with shamisen, noh flute, and *ko tsuzumi*. Many of Okina's lines are accompanied by *ōzatusma* patterns on the shamisen. These are designed to accompany narrative passages, but what one reads is disconnected ancient ritual phrases such as "long life," "crane and tortoise," and "sounds of the waterfall." The latter is said to be from a fourteenth-century popular song. The words *tōtari aridōdō* are imitations of the sound of the waterfall. A rare passage is heard in three beats instead the standard two. In another reference to long life, Hagoromo is mentioned. This is a robed angel in a well-known noh drama of that title, who presumably lived forever as an angel once she was given back her robes by a fisherman who had stolen them.

The *agemaki* section of text is said to be derived from a horse pack song. The syllables *ya tondoya* are *hayashi kotoba*, rhythmic patterns, either clapped or sung. The text defies direct translation. It refers to a well-known Yoshiwara geisha, Agemaki in the play *Sukeroku*. The word *hirobakari* implies that she and her lover are not sleeping or sitting together. More mnemonics appear as the crane sings out "banzeiraku," a variant name for a music that soon becomes "manzairaku" (see below). The three terms inscribed on the tortoise's shell are common in many congratulatory symbols.

The positive text leads to a congratulatory dance. Both the drums and the shamisen line emphasize a rhythm pattern (ton, rest, ton, rest, rest, to ton). It is played only is *Okina Sanbaso* music. When Okina sings congratulation, the shamisen play the double-stop pattern in the same rhythm to depict some imperial court setting.

The term *manzairaku* prepares one for the second half of the piece, which is subtitled Sanbasō. The genre *manzai* continues as a street theatrical that consists of dialogues between actors often dressed in Sanbasō or Okina costumes. Itinerant performers can be still found in some rural locations, where they appear, traveling from house to house, with congratulatory songs to bring in the new year.

A complete *tsuzumi* and flute interlude using the repetitive drum pattern heard at the start of the piece usually precedes the beginning of the Sanbasō section as well. The *ō tsuzumi* enters to complete the rhythm. In some performances, only the continuing *hayashi* is used to accompany the first words of Sanbasō. This is followed by the congratulatory dance music for shamisen and *hayashi*. The next section is a dialogue between the character Sanbasō and a Lord Ado. It is in the style of the *kyōgen* comic interludes found between acts in most noh plays. Lord Ado is usually the lord of a house who meets with his servant to issue instructions that are later disobeyed. The conventional opening text can be seen in the *nagauta* piece

Suehirogari (p. 123). In this composition, Sanbasō is the second character. The noh-style *mondō* text is accompanied by *ōzatsuma* shamisen patterns A second *mondō* dialogue is found in text collections but is not included in contemporary performances. Instead, after "saraba suzu o marirashō" a long interlude is played called the *suzu no dan,* named after the shaken bell tree (*suzu*) used by the dancer. This is a basic instrument in Shinto ceremonies, although it is not used in the interlude. The notation of this *aikata* is often found at the end of the piece and can be inserted if desired. The text of the second dialogue is shown in the translation. It does not match the interest of the long instrumental *aikata* that replaces it. After this long *aikata*, a series interlude, text, interlude, text, and interlude is used to describe the treasure boat of the gods (see *Takarabune,* p. 105). The *hayashi* uses noh patterns plus a bamboo flute, which follows the melody. This gives it a *taiko ji* sound. A new tuning (*niagari*), full *hayashi* with noh flute, and busier singing signal a short *chirashi* section and a *dangire.*

Professor and Mrs. Reinhard Zöllner are thanked for helping with the translation of many archaic passages in this text. Reading it, the piece seems chaotic, but in performance it is an exciting example of prekabuki theatrical music.

MAEBIKI (*honchōshi* tuning)	Length 37'
(Okina) tōdōtarari tarari ira	(flute mnemonic only)
tarari agari ta(ra) raridō	
(*ji*)	
chiriya tarari tararira tarari agari rararidō	
(Okina)	
tokoro chiyo made owashimase	enjoy a long life
(*ji*) wareramo senshū samura hō	we maintain a long life and continuing service.
(Okina) tsuru to kame to no yowai nite	Like the tortoise and the crane, joy fills our hearts.
(*ji*) saiwai kokoro ni makasetari	
AIKATA	
(Okina) naru wa taki no mizu	The sounds of the waterfall.
naru wa taki no mizu	The sound of waterfalls.
naru wa taki no mizu (*ai*)	The sound of waterfalls.
hiwa teru tomo	Even in dry weather,
taezu tōtari ariudōdō	the falls always flow.
kimi no chitose o henkotowa	I hope you live a long life
amatsu otome no hagoromo yo	like the angel in Hagoromo.
naru wa taki no mizu	The sounds of the waterfall.

hiwa terutomo	Even in dry weather,
(*ji*) taezu tōtari ariudōdō	the falls always flow.

AIKATA

(Okina)

agemaki ya tondoya	agemaki,
hirobakari ya tondoya	separated
(*ji*) zashite itaredomo	sits with lover
mai roren	love affair
geri ya tondoya	

(Okina)

chihayofuru kami no hikosa no	The kami and hikosa
mukashi yori	since ancient times.
hisashikare tozo	Long life to you
iwai	celebrate
(*ji*) soyoya reichiya tondoya	(rhythmic syllables)

(Okina)

oyoso sennen no tsuru wa	an ancient crane is calling out.
manzeiraku to uta utōtari	Still, an ancient tortoise in the
mata mandai no ike no kame wa	pond reveals the words *"heaven,*
kō ni sankyoku o itadaitari (*ai*)	*earth, mankind"* on his shell.
(*ji*) taki no mizu	The water of the falls is pure and
(Okina) reirei to ochite	cool.
yoru no tsuki	In the sky the night moon
(*ji*) azaya ka ni ukandari	is very clear.
nagisa no isago sakusaku toshite	beach sound (*saku* = sound)
ashita no hi no iro o rōsu	Morning light reflects.
tenga taihei kokudo anran no	Today's prayer is for peace in
konnichi gokitō nari	the realm and for safety in the country.

(Okina *utaigakari*)	
ariharaya najō no Okinatomo	Even if you don't know where Okina comes from,
(*ji*) arewa najō no Okinatomo	Okina comes from a strange
soyo ya izuku najō no	place. Indeed, we don't know
Okinatomo	where he came from.
(Okina) soyan	Indeed.

AIKATA	Dance (*mai*)
(Okina) senshūbanzei no	Let's do dances of joy and long

yorokobi no mai nareba

hitosashi maō manzeiraku

(*ji*) manzeiraku

(Okina) manzeiraku

AIKATA (*honchōshi* tuning)

(Sanbaso) (*kyōgengakari*)

osae osaeo yorokobi aiya waga

kono tokoro yori

hoka e wa yarajito zo omō

AIKATA

MONDŌ

(Sanbasō) ara medetaya mono ni

kokoro etaru

Ado no taifudono ni

soto genzō mōsō

(Ado) chōdo naitte sōrō

(Sanbasō) taga otachi nite sōzo

(Ado) Ado to ōse sōrō hodo ni

onmi ado no tama ni makaritatte sōrō

konnichi no sanbasō senshū

banzei to mōtte orisoe

iro no kuroi jōdono

kono iro no kuroi jō

ga konnichi no sanbasō

senshū banzei tokoro hanjō to

mai osemyozuru to wa

naniyori motte yasuu sōrō

(Sanbasō) mazu Ado no taikdono

wa moto no zashiki e omo omo

to onaori sōraoe

(Ado) sore gashi zashiki e naorō

zurukoto wa

jōdono mai yori ito

yasū sōro

onmai nōte wa naori sōrō maji

(Sanbasō) ara yōgamashiya

---

life.

Let's dance manzairaku

manzairaku

manzairaku

Sanbasō section kyōgen style

osae, osae

This is so much fun.

I think that this happiness will never depart from us.

Yorokobi dance

I bring good wishes and would like to greet the great and wise Lord Ado to wish him well.

I have just arrived.

Who might you be?

I am Ado. Is it for my sake that you have come?

Today Sanbasō comes with his black mask to dance "Senshū Banzei" With his black mask Today Sanbasō is going to dedicate his "Senshū Banzei" dance for the prosperity of this place. This is very easy.

First, Lord Ado, please go back to your original seat.

For me to go back to my seat is indeed much simpler than dancing with a mask.

But I want to dance, so I won't sit sit down.

You demand too much.

(Ado) sa araba suzu o marirashō

Then let me give you the *suzu.*

AIKATA

Suzu dance

[deleted section]

[deleted section]

(Sanbasō) Ado no taifudono ni

Lord Ado, I have something to tell you.

mōsubeki koto no sōrō

What could it be?

(Ado) nanigoto nite sōrō zo

Wouldn't it be funny if in May

(Sanbasō) satsuki no nyobō ga

the wives lined up the edges of

kasa no ha o tsurane

their caps and, hastily gripping

sanae ottote

the seedlings, threw them into

uchiagete utō wa

the air and sang.

omoshirō wa naku sōrō ka

That would be truly funny?

(Ado) geni omoshiroki koto nite

If so, let's have the lord

sōrō

listen to my song.

(Sanbaso) saraba taifudono nu

It would be interesting

utōte kikase mōsō

Indeed, great lord, listen to my song

AIKATA

(Next section starts at this interlude)

kore nonnanna

They say that the treasure boat

ike no migi wa ni takara mifune ga

is pulling into the pier at the

ga tuku ton no

lake.

AIKATA

tomo e ni wanna

In the stern are the wealthy

ebisu daikoku naka wa

Ebisu and Daikoko, the beautiful

bishiyamon kichiyō tennyo

Kichijōtennyo.

AIKATA

CHIRASHI (*niagari* tuning)

shikai nami kaze shizukeki

The peaceful winds on the waves

kimi ga

of the four seas bless us.

miyo wa kashikoki Amaterasu

Through the presence of the

kami no

goddess Amaterasu, all enemies

kage mo mumorazu

in the shadows of the clouds are

ontekitaisan

vanquished.

gokoku jōjiju tamiyutaka

Plentiful harvests, and thriving people.

DANGIRE

yayo yorozuyo mo

For centuries

kuni ya sekaen

our country flourishes.

.ᴗ ᴗ.

Niwakajishi, 1834
"The Improvised Lion"

Composer: Kineya Rokusaburō IV
Text: Unknown
Recordings: Ocora C 560144; NHK 2-16-2; Toshiba TOCF 4008
Notation: Bunka 3354

The "nightless city" of the Yoshiwara was equally busy in the daytime, particularly at festival time. This dance piece is set during the annual ninth-month festival when all the pleasure houses showed off their finery in a parade. Prancing improvising lions and fireman's songs (*kiyari*) were part of the event. All of these elements are mixed with short verbal images and Yoshiwara-related music to create a piece as colorful as the dance finale of a Western musical. Another view of the same location is seen in *Kuruma Tanzen* (p. 135).

Text. The term *gochō* (five blocks) means the five sections in Yoshiwara: Edochō, Fushimikchō, Sumichō, Ageyamachi, and Kyōmachi. *Kamuro* is a beginning rank in a geisha house. *Niwaka* implies something offhand such as a lion dance created during a young geishaís dance lesson. The structure of the piece is equally offhand as it creates short images to entertain the audience. The lion-related text seems to have been borrowed from another lion piece, *Aioijishi*. Double entendres throughout the text add to the games one can play in this piece. The frequent topic changes from famous spots to sensual scenes must generate an equal variety in the choreography.

Nakanochō is the main avenue of the Yoshiwara district. "Mountains of bedding" refers to the festival tradition of spreading out bedding to air. This allows the houses to show off some of the opulent materials used by the better girls. The first *kiyari* song refers to a shop that sells a moon-shaped sweet special to the area, and the second (at "yai no yamaya") contains a local saying. The third text notes another cite near *nakanochō* and adds a lewd remark of the type made by the house comics (*taikomochi*) who were part of every geisha party. "Yoi yoi" is a standard ending sung by other firemen at the end of a verse. The text of the *chirashi* section is derived from that of the *Shakkyō* (see p. 60), a lion piece based on noh drama.

Music. Oki. As basically a dance piece, offstage music might begin the *oki* with a performance with *wataribyōshi* patterns (see p. 18) that identify the location as Yoshiwara. The voice and shamisen then set the scene.

The same kinds of drum patterns begin the *michiyuki* section. The *hayashi* style can be compared to those of pieces set in the same location such as *Gorō, Yoshiwara Suzume* or *Kuruwa Tanzen.*

Shamisen and voice begin the lyric *kudoki* section, but two *tsuzumi* soon enter in lively *chiri kara* patterns. The interlude leads to the lion dance, during which the *taiko* is added in dialogue with the *tsuzumi* plus the noh flute.

In the next interlude, after "shirami ya," the festival spirit is enhanced by the sound of the bamboo flute and the use of thinner sticks on the *taiko*. They begin with the standard *wataribyōshi* but then move on to a pattern imitating festival *hayashi*. If an offstage *ōdaiko* is added, call-and-response patterns are heard.

The alternation of *kiyari* and *kudoki* is unusual. The *kiyari* are songs sung by groups of firemen, and they follow the folk tradition of a text and a group *hayashi kotoba* response ("yoi yoi" in this case). The *tsuzumi* is used for the *kiyari* songs while the *kudoki* have no percussion.

The third *kiyari* returns to *taiko* and flute festival music.

The comedian's joke is in the *serifu* dialogue style.

The next section could be called either an *odori ji* or another *kudoki* because no *taiko* is used and only a bamboo flute adds support to the lyrical vocal line. When the topic changes to the lion (at "shishi ni soite"), the tempo becomes faster and the *tsuzumi* return. The *aikata* is fast festival *hayashi* music. It is used to give the dancers time to change costumes. When the dancers return, the full *hayashi* ensemble and shamisen play lively music. Since the first part of the *chirashi* text is from a lion noh drama, the *hayashi* play the sequence called *sandame* (see *Suehirogari*, p. 123), which is based on a noh drama dance music. If the performance is a dance concert, the *dangire* is followed by more dramatic *hayashi* music as the curtain closes.

OKI (*niagari* tuning)	Length 14'57"
hana to mitsu gochō	There's no one who isn't delighted
odorikanu hito mo nashi	at seeing the flowers of the Five
nare mo mayou ya samazama ni	Blocks.
shiki oriori no tawamure wa	You, too, will be seduced by it all,
monbi monbi no kakekotoba	the seasonal pleasures and double
	entendres of festival days.
MICHIYUKI	
chō ya kochō no kamuro niwaka	There are the dances improvised by
no	*kamuro* with butterflies and
ukarejishi mikaereba hana no	frolicking lions.
yatai ni mietsu kakuretsu iro iro	When you look back there are

no sugata yasashiki nakanochō
(*ai*)

KUDOKI
kokorozukushi no na
sono tamazusa mo
itsuka watasan sode no uchi
kokoro hitotsu ni omoigusa
yoshiya yo no naka (*ai*)
kurui midaruru mejishi ojishi no
anata e hirari konata e hirari
hira hira hira
shinobu no mine ka kasane yagu
makura no iwama
takitsuse no
sake ni midarete ashi mo tamarazu
yoso no miru me mo
shirami ya

AIKATA
KIYARI
yaa, aki no monaka no
tsuki wa Takemura fukete au no ga
mabu no kyaku yoi yoi

KUDOKI
itsuji ura migoto kurikaeshi
naze kono yō wasurarenu
hazukashii hodo guchi ni naru

KIYARI
to iu cha murizake ni
nandemo kotchino machibito
koinona
koi no yamaya ga
tōfu ni kasugai
shimari no nai node nurakura
fuwatsuku uso bakari yoi ya na

flowers—the various gentle figures
of Nakanochō.

What attentiveness! Even those
letters soon to be delivered tucked in
their sleeves. Their thoughts are as
one.
What in the world?
Wild lions, male and female,
cavorting, fluttering here and there,
flutter, flutter, flutter.
Like hidden mountain peaks,
bedding is piled high, and the pillows
seem stacked like boulders.
The gushing waterfall of sake
intoxicates, and everyone staggers
along while the watchful eyes of
        others seem like white waves.

Hey, for midautumn's Monaka
sweets come to Takemura's.
It is now late at night, and the one
        she'll meet is her lover. yoi yoi.

"Just my foolish luck once again.
Why can't I get him out of my
mind? It's almost embarrassing. Still
        what can I do but complain?"

she says, making herself drink.
Saying, "the love of Yamaya' is like
putting a key in tofu. You just can't
hold a guy down. Men are slippery,
wishy-washy, and full of lies."
Yoi ya na.

95

KUDOKI

yoi kara matasete	"He's kept me waiting since dusk,
mata yukō to wa	and now he's about to go again.
ee ammari na to	Hey, it's not fair!"
hiza tatenaoshi	she says, drawing her knees up.

KIYARI

shimero yare, tanda ute ya ute	Cut it out! Hit it hit it!
utsu wa taiko ga	Strike up the drums, yet play the
torimochigao ka	go-between. Pouting, she looks
sunete ura muku Suidojiri ni	back at Suidojiri. "If she were a
okagura soba nara sukoshi nobita	noodle, she'd be soggy by now,"
to hayasarete	says the house jester.
chinchin kamo no toko no uchi	Now loving ducks in bed playing
tantan tanuki no soraneiri	'possum. They pretend to be
tsunetta ato no	asleep. Their pinch marks have
yukari no iro ni	turned black and purple, and they
utte kawatta nakanaori	have totally changed and made up.
are wa sa, kore wa sa	"There's this and that, y'know.
yoi koekake ya	My what a good time that was."
yoi ya na shidomonaya	yoi ya na! She's a mess.

ODORI JI (*sansagari* tuning)

hitome shinobu wa urajaya ni	To avoid public view, in the back
tame ni naru no o furisutete	teahouse she casts away that
fukaku shizumi shi koi no fuchi	which is good for her and sinks
kokorogara naru mi no usa wa	deeply into this pit of love.
isso tsurai ja nai ai na	This state of melancholy she's in,
awanu mukashi ga	my god, isn't it painful? Her past,
natsukashi ya	before they met, now seems so dear.
shishi ni soite ya tawamure asobu	Along with the lion, everyone frolics
ukitatsu iro no muragarite	and plays in an exhilarating orgy.
yūhi hana saku satogeshiki	The flowering beauty of the brothels
mokuzen to kisen	is set against the evening sun.
utsutsu nari	Both high and low, all are in ecstasy
shibaraku matase tamae ya	with what is before our eyes. Wait
yoi no yakusoku ima iku hodo ni	awhile for this evening's engagement,
yo mo fukeji	which you will now attend; the night
	will grow late.

AIKATA

CHIRASHI

shishi toraden no bugaku mo	(*kurui*)
kakuya	Is the lion *toraden* dance music
isamu massha no	also this way? Their stirred-up
hana ni tawamure	followers romp among the flowers
sake ni fushi	and are felled by drink.
taikin chirasu kimitachi no	Those of you who flaunt your
uteya ōmon zensei no	wealth, hiring all the geishas, with
kōkin no kidoku arawarete	with this miracle of big money coming
nabikanu kusaki mo	forth, surely this is a time when
naki toki nare ya	even the plants and trees are
senshū banzei banbanzei to	swayed by it all.
	For a thousand autumns, ten
	thousand years, an eternity.

DANGIRE

yutaka ni shukusu shishi gashira   Celebrate abundantly, the lion's head.

Kanjinchō, 1840
"The Subscription List"

Composer: Kineya Rokusaburō IV
Text: Namiki Gohei III
Recordings: Columbia COCF 70107; NHK 1-1
Video: NHK NSDS 7860, DVD
Notation: Bunka 3318; Kineya 77; Yoshizumi, vol. 5

The source of this famous kabuki play is the noh drama *Ataka*. The story concerns the successful passage through the barrier at *Ataka* by the young Yoshitsune fugitive, his faithful warrior priest protector Benkei, and their followers, who were disguised as *yamabushi* priests. The major event in the plot is when Benkei reads a nonexistent list (*kanjinchō*) of contributors to a temple to the suspicious barrier guard and his warriors. There are three versions of the story still in the *nagauta* repertory: the 1769 *Kumadori Ataka no Matsu* by Fujita Kichiji; the 1840 *Kanjinchō*, reproduced in this anthology; and a long, noh-style 1870 concert piece, *Ataka no Matsu*, by Kineya Katsusaburō.

The kabuki production of *Kanjinchō* places onstage at least nine shamisen, nine singers, and five *ko tsuzumi* plus one each of *ō tsuzumi*, *taiko*, and *nōkan*. This creates an impressive accompaniment to the mass of actors onstage. It feels rather like a Steven Spielberg production of *Swan Lake*. The play is one of eighteen standard (*juhachiban*) kabuki pieces and can be seen annually in various productions. Because of its popularity, and the popularity of the actors who perform in it, there are many translations of the play (see Brandon 1992; and Scott 1953), but the music is seldom discussed. This commentary deals primarily with the music of the *nagauta* concert version of the composition.

In such performances, the ensemble seldom exceeds three singers, three shamisen, and a normal *hayashi*.

Okiuta. Like most noh-derived *nagauta* pieces, the music opens with noh *hayashi* and the text begins with direct quotes from the original play sung in an imitation of the noh style (*utaigakari*). At "tokishimo," the shamisen enter with *ōzatuma* patterns. Throughout this performance, one should remember that most dialogue sections in an actual kabuki performance were spoken by the actors rather than sung by the singers.

Michiyuki. The *tsuzumi* shamisen accompany the "mustering" (*yose*) action of the actors, who would be coming down the *hanamichi* ramp. Although the mood of the piece resembles that of noh, the shamisen and *chiri kara* drumming rhythms are derived from those of the actor's movements in a kabuki performance. Some copies of the text include instructions to play the opening of the *michiyuki* in the style of *gekibushi* (*gekigakari*), an older narrative genre. Additional "*gakari*" style indications in the text name other archaic shamisen musics; *itchū, sekkyō,* and *handayū.* They are shown in parentheses in this translation though their musical meaning is unknown today. Only *sekkyō* seems germane because it was originally music for Buddhist stories.

The tempo is faster in this concert performance. The *hayashi* return to the noh style when the singer enters at "kore ya" in the *notto* section. The long explanation of *yamabushi* is delivered over a steady ostinato of *tsuzumi* (*pu pon pu pon*) and long, menacing, noh flute sounds such as one hears in supernatural kabuki scenes. Syllabic singing and *serifu* declamations absorb this long lesson. The rolling of Benkei's rosary is heard in fast up-and-down strokes on a high shamisen pitch.

At "moto yori," another speech by Benkei combines *serifu* and *ōzatsuma* shamisen patterns. Dialogues between the Hogan and Benkei continue in such combinations until "oretsu mie ni keru." All of this in a kabuki performance would not be music. When the power of swords is mentioned the shamisen walk in fourths down a chromatic scale. The *tsuzumi* also intensify the excitement with *chiri kara* playing. The tonalities throughout this violent text is in the new sound of F-sharp and C-sharp, the traditional arena of *ōzatsuma* patterns. At "shitsutsu o," the pitch centers move to the *in* scale on B an E. The music moves toward a *kudoki* song about Benkei's concern for his master at "tsui ni nakanu Benkei." Before this text, there is a slow call-and-response of the shamisen and *tsuzumi.* This is the "echo" (*kodama*) convention, which represents the sounds of mountain valley scenes or analogous atmospheres. We are at a barrier on a mountain road. Unlike the fast pace of syllables in the previous section, the vocal line is slow and lyrical and set against a typically thin *kudoki* shamisen accompaniment. Benkei pantomimes the story of their flight.

A fast tempo returns. At "oroi ni," the *tsuzumi* enter with the *mitsuji* pattern and change to *chiri kara* in the next interlude. At "okaku," the tempo slows. The text and the several rubato passages in this section would accompany dance in kabuki.

The tuning changes, and another voice/shamisen dance accompaniment is used. The notation calls it a *sekkyōgakari*, a genre mentioned earlier. Tonal centers of F-sharp and B give us a fresh set of sounds. There is even a *tataki* pattern on G. The *odori ji* returns to *honchōshi*, and the tuning brings back an E pitch center, a faster tempo, and the *tsuzumi* in the noh style. The next *aikata* begins with noh flute and *tsuzumi* because it is *ennen no mai*, the major dance by Benkei in the original noh drama. In the concert version, it is followed by a shamisen/*hayashi* interlude that becomes very fast. In the *chirashi*, the *tsuzumi* change to kabuki-style drumming. In concerts, the previous *aikata* may be moved to this spot. The next *aikata* is also movable. It varies with the performers.

Kanjinchō is so popular as a shamisen showpiece that it can be heard in excerpts on a 1980 Nonesuch CD (H-72084) and a 1989 UNESCO collection (Auvidis D 8016). The analogy to the waterfall that never dries up is seen as well in *Okina Sanbasō* (see p. 90). Whether in the kabuki or a concert performance, *Kanjinchō* continues to flourish.

OKIUTA (UTAIGAKARI)	Length 31'18"
tabi no koromo wa suzukake no	We set out on a journey wearing monks' robes.
tabi ni koromo wa suzukake no	We set out on a journey wearing monks' robes.
tsuyu keki sode ya shioru ran	Because our expedition is sad,
(GEKIGAKARI)	
tokishimo koro wa kisaragi no (*ai*)	our sleeves are wet with tears as well as dew.
kisaragi no tōka no yo	Around the time of the new moon
tsuki no miyako o tachi idete	in the moonlight of the tenth of the month we left the capital.
yose no aikata	
MICHIYUKI (AIKATA)	
kore ya kono yuku mo kaeru mo	Crossing Mount Osaka and
wakarete wa	looking back, we regretted
shiru mo shiranu mo	that we could not see
ōsaka no yama kakusu (*ai*)	over the mountains
kasumi zo haru wa yukashi keru (*ai*)	because of the spring mist.
namiji haruka ni yuku fune no	Having crossed Lake Biwa by
Kaizu no ura ni tsuki ni keri.	boat, we arrived at Kaizu.
INAORI	
iza tōran to tabi goromo	They agree to pass the barrier
seki no konata ni tachi kakaru (*ai*)	and now they are before it.
NOTTO	
sore yamabushi o ippa	Yamabushi follow the
En no Ubasoku no gyōgi o uke	teaching of En-no Ubasoku.
sokushin sokubutsu no hnohnohontai o	As they are his disciples, they

koko nite uchitome tamawan koto
myō-ō no shōran hakari gatō
Yuya no Gongen no gobatsu
ataran koto
tachidokoro ni oite utagai

arubekarazu, on abiran unken to
juzu sara sara to oshimondari
motoyori kanjinchō no araba
koso oi no uchi yori ōrai no
makimono ikken tori-dashi
kanjinchō to natsuketsu
takaraga ni koso yomiagegekere
ten mo hibike to yomiagetari
kanshin shite zo mienikeru
osoretsu ga hakobu hirodai ni
shira aya bakama hitokasa ne
kagakiinu amata torisoroe
gozen e koso wa naoshitere

ko wa ureshiyato yamabushi mo

shizu shizu tatte ayumarekeri
suwaya wagakimi ayashimuru wa
ichigo no fuchin kokonari to
onono ato e
tachikaeru
kongō zue o ottotte

sanzan ni chōchakusu
tōre to koso wa nonoshirinu
katagata wa nani yue ni
kahodo iya shiki gōriki ni
tachigata nao nukitamō wa
metare gao no furumai
okubyō no itarikato
mina yamabushi wa
uchikatana nukigatete (ai)

represent Buddha himself
while they live. Myō-ō will
guard our destiny. If you kill
us here, we cannot tell what
he may do, but Yuya no Gongen will
punish you instantly. We pray to
them to help.

So saying, Benkei rolled his
rosary (*juzu*).
Of course, he has no
subscription list, but, taking
out a scroll from his box,
he pretends to read.
He read so loudly that it
echoed in the heavens.
The guard looked impressed.
The retainers brought in
wooden stands.
Dressed in their white
ceremonial costumes with silks
from Kaga and other things, they
placed the gifts on them.

Quietly rejoicing, the *yamabushi* stood
up and went
on their way.
They worried for their master.
It is a critical moment.
They all step back in anxious
suspense.
With his staff he gives the servant
(Yoshitsune) a good beating.
We cannot let him pass.
Why do you all try to draw
your swords to fight over a
servant?
With fierce expressions and
postures, but full of worry
and concerns,
all the *yamabushi*
begin to pull their swords

(GEKIGAKARI)

isami gagareru arisama wa
ikanaru tenma onikami mo ō (*ai*)
obyōszoretsu asu mie ni teru ((*ai*)
shisotsu o hikitsure
sekimori wa kado no uchi e zo
iri ni keru

gallantly holding together,
looking as frightening as the
devils of hell.
The keeper of the barrier,
accompanied by his retainers
enters the gate,

AIKATA
KUDOKI
tsui ni nakanu Benkei mo
ichigo no namida zo shushō naru
(itchūgakari)
Hōgan onte o tori tamai (*ai*)

Benkei has never wept before
but at this moment he weeps.

It is touching and Hōgan (Yoshitsune)
     takes his hand.

yoroi ni soishi sode makura
katashiku himamo nami no ue
arutoki wa fune ni ukabi
fūha ni mi o makase
mata arutoki wa sanseki no
batei mo mienu yuki no naka ni
uma sukoshi ari yūnami no
sukoshi ari yūnami no
tachikuru otoya Suma Akashi (*ai*)
tokaku mitose no hodo mo
nakunaku
itahwashi ya to
to shiore kakarishi
oni azami shimo ni tsuyu oku
bakari nari
tagai ni sode o hikitsurete
izasase tamae no orikara ni

We slept on our sleeves in full
armor.
Aboard a ship our fates were
fates were once at the mercy of the
waves.
Once high in the mountains
We met a snowstorm which
covered our horses to their
knees.
The few evening waves made
the lapping sound of Suma
and Akashi
Three years have passed.
Our plight is unfortunate.
(Benkei's) look was as a thistle
beaten down by frost and
rain. Tugging each other's sleeves,
     they were about to leave.

(*niagari* tuning, sekkyōbushi)
geni geni kore mo kokoro etari
hito no nasake no sakatsuki o
ukete kokoro o todomuto kaya
ima wa mukashi no katarigusa

Wait! Wait! I was impolite to
you.
Please take this sake cup and we shall
have a drink. I will tell a story from
     long ago,

ara hazukashi no waga kokoro

though it embarrasses me to speak of it,

ichido mamieshi onnasae

about a girl I once met and had to cross a barrier on the path of love.

mayoi no michi no seki koete
ima mata koko ni koekanuru
(HANDAYŪKAGARI)
hitome no seki no yaruse naya
a a satorarenu koso
ukiyonare

Once again in trouble, I have
to cross another barrier,

unenlightened, into this
floating world.

ODORI JI (*honchōshi* tuning)
omoshiroya yama mizu ni
omoshirya yamamizu ni
sagazuki o ukabete wa
ryu ni hikaruru kyoku sui no
to mazu saegiru sode furete
izaya mai o mao yo

How enjoyable in a mountain stream.
How enjoyable in a mountain
stream to float wine cups. My
dampened sleeve moves to
the rhythm of the winding
stream. Come on, let's dance.

ENNEN O MAI
CHIRASHI
moto yori Benkei wa santō no
yūso
mai ennen no toki no waka (*ai*)
kore naru yamamizu no
ochite iwao ni hibiku koso
naru wa taki no mizu
naru wa taki no mizu

(*ennen* dance)

Benkei had originally been a
pleasure-loving priest of
Santo. He performs an *ennen*
dance to a poem ("The Falling
Mountain Stream Resounds on
the Giant Rock.").
The sound of the waterfall.

AIKATA
naru wa taki no mizu
hi wa teru to mo
taezutōtari toku toku
tateya tatsukayumi no
kokoro yurusu na
sekimori no hno hitobito
itoma mōshite saraba yotote
oi o ottori kata ni uchikake
(*ai*)

The sound of the waterfall.
Although the sun shines,
the water never dries up."

Now let us depart quickly.
Be careful of the border
guards.
This is now our good-bye.
They slung their goods over their
shoulders.

tora no o o fumi dokuja no
kuchi o nogaretaru kokoji shite
mutsu o kuni e zo kudari keru

Feeling as if they had
escaped the fangs of a
poisonous snake and stepped on a
tiger's tail, they depart from Mutsu
[Michinoku].

Takarabune, circa 1840
"The Treasure Boat"

Composer: Kineya Rokusaburō IV
Text: Unknown
Recordings: NHK 3-18-4; Columbia COTF 4166;
      Columbia cassette CAK 9223
Notation: Bunka 3334, 3362

A popular dance recital piece, *Takarabune*'s date of origin is uncertain. It has been placed between 1818 and 1843. The treasure ship is a standard palindrome for good luck and good fortune in the pleasure quarters, particularly on the second day of the new year. The seven lucky gods are shown at the bow with a sail behind them displaying the character for money. Placing the picture under one's pillow on the first or second night brings good dreams and good fortune for the year ahead.

The text describes the seven gods in the context of the Yoshiwara. The music is lightweight and the shamisen line simple. The formal sections have been noted to show how even this short piece is influenced by traditional needs for a sense of progress and change. The first three gods' *hayashi* part uses *taiko, tsuzumi,* and noh flute in slow formal noh style. The next three are more clearly in the Yoshiwara spirit with *chiri kara tsuzumi* and kabuki patterns for the flute and *taiko.* Just the *tsuzumi* are heard from "kore wa tamaranu" on. For variety's sake, a *kudoki*-like section for shamisen and voice alone begins at "taiko massha no."

A *taiko ji* section begins at "sode ni kamuro" with the standard *wataribyōshi* pattern for *taiko* and flute.

The *chirashi* brings in the entire ensemble in kabuki patterns, and the *dangire* is standard. In all, the piece is suitable for beginners.

MICHIYUKI (*ni agari* tuning)	Length 5'46"
nagakiyo no	From the distant slumber of a
tō no nemuri	long New Year's night,
mina mezame	everyone awakes.
ehō ni ataru	Oh, to be forever enchanted by
Benten no egoa ni mitorete	the smiling faces of the felicitous
itsu made ka	Benten.
chaya ga shōgi ni	Rooted to a stool and flirting

ne ga haenuki no
Bishamonsanno jaratsuki o
mikanete Hotei ga
nossa no sa
Sō wa naranu to
oshiau naka e
tsuredatsu isami no
Daikoku Ebisu
kore wa tamaranu
korya dō ja koi arasoi wa
Yoshiwara no rippa na daijin
Fukurokuju

somsomo kuruwa no
zensei wa

with the girls is Bishamon, an
habitué of teahouses, and with
him is Hotei. How thrilling to see
them here.
And if that is not enough for
you, there, making their way
through the jostling throng, are
the bold pair Daikoku and Ebisu.
It's too good to be true! How will
this do? For the contests of love,
nothing surpasses the Yoshiwara
and the splendid spendthrift
    Fukurokuju.

At the height of the festivities
here in the pleasure quarters,

KUDOKI
taiko massha no
ō ichiza
mikka wa kyaku no
kiso hajime
konata ni hige no Ikyū to
mitaru wa kokoro yasashiki
Jurōjin

jester and hangers-on entertain
the large crowds. Everyone on
this auspicious day sports his
newest finery.
Over there the one who looks
like the bearded Ikyū is the kind-
hearted Jurōjin.

TAIKO JI
sode ni kamuro ga
shika no nui
kore mo shikise no
date moyō

On the sleeve of a young geisha
to be is embroidered the figure
of a deer. She wears her new
kimono proudly.

CHIRASHI
minna sazame kite isamashiku
kuruwa no uchi ni iryu wa

The procession moves gallantly
through the pleasure quarters to the
    docks.

DANGIRE
nami no norifune no
oto no yokigana.

The sounds of the passenger
boat waves are loud.

Gorō Tokimune, 1841

Music: Kineya Rokuzemon X
Text: Mieya Nimidai
Recordings: Columbia COCF 70108; NHK 1-7-3
Video: Victor PEUT 1122
Notation: Bunka 3303; Kineya 10; Yoshizumi, vol. 1
Audio Excerpt in Malm 96 and Malm 2000

Originally part of a nine-part (*hengemono*) performance by one actor, *Gorō Tokimune* now usually is a single performance in a kabuki or dance program. The original performance was by Ichikawa Danjurō at the Edo Nakamura za. The plot is derived from the popular Soga story about two brothers who in 1193 attempted vengeance for the death of the their father. The brother was killed, and Gorō was condemned to suicide. The variety of plays, poems, and legends about the event can be seen in Kominz 1995.

Text. As a dance piece linked to a well-known story, much of the text is narrative. However, many double-meaning pivot words common to Japanese poetry are present. One example in the *oki* is *kuruwa*, where *kuru* means to come and *kuruwa* is a word for the brothel quarters. A literal translation of Kewaizaka is "Makeup Hill." The most exotic pun is the name Shōshō, which is a Japanese pronunciation of a place in China famous for its beauty in the rain (the dancer is using an umbrella). In the *kudoki*, the term *kari* means both "false" and "goose." The latter relates to a Chinese legend about a captive who sends a message home by tying it to a migrating goose. Thus the term *kari no tsute* can mean "message from afar." The term *yoi* means both "drunk" and "evening." The plot returns at "Ide ō sore yo." The text that follows is related to the masculine *aragoto* choreography that dominates the dance piece. The decorations on the kimono are seen by the audience while the dancer poses (a *mie*) and assistants (*kōken*) hold out the costume. The bird and plum tree are standard symbols for romantic texts as are the flowers and the "drenched" things, which imply that lovemaking has happened. The location of the main street (Nakanochō) of the Yoshiwara confirms the event.

   Gorō is commonly used for early shamisen lessons, and so it is well known. Since an analysis and full score in Western notation of it are found in Malm 1963, comments here will be short. The *oki* is a good example of the *ōzatsuma* patterns (see p. 16). The *taiko*/flute part that opens the *michiyuki* is *wataribyōshi* (see p. 18; or Malm 1996, 242).

The return to declamations (*serifu*) is accompanied by *ōzsatsuma* patterns and the noh pattern *mitsuji* (see p. 17) on the *tsuzumi* drums. It is followed by *chiri kara* kabuki patterns on the drums (see Malm 2000, 233). All the *hayashi* play a special pattern, *hige soru* (scrape the beard), to accompany a dance gesture that is just that. The *odori ji* follows the traditional accompaniment of *taiko* and flute followed by *tsuzumi* and then a call-and-response between the drums. The *chirashi taiko*/flute pattern is called *sarashi*, a term that means the waving of long strips of cloth in the piece *Echigojishi*. Although the dancer does not do this in *Gorō*, the fast tempo of the music is appropriate for a male dance.

OKI (*honchōshi* tuning)

Saruhodo ni Soga no Gorō
Tokimune
wa gufu taiten no, chichi no ada
uranzu mono to, tayumi naki
yatakegokoro mo
harusame ni, nureta kuruwa no
Kewaizaka, nauta to kikishi
Shōshō no

Length 11'36"

Well, Gorō Tokimune of the Soga family harbors an implacable will to strike down his father's killer. With unflagging boldness of spirit, his heart is springing, as through the spring shower has comes soaking, to Kewaizaka in the licensed quarters. He comes to see Shōshō, whose name is known far and wide.

MICHIYUKI (*ai*)

ame no fuyu yo yuki no hui mo
kayoi kayoite ōiso ya.

On rainy nights or snowy days,
still he comes to meet her at Oiso.

KUDOKI

Sato no showake no
hodasareya suku. tare ni
kari no tsute.
yabo na kuzetsu o kaesugaki.
sui na tekuda ni tsui nosarete
uwaki na sake ni
yoi no tsuki.
harete yokaro ka harenu ga yoi
ka
tokaku kasumu ga haru no kuse.

He is easily ensnared by the affairs of the quarters. A letter comes from someone: false tidings on the leg of a goose. He writes a rude reply. Taken in, in spite of himself, by the elegant coquetry and the fickle rice wine, he lies drunk, mooning beneath the evening moon. Will it clear or is it better clouded over? Anyway, it's always foggy in the spring.

Ide! ō sore yo ware mo mata itsu
ka harasan chichi no ada
jūhachi nen no amatsukaze, ima
fukiaesu nenriki ni nogasaji
yararji to
ima fukikaesu nenriki ni nogasaji
yaraji to yūnō kekki.
Sono arisama wa, botanka ni
stubasa hirameku kochō no
gotoku isamashiki
mo mata kenge nari,

Hey! What am I doing? I've got to
clear this thing up soon—avenge
my father!
The winds of eighteen year ago
blow once again, strengthening
his determination not to let the
enemy escape. Dauntless and
blood-lusting, he cuts a manly
and brave figure with
peonies and wing-spreading
butterflies on his kimono.

ODORI JI (*niagari* tuning)
Yabu no uguisu, kimama no natte

The bush warbler sings
    self-indulgently in the mountain
    thicket, envying

utayamashisa no, niwa no ume.
are soyosoyo to, harukaze ga
ukina tatse ni fukikuru.
tsutsumi no sumire saitazuma
tsuyu no nasaki ni, nureta dōshi
iro ro koi to no, jitsu kurabe. jitsu
uita Nakanochō yoshi ya yoshi.

the plum tree in the garden.
Gently the spring breeze spreads
rumors of love.
Along the earthen dikes, the
violet and the knotweed are
together drenched by the sympathetic
dew. A true meeting of love and
    affection in gay Nakanochō.
    All is well.

CHIRASHI
Kōyū busō no isaoshi wa
arahitogami to, sue no yo mo
osore agamete,
kotoshi mata
hana no o Edo no Asakusa ni

For his matchless deed of filial
piety, he will be praised with awe,
like a god in man's form, until the
end of time.
This year, too, in flowery Asakusa in
    Edo. (Tokyo).

DANGIRE
kaichō aru zo
nigiwashiki.

We bring out the god's image
and honor him merrily.

·ɔ ぃ·

Aki no Irogusa, 1845
"The Colors of Autumn"

Composer: Kineya Rokuzaemon X
Text: Lord Nambu
Recordings: Columbia COCF-0108; NHK 1-3-1
Notation: Bunka 3316; Yoshizumi 1955, vol. 3

In many ways, the musical world of nineteenth-century Edo was like that of eighteenth-century Vienna. Music for the theater (kabuki and opera) was all the rage, and middle- and upper-class women took lessons in it. Rich patrons hired musicians and commissioned music for their own enjoyment. (Esterhazy for Haydn, Lord Nambu for Kineya.) In this context, the Lord of Nambu is said to have brought the texts of *Aki no Irokusa* to Kineya Rokuzaemon X, who was the *nagauta* teacher of the women in the Nambu mansion of Edo. The author of the text is sometimes listed as Satake Toshinari, Lord Nambu. Historically, such a person did not exist. Satake may have been Nambu's nom de plume, a common feature of aristocratic poets. As in other Nambu compositions, *Shiki no Yamamba* (p. 145) and *Azuma Hakkei* (p. 80), the text may have been written by Kineya's female students in the mansion. Whatever the origin of the text, the composition has remained a favorite in the *nagauta* repertory.

The composer is said to have been inspired by the concert piece *Azuma Hakkei*, written ten years earlier by Kineya Rokusaburō. Both pieces became popular because of their long shamisen interludes. While it has been borrowed by dancers and the conventional dance section's terms could be applied, the piece is better thought of as being in the *kumiuta* form (see p. 13) with its alternations of instrumental interludes and sets of unrelated poems.

Text. After a prelude, the four seasons imagery is sung quickly and the conventional listing of flowers and scenic locations fills in the text. The image of the wild geese (*karigane*) and sails (*ho*) is taken from the *Kokinshū*, poem 212. The dew on the reeds (*tsuyu no dani*) is from poem 167. It leads to a flower that represents the bond between husband and wife. After the insect interlude, the text is composed of a series of unrelated images, from a Chinese myth about an emperor's dream to a love scene, and then the sounds of nature lead to the next shamisen interlude, which is based on koto music. The wind blowing through the summit pines (at "mine no matsu kaze") is derived from a *Shūishū* poem that compares the sound to that of the koto. All the images that follow are conventional ones for seasons and finales. There is a pine tree that is said to flower once every hundred years, an image that is often found in final phrases (see *Takasago Tanzen*, p. 44).

Music. The *hayashi* instruments are seldom used in performances of this piece, but a second *(uwajōshi)* shamisen line is common. The shamisen's neck has an attachment *(kase)*. Like a guitar capo, this makes it possible to play the melody an octave higher and add light ornamentations or ostinatos.

The long *maebiki* is said to represent autumn. There is an imitation of insect sounds when the singers say "mushi no ne" before the first long interlude, which is entitled "The Sound of Insects." When the singer returns, the shamisen uses the virtuosic *ōzatsuma* pattern *honte*. A change of tuning leads to what could be considered a *kudoki* section or the middle song *(nakauta)* of the *kumiuta* form.

The next long instrumental interlude about koto music begins with the conventional *kangen* pattern. It is meant to imply courtly music. After that, virtuoso music flows over an ostinato played by the second shamisen. The next change of tuning *(sansagari)* leads to the final song with conventional text and accompaniment. Understandably, the piece is more popular with shamisen players than it is with singers.

MAEBIKI (*honchōshi* tuning)	Length 21'43"
MAEUTA	
aki kusa no azuma no nobe	Among the grasses of autumn
no shinogusa	and the ferns of the Azuma
shinobu mukashi ya	Plains, I recall the past, returning
inishieburi ni sumitsuku	to the village in summer after a
sato wa natsu ohiku	long absence.
azabu no yama no tani no	The Azabu mountains and
to ni asayū mukō tsukiyuki no	valleys under the moonlight look like the snow that, day and night, blankets the valley.
haru tsugedori no	In spring, the nightingale is
atowakete	known by its call.
namameku hagi ga hanazuri no	Fresh bush clover colors our
koromo karigane	borrowed garments.
koe o ho ni	Now the cry of passing geese
agete oroshite	sounds over the raised sails of
tamasudare	ships.
hashii no noki no niwa magaki	From the garden veranda's lowered bead blinds are seen

ukera, murasaki, kuzu,	morning glories [*ukera*], violets, [*murasaki*] arrowroot [*kuzu*], and
obana na	pompous pampas grass [*obana*].
tomone no yowa ni	We pass the night together.
ogi no ha no kaze wa	Even the midnight wind shall not
fukutomotsuyu o dani	disturb the dew on the reeds.
sueji tochigiru ominaeshi	Constant are my pledges to a "maidenflower."
sono akatsuki no	Here, at daybreak, I've made a
tamakura	pillow of my arm.
matsumushi no ne zo	The sounds of pine crickets.
AIKATA (*mushi no ne*)	("The Sound of Insects")
tanoshiki	How fine!
hentai hinpun tari	A sweet cacophony!
shinnari mata shinnari	Supple and mellifluous is their
shinsei enten su	strange music.
(*niagari* tuning)	
yume wa fuzan no	In a dream, the Divine Woman of
kumo no kyokun	Mount Wu appeared.
kumo no akebono	"In the morning I will be clouds,
ame ni yo ni utsusu ya	in the evening rain, and will come to you."
sode no ranjatai (*ai*)	The scent of incense scents fills the sleeves of our robes,
tometsu utsushitsu	kindling the fragrant substance.
mutsugoto mo	We exchange whispered
itsuka shijima no kanete yori	intimacies.
kotoba no masago shikishima no	Silence. Then a verse or two known from ages past as a
michi no yukute no tomoguruma	steadfast companion of love.
kuruto akuto ni	Day and night pass in this
kayuramu	fashion.
mine no matsu kaze	With the wind that blows through the summit pines
iwa kosu nami ni	and the sound of waves breaking,
sugagaku koto no	I play my koto,
tsumashirabe	setting first the pitch.
AIKATA (koto *tegoto*)	("koto music")
ATOUTA (*sangarari* tuning)	

112

utsushi gokoro ni	In this world, the flowers of
hana no haru tsukiwa	spring, the moon and the winds
aki kaze hototogisu	of autumn, and summer's song,
yuki ni kiesenu tanoshimi wa	the thrush, are the everlasting
tsukiseji tsuinu	joys of a thousand ages, joys that
chiyō yachiyō	remain after the winter snows have disappeared.
tokiwa kaki wa no	A thousand years, eight thousand
matsu no iro (*ai*)	years.
	Firm upon the rocks, the pine tree's color symbolizes longevity.

DANGIRE

iku tokaeri no	It blooms once in a hundred
hana ni utawan	years. This I sing.

Tokiwa no Niwa, 1851
"The Garden of Eternity"

Composer: Kineya Rokuzaemon X
Text: Mōrikō no Inkyo
Recording: NHK 1-6-2
Notation: Bunka 348 and vol. 18; Yoshizumi, vol. 3

The text is said to have been begun by the daimyo of the Namba clan and completed by his widow, Mōrikō, in their Edo residence. This was a major center for *nagauta* patronage during the mid–nineteenth century. Other pieces commissioned by the daimyo were *Azuma Hakkei* by Rokusaburō IV (see p. 80) and *Aki no Irogusa* by Rokuzaemon X (see p. 110). The text was inspired by seaside settings of the four seasons.

The text was jointly composed. It is a combination of stereotypical images of famous places and scenes. Thus, the words and music will be discussed together. In the Western calendar, the accepted date of the construction of the shrine mentioned in the first line of the text is 1168. Its mass of lanterns still shine. The *maebiki* is a delicate, free rhythm, shamisen solo. The opening vocal line is equally rubato. The tale of the reconstruction of the shrine is declaimed in *serifu* over *ōzatsuma* shamisen patterns. At a walking tempo, the full ensemble begins a *michiyuki*-style section, although there is no actor to enter. The *hayashi* adopts a formal noh drama style to help support the impressive views of the sea. The *hayashi* drops out at the interlude after "usugasumi" as the scene changes. The singer uses a long melisma on the word *no* while the listener pauses to imagine a view of Mount Fuji.

An instrumental prelude sets a new tuning and introduces two poems about seashells. They are divided by another interlude. After "kawairashi," a faster interlude using *tsuzumi chiri kara* patterns provides a transition to the next scene and tuning. The *taiko* and flute are typical signs that an *odori ji* (or *taiko ji*) has begun. The boat image returns with bright kabuki rhythms. The interlude after "feats" returns the *tsuzumi* to kabuki style. An *ondo* is a genre of folk songs, so the shamisen play a slow ostinato as the singer depicts a village scene with bamboo flute for support. The same kind of interjection (a *hamauta*, "beach song") is heard in another Namba-composed piece, *Shiki no Yamamba* (see p. 145).

The flute drops out at "koko," and the music picks up with a more kabuki, non-folk-song style. The *taiko* returns at "hatsufuyu" along with the bamboo flute, which supports the melody. The sounds of fluttering birds in this piece is the same as that in *Shiki no Yamaba* for the sound (*potto*) of a clump of dropping snow. One wonders what it means here. The *aikata* gives the shamisen room for virtuosic playing.

A new tuning returns us to the garden, which is filled with longevity signs such as pine trees. The *tsuzumi* play respectful noh patterns but soon return to the more lively *chiri kara* kabuki style when the lucky goddess Benziten is mentioned. The "secret piece" (*hikyoku*) is a long instrumental interlude that represents Shinto ritual music and then Shinto *kagura* dancing. It begins slowly with an ostinato by the second shamisen and noh pattern drums. The noh flute imitates the sound of the *kagurabue*, the flute used in Shinto ritual dances. Compare this part to that of the Shinto-based piece *Okina Sanbasō* (see p. 87). The tempo increases for the *kagura* dance music, showing off the skills of the shamisen rather than those of a dancer, who is not there.

The *chirashi* is conventional with double-stroke ostinatos before the singers enter. Only the *tsuzumi* in kabuki style are added, the *taiko* and flute being reserved for the final cadence.

A fine example of concert music at its best, listeners of *nagauta* still enjoy this product of the Edo period and its patronage of the arts.

OKI (*honchōshi* tuning)	Length 24'1"
somsomo itsukushima no	Hear now! The sacred shrine at
moyasjiro wa	Itsukushima, during the seventy-fourth
ninnō shhichijūyo	emperor's reign, it is said,
gyou ka to yo saikon arishi	was reconstructed with all its
miyabashira ikumno tose ka	pillars, how so many hundreds of
shiranami ni	years amid the white waves.
MICHIYUKI (*ai*)	
kazu no tomoshibi teriwatari	Countless lanterns shining across
sono omoklage o azuma naru (*ai*)	the waters reminding one of eastern
nagame wa tsukiji unabara no	Japan and a view without end: the sea
minami wa sōkiai kumo ni tsuzuki (*ai*)	[at Tsukiji] stretching southward, the
tōyama haruka ni	azure ocean climbing to the clouds;
usugasumi (*ai*)	the distant hills clothed in a cloak of
chifune momofune	mist; ships by the hundreds, by the
ikikatou haru no akebono	thousands, coming and going through
fuji no yuki nodoka ni nioou	the spring dawn; snow on Mount Fuji,
asahikage	and the balmy scent of morning sunlight.

KUDOKI (*niagari* tuning)
ada to koi o utsuse gai moshi ya
miru me o uchiyoru miru me o
uchiyoru nami ni sui na sugai no
sono osugata o itsu ka wasuren
wasuegai kao wa kazukashi

Vengeance and love as an empty
sea-shell are seen.
If one should "see" weed
pounded by the waves, the chic
tipsy-shell showing its shape
among them. Who could forget it,
who shall forget it?

monijigaii nadeshikogai no
kawairtashi (*ai*)
sashikuru shio ni kogi izuru

The shamefaced, blushing, red maple
shell, the maiden flower-shell so
charming. Rowing out over the
incoming tide,

ODORI JI (*sansagari* tuning)
yukashiki fune no aosudare (*ai*)
nejime mo tataki takanawa ni (*ai*)
narete kamome no
mitsu yotsu futatesu mutsu (*ai*)
mutsumutsushi takeshiba ni (*ai*)
mietsu kakuretsu okisu
no ashi ni tsubasa suzushiki
yūmagure miji ni shimu koro wa
tatsu aki no

a lovely boat, with its sky blue
blinds, the high-pitched strains
of high-strung bird-trap lines;
undeceived, the sea gulls—three,
four, two, six. In harmony
off Takeshiba one sees, then
cannot see them, the shifting
shoals where they cool their
wings among the reeds in the
twilight. One feels the chill on this
first day of autumn.

ONDO
tomaya no kemuri kuna dorite
ejima ga saki ya akashigata
suma no urabe de shio kumu
ama wa shinkirashi ja nai kai na
yoi yoi yoi
yoiyawsa sore (*ai*)

The smoke from the thatched
hut, in delicate shades of gray; at
Picture Island's cape, Akashi's
lagoon, or Suma's beach, the
fisherfolk making salt—aren't
they provoking? Yoi yoi yoi yoi
yoiyasa sore.

koko wa ohama no tsuki o mede
shimo o kasanete utsu kinuta

Here one can admire the moon
above the beach, the sound of the
fulling block.

hatsufuyu no itaya o tataku tama
aware (*ai*)
oto mo samukeki meya no to o (*a*)

On a frosty eve, the
tintinnabulation of hail on a
board roof in early winter—even
the sound makes one shiver, the
bed chamber door left ajar with

sasade nagusamu tomochidori chiya
chirichiri (*ai*)
chirichi chiri patto
yahan no izaribi yotsude ami
yo wataru waza no shinajima wa
koto no hagusa no oyobi naki

rice wine for consolation
with gregarious plovers
fluttering chiri ya chirichiri chirichiri
patto and suddenly in the night a
fisherman's flickering fire, a fishnet
being paid out—truly the myriad
skills of this world cannot be
described in words.

AIKATA (*honchōshi* tuning)
tada kono niwa wa toshigoto ni
matsu o midori no oishigen
shikioriori no fūkei wa
Benzaiten nyuo no onmegumi
fuku enman kagiri naki mai no
hikyoku no omoshiroua

Meanwhile, in this garden, year
by year the young pines mature
and flourish and each season's
scenic sights are the blessed gifts
of the goddess Benzaiten:
happiness, longevity, and harmony
without limit, and a secret dance
piece so wonderful!

AIKATA
CHIRASHI
namki no tsuzumi ni fuetake no
jūni no ritsu o misuji no ito ni
shirabe totonou hitofushi wa
shunka shūtō tanoshimi no
chiyo ni yorozuyo

(*Miho kagura* music)

The drumming of the waves, the
bamboo of the pitch pipes, the
twelve pitches on the three
strings: the melody thus properly
performed is "Spring-Summer-
Autumn-Winter Music"; through a
thousand ages, ten thousand ages,

DANGIRE
shukushi shukushite

let us celebrate.

Tsuru Kame, 1851
"The Tortoise and the Crane"

Composer: Kineya Roukuzaemon X
Text: Noh drama *Gekkyuden*
Recording: Columbia COCF 70109, NHK 2-1-1
Notation: Bunka 3305; Yoshizumi, vol. 1

BOOK CD: 2–1

Originally a concert piece, *Tsuru Kame* later was used to accompany dance. The formal divisions of the piece mix noh terms such as *ageuta*, *mondō*, and *kiri* with those of traditional kabuki dance. After a *nagauta* imitation of noh chant, the shamisen enters with a noh-style percussion and flute ensemble. With the end of the *oki* section (*tsuranu*) and its imperial setting, the shamisen play a double-stop pattern called *kangen* (winds and strings), which is an imitation of the thicker texture of *gagaku* court music. The *ageuta* section begins with kabuki *chiri kara* drumming until the mythical mountain Hōrai is described. To see the same place described in a geisha house context, look at the piece *Hōrai* (p. 84).

During the *mondō* dialogue of the noh drama text, the shamisen uses the *ōzatsuma* patterns that had become the standard method of accompanying narrative rather than lyrical music (see p. 15). It is followed by a *kudoki*-style solo song that contains Japan's best-known symbols of long life and prosperity, the tortoise and the crane. With the change of tuning (*niagari*) comes the text of a dance. In addition to a slow shamisen, the lyrical vocal part, the *hayashi*, plays music derived from a "Chū no Mai" dance, which was part of the original noh drama. The section (at "sumeru") that provides the transition to the *kiri* uses kabuki drum patterns for textural contrast. The *kiri* section contains the major dance of the play. The *hayashi* is taken directly from the noh music of the dance *Gaku* and is meant to represent an imperial setting. Note that the shamisen uses a few double stops as well as a second (*uwajōshi*) shamisen line to thicken the texture. Analysis and the Western score of a full performance can be found in Malm 1963.

Oᴋɪ (*honchōshi* tuning)	Length 19'4"
sore seiyo no naru ni nareba	Since this is the season of
shiki no sechi e no koto hajime (*ai*)	early spring, we begin the ceremonies of the four

furōmon nite, jistu getsu no
hikari o kimi no (*ai*)
eiran nite (*ai*)
hyakan keishō sode o tsuranu (*ai*)
sono kazu ichioku, kyakuyo nin
hai o susumuru, manko no koe
ichidō ni hai suru sono oto wa
ten ni (*ai*)
hibikite obita dashi

seasons as our lord views
the light of the sun and
moon by the Gate of Eternal Youth.
Hundreds of officials and
the ministers of state
accompany him, millions of
people lift up their prayers,
and the sound of ten
thousand families praying as one
  resound to the heavens.

AGEUTA

niwa no isago wa, kin gin no

tama o tsurante, shikitae no

ioe no nishikiya, ruri no toboso shako no
yukigeta, menō no hashi
ike no migiwa no, tsuru kame wa hōraisan
mo, yoso natazu

kimi mo megumizo (*ai*)

arigataki

The gardens are arrayed in jewels of
  gold and silver, numberless as
grains of sand; marvelous
  five-hundred-fold
brocade is spread about. Gates of lapis
lazuli, roof beams of mother-of-pearl,
stairways of agate. The crane and the
tortoise at the brink of the pond
  gratefully
 receive our lord's favor; it is as if the
  holy
mountain of P'ing Lai were in this
  place.

MONDŌ

Ikani sōmon mosubeki
koto no sōrō
somon towa nanigoto zo
mainen no karei no gotoku
tsuru kame o mawaserare
sono nochi gekkyuden,
nite bugaku o
so seraryo zuru nite sōrō
tomokaku mo hakarai sorae

How should we appear
before the throne? What
message shall we bring? In
keeping with our yearly
custom, we dance the
Crane and Tortoise Dance
and afterward, at the
Moon Palace, present our
lord with court dancing (*bugaku*). Let
  us see that this is suitably
  arranged.

AIKATA
kame wa manen no yowaione

(*chū no mai*)
The tortoise lives to the age

119

tsuru mo chioya kasanuran

of ten thousand years; the crane's years mount up to one thousand.

ODORI JI (*niagari* tuning)
chiyo no tameshi no
kazu kazu ni
nani o hikamashi, hime komatsu (*ai*)
yowai ni tagū tanchō no
tsuru mo hasode o taoyaka ni
chiyō o kasanete,

From the many paragons of long life, let us choose the small pine tree. And alike in its life is the sacred crane, gracefully disporting its sleeves, time and again for thousands of

mai asobu (*ai*)
migiri ni shigeru,
kure take no midori no
kame no iku yorozu yomo
ike mizu ni
sumeru mo yasuki,
kimi ga yoi aogi kanadete
tsuru to kame yowaio sazuke tate
matsureba kimi mo gyokan no
amari ni ya
bugaku o so shite, mai tamo o

years there are pleasurable dances. As the green bamboo flourishes by the garden path, As the tortoise dwells many

thousands of years in the depths of the pond, so, when the crane and tortoise present their long lives amid dance and song and pay homage to our lord's tranquil life, his feelings seem to overflow and he himself joins in the music and dance.

AIKATA
KIRI
gekkyuden no hyakue no tamoto
gekkyuden no hyakue no tamoto
iro iro taenaru, nan no sode

(*Gaku* interlude)

The sleeves of the white robe in the Moon Palace, the myriad flowerlike sleeves,

AIKATA
aki wa shigure no mamiji no hasode
fuyu wa saeyuki,
yuki no tamoto o
hirugaesu koromomo,
usumursaki no kumo no eubito no,

like maple leaves in the showers of autumn, the sleeves like the snows of winter . . . the waving garments of cloudy purple as voices of those above the clouds join in the song

120

bugaku no koegoe ni
geisho ui no, kyoku naseba

of the rainbow-skirted robe
of feathers.

AIKATA

CHIRASHI

san kasomoku, kokuto yutaka ni chiyo
yorozu yoto, mai tamaeba
kannin kayochyo,
mikoshi o hayame
kimi no yowai mo, chyoseiden ni
kimi no yowai mo, chyoseiden ni

Our dance brings
thousands upon thousands
of years of prosperity to
this land, rich in
mountains, rivers, plains,
and forests. Then courtier and
commoner alike speed our lord's
chariot, and his reign itself, into the
Palace of Longevity.

DANGIRE

kangyo naru koso
medetakere

For an auspicious
congratulatory event.

Late-Nineteenth-Century Compositions

·⌣ ⌣·

Suehirogari, 1854
"The Open Fan"

Composer: Kineya Rokuzaemon X
Text: Sakurada Jitsuke III
Recordings: Columbia COCF 70116; NHK 2-19-2; Toshiba TOCF 4045
Notation: Bunka 3302; Kineya 1; Yoshizumi, vol. 1

This piece is most often heard at a beginner's concert. It is such a clear, short example of the kabuki dance form that it was used for an educational video (Malm 1994). The origin of the story is a comic *kyōgen* from noh. In it, a lord sends his servant to buy a fan after describing its shape and structure. The servant returns from the market drunk and happy with an umbrella. In the *nagauta* version, the dance ends with an open fan, a symbol of good fortune. *Shite* and *ado* are dramatic terms for actors on stage.

Text. The *oki* describes the setting of a noh stage and identifies the *kyōgen* actors, who appear in the *michiyuki* as the *hayashi* enters. At "tanoda," there is a sensual diversion from the plot. In keeping with its lyric function, the *kudoki* is more romantic. The *taiko ji* can be called the *odori ji* because it is here that dance (*odori*) is emphasized. The text of the *chirashi* is typical of congratulatory pieces, and the *dangire* refers to the meaning of the title.

Music. The *oki* uses voice and shamisen. The *hayashi* enters at the *michiyuki* using basic noh-style patterns: *mitsuji* (fig. 15, p. 17) for the *tsuzumi* and *koiai* for the *taiko.* The standard opening text in *kyōgen* of the lord and his servant's reply is declaimed in *serifu.* After "omae ni," the *tsuzumi* change to *chiri kara* patterns (fig. 16, p. 17). The *taiko* and noh flute then play the kabuki pattern *bungo sagari ha* (fig. 19, p. 18), twice, plus a *kuse.* This first section of the piece actually introduces the basic styles of *hayashi* music in *nagauta.*

The *kudoki* is correctly set for voice and shamisen only. Melodic tension is created by means of stops on pitches above tone centers. If one thinks of B, E, and F-sharp as tone centers, then the melody will stop on C, F, or G (see fig. 12).

Note. Since this piece is used so much in education, it seems appropriate to list all the patterns when they appear.

The *taiko ji* begins with the *taiko* playing *ten ten ten* while the shamisen play E, E, E. This *taiko ji* entrance is standard. At the instrumental interlude (*aikata*), the noh flute and *taiko* play the kabuki pattern *kyōgen gakko* (fig. 18, p. 18). The rhythm of the shamisen line matches that of the pattern. The *tsuzumi* enter in *chiri kara* and one *mitsuij*. The text is declaimed (*serifu*). The *aikata* is repeated with the same *hayashi*. This repeat is rare in *nagauta*, but it helps in an educational piece.

A *taiko* cadence (*kashira*) is the standard beginning for a *chirashi* section. The *hayashi* plays a noh drama unit of patterns called *sandame*, the "third *dan*." It only appears near an ending in noh or kabuki pieces (see Malm 1978, 164). The *dangire* (fig. 14, p. 17) use of stock melody and *hayashi* cadence confirms an ending. This pedagogically perfect example is a good beginner's piece and pleasant listening.

OKI (*honchōshi* tuning)	Length 8'35"
egaku butai no, matsu take mo	Like pines and bamboo upon the
chiyo o kametaru, saishiki no	stage, like these painted
wakamidori naru, shite to ado	emblems of longevity, is the youthful greenness of the *shite* and *ado*.

MICHIYUKI

makari ide shimo, hazukashisō	Bashfully he makes his
ni	appearance, and a voice calls,
koe hariagete	"Tarōkaja, are you there?"
Tarōkaja, aru ka, omai ni.	"I am before you."
nen no hayakatta.	"You are quick."
tanoda hito wa,	Today the gentleman again has a
kyō mo mata koi no	request to make. Is it an errand of
yakko no mo no otsukai ka	a slave of love, love that awaits a
henji matsu koi, shinobu koi	reply, stealthy love that cheers
harete ōgi mo na nomi nite	him. Even the word *"fan."*

KUDOKI

hon ni kokoro mo, shiraōgi	His heart is truly like a white fan,
itsuka shubi shite, aobone no	with blue ribs held firmly at
yurugumai tono, kaname no	their pivot, secure as lovers'
chigiri	vows when they arrange to meet.
kataku shimeo no,	The lovers's knot,
en musubi kami o	firmly tied,
tanomu no, chikaigoto	when they call upon the gods
nurete iro masu,	in their pledge.
hana no ame	The colors of the flowers are brighter, drenched with rain, a rain of flowers.

TAIKO JI

Kasa o sasu nara, Kasugayama	And he holds an umbrella at
(ai)	Mount Kasuga. It is like a flower-
kore mo hana no, en tote hito	viewing party.
ga	People drink and pour wine.
nomite sasu nara sasōyo	"I think I'll do the same."
hana no saka	The wine cups of flowers. The
hannagasa	hats bedecked with flowers.
genimo sōyono, geni makoto	Thus it is, indeed, it is.

CHIRASHI

Yotsu no umi,ima zo osamaru	Even now, a favorable wind
tokitsukaze nami no tsuzumi	calms the four seas; the voices of
no	the drumming waves are stilled,
koe sumite utotsu mōtsu,	while we sing and dance.
kimi ga yo wa ban, banzai mo,	Our lord's reign for ten thousand
kagiri naku suehiro gari koso,	years unending spreads out
medetakere.	before us like our fans as we wish
	him joy.

DANGIRE

Suehiro gari koso, medetakere	Spreads out like our fans, as we wish
	him joy.

Funazoroi, 1856
"A Pageant of Boats"

Composer: Kineya Katsusaburō II
Text: Unknown
Recording: Columbia CAK 9223
Notation: Bunka, vol. 19

Funazoroi is a *buyō* (classical dance) rather than a kabuki composition. It probably was performed on a stage near the Sumida River. The music is relatively simple and functional as a support for dance. It can be heard in beginning dance or shamisen concerts.

Text. After reciting a novel fiction about the ancient invention of boats, the words lead us through a series of boat scenes and locations along the shore of the Sumida and other rivers. All the names dropped and the styles of passenger boats would have been nostalgic to audiences familiar with the lifestyle of the Yoshiwara entertainment district. The pleasure boats can still be seen during holidays on the river in Tokyo. Although nowadays they have motors rather than poles and recordings rather than geishas, many a song can be heard along the banks of the Sumida. Chichibu is the source of the river. The singer performs a long melisma on the *wa* of "Sumidagawa," perhaps to emulate the flowing waters. The "village of love" is obviously part of the chain of brothels located along the river.

Music. As dance accompaniment, the musical form is fairly predicable. The opening *maebiki* is for shamisen alone. The first line of the *oki* is sung rubato with brief shamisen support. Note that the shamisen does *not* use introductory *ōzatsuma* patterns. The function of this music is not to show off the singer but to get on with the dance. At "morokoshi," a steady beat and full orchestration enter and continue up to "fuku kaze." Given its function of supporting the dance movement, it is interesting that the *tsuzumi* first play the exact rhythm of the shamisen line before entering into the noh drama style with a few noh flute sounds added to evoke the atmosphere of ancient times. The dancer no doubt appreciates such clear guides to the beat. The legend begins (at "niwa no ike") with just a singer and shamisen. From "sasagani" to the cadence, the tempo is rubato and *ōzatsuma*-style patterns are used. The first *aikata* includes noh-style *tsuzumi* and noh flute. At "miwataseba," the orchestration changes to *taiko*, bamboo flute, and hand gong. They provide an active, plebian atmosphere as we have changed from the Chinese imperial scene to a busy line of Edo ships. After "ukisugata," the *tsuzumi* enter with kabuki *chiri kara* patterns as the birds are in flight.

A change of tuning and orchestration introduces other nautical scenes with a bamboo flute embellishing the lyrical *kudoki* melody.

The next brief *aikata* is a prelude to the scene of boats, which are about to appear, with the *taiko* and flute play playing *wataribyōshi* patterns (fig. 17, p. 18). They drop out at "haruka mukau o." The music stops while voice alone sings out "Takeya" like a melismatic folk song. At "noki o" the *wataribyōshi* pattern returns. However, this time it is played on a folk *odeko* drum, bamboo flute, and hand gong because we are moving toward Tsukuda, another party area on the river.

The next *aikata* is played by shamisen and *chiri kara tsuzumi*. Both parts match rhythms as, probably, do the dance movements.

A slow lyrical voice and shamisen section begins at "moshi ya" in imitation of a geisha *hauta* genre piece. The shamisen then tune to the popular "geisha tuning" (*sansagari*) and perform part of a lively popular song. The shamisen then play the Tsukuda pattern (fig. 13, p. 16) while the previous flute and percussion group returns with more party music as the scene enters the Tsukuda brothels. The *aikata* uses a jaunty, slightly dotted rhythm for both the shamisen and a *chiri kara tsuzumi* line. They mix with the bamboo flute and hand gong to support the gay image of the teahouse.

Following the text about two shamisen playing, a slower interlude occurs with two shamisen parts and *tsuzumi*. It continues as a geisha-style popular song is sung. The boat scene returns (at "fune no yoko"), and the same ensemble plays, again matching rhythms. However, there are two shamisen lines that do not seem to coincide. Perhaps this is the mix of musical sounds emanating from the many boats.

A faster tempo supports the song of the drunken customers or girls. Much of the dialogue is declaimed (*serifu*). The festival drum and flute music returns as the boatful of drunken guests gambles and dances to a lively *aikata*. The last syllable of *yara* is extended like a drunk unable to beat his fan.

The *chirashi* section opens with the traditional three beats of the *taiko*. The *hayashi* plays the standard *sandame* patterns (see p. 18).

The standard *dangire* is delayed until the repeated last line, during which time the actor will have struck his final *mie* pose. On recordings meant for dance, other standard items may be added. One is kabuki curtain-closing (*makigai*) music. Another piece (*kata shagiri*) is played after the curtain closes while the audience departs.

MAEBIKI (*honchōshi* tuning)	Length 42'
OKI	
somosomo fune ajimari wa	Hear now: the first boat was invented

morokoshi hōtai ni tsukasehi
kateki to ieru ari chiriku yanagi no
hitoha no ue ni chichiu no norite
sasagani no ito hikihaeshi sugata yori
takumi idseshi fune to ka ya

in the court of the Yellow Emperor of China by one Huo-di, a retainer. In a garden pond, blown by the autumn wind, floated a single willow leaf, and on it rode a spider, spinning its web. Inspired by this scene, it is said he cleverly created the first boat.

AIKATA (MICHIYUKI)
miwataseba unabara tōku
maho kataho
yukikō fune no kazukazu wa
kasumi no urani miegakure (*ai*)

Looking far out to sea, one sees the sails, full or half furled, of numerous ships running hither and thither then disappearing from view in fog-filled inlets.

shiranami yosuru iso chikaku
chidori kamome no ukisugata

White waves wash the sandy strand, and nearby plovers and seagulls bob and float.

AIKATA
ami hiku fune ya tsuribune no
minakogi tsurete yuki kayō
nagame nodokeki haru geshiki
omoshiroya

Boats hauling nets, boats trawling, all rowing, coming and going.
How pleasant to behold.
How interesting.

KUDOKI (*niagari* tuning)
Tsukuba ne no
mineyori otsuru mitsuzuji mo
tsumori tsumori te Chichibu yori
kiyoku nagaruru Sumidagawa
tsukiyo (to)hana yo to
kogi idasu

As the thread of water falling from Tsukuba's peak, so flows from the mountains of Chichibu the crystal-clear Sumida River.
It's moon-viewing time! It's blossom-viewing time!

AIKATA
yakata yanefune (*ai*)
chiyoki nitari
Omaya Suda no watashibune

They go rowing out in
salon boats, roofed boats,
swift boar's tusks light cargo boats, the ferries at Omaya and Suda.

haruka mukau o

From over on the bank someone calls out

Takeya to yobukoe ni
sanya ori o nori idasu

"Takeya." As we head into Sanya, the canal

koi no seiki ya no sato chigaku	not far from the village of love,
sanami no fune no Mukōjima	the blossom-viewing vessels cluster at Mukōjima.
noki o narabeshi yanefune no	The eaves of the drifting salon boats
sudare no	nearly touch. A gentle sound is heard
uchi no tsumebiki wa	from behind the bamboo curtains.

AIKATA — Who could the player be?

moshiya sorekato hitoshirazu	Aflame with curiosity, scarlet kimono
kiomomi ura o fukikaeshi	linings exposed by the trailing breeze
oite no kaze ni	and borne by the incoming tide,

ODORI JI (*sansagari* tuning)

ageshi oni (*ai*) Tsukuda Tsukuda to isoida oseba	"To Tsukuda, Tsukuda, quickly we row."

AIKATA

mata kamite kara	while from upstream are heard
nichō samisen hiki tsurete	two shamisen playing in tandem:
sama wa Sanya no mikazukisama yo	"You're the crescent moon over Sanya.
yoi ni chirari to mitabakari	I only see you fleetingly in the night.
shōngai na (*ai*)	Isn't so?
makezu otoranu (ai) yukiai no	Not to be outdone, from a passing
fune no yoko kara misuji no ito ni	vessel comes, added to the three strings,

AIKATA

nichō tsuzumi o utsuyōtsutsu no	the sound of two hand drums
nami no fune (*ai*)	unreeling in this unreal wave-borne boat world.
jitai warera wa miyako no umare	Originally we're all from the capital, but, drawn by debauchery, we've
iro ni soyasare konna nari ni narareta	ended up like this. There are many
migoto na sake wa ōkeredo	great rice wines, but I was surprised to
kiite bikkuri mara sanbai nonda	hear that I'd drunk three whole
sakazuki tsu,tsu, tsu no tsu	cups—I hadn't noticed."
omokaji torikachi koegoe ni	A voice calls out, "Steer to the right,
norishi	steer to the left."
okyaku no kimo ukare (*ai*)	The passengers, too, find their spirits afloat.
rōchiei bamakai haratte ikken osaemashō	Let's settle up and finish the game.
kenuchi yamete odoruyara	Ending the hand game, they dance;

129

AIKATA

ōgi narashite uto oya aaa ra

beating the rhythm with their fans,
    they sing.

CHIRASHI

shido mo naya

Such gay revelry out on the bustling

nigiō suda no kawazura wa

surface of the river.

kore zo makoto no Edo no ana

This is the true flower of Edo

sako oru miyo koso

blooming in auspicious profusion for

medetakere

all ages to come in auspicious
    profusion.

DANGIRE

sako oru miyo koso medetakere

[repeated phrase]

Kuramayama, 1856
"Mount Kurama"

Composer: Kineya Katsusaburō II
Text: Unknown
Recordings: NHK 1-2-15; Toshiba TOCF 4015
Notation: Bunka 3310; Yoshizumi 1, vol. 1

The text tells a mythical story about the youth of Minamoto Yoshitsune, the tragic hero of many tales about the Minamoto/Taira (Genji/Heike) civil war in the twelfth century. The tale of his fights with demons in the mountains makes for dramatic kabuki dancing and music, but the words are more functional than poetic.

Text. Mount Kurama, north of Kyoto, is the site of the Kuruma temple. According to folklore, it was filled with *tengu*. These are supernatural beings with red faces and long noses. Their masked figures are seen at many folk festivals. Originally considered malevolent, they appear in this story as protectors of good in the face of evil.

Ushiwakamaru is the childhood name of Yoshitsune. His family name is written here as Genke (Genji) no Saidōtaru. His father was slain for the Heike by a traitorous retainer. Heike is an alternate name for the Taira clan.

Tamoten (also known as Bishimonten) is the principal deity worshipped at the Kurama temple. Munekiyo was a Taira warrior who took pity on Yoshitsune's mother, Tokiwa, and helped her to safety.

Shōjōbō was a famous *tengu* said to be at the Kurama temple. In this story he has arranged a mock attack on Ushiwaka as a teaching device and a test.

Music. There were several attempts to make *nagauta* more narrative than lyrical. This is an example of the usual way to do so, the use of *ōsatsuma* patterns.

The opening *maebiki* ends with the *jo* pattern notated earlier (fig. 11A, p. 15). All the music up to "osoroshi" is in *ōsatsuma* patterns. A similar music is found at the start of the piece *Gorō Tokimune* (see p. 107). Kabuki-style *serifu* declamations appear throughout the piece. The first is occurs at "tengu."

In the *michiyuki*, the entrance of the actor is supported by normal shamisen music plus the sound of *tsuzumi* drums playing noh patterns and the noh flute. The shamisen stops suddenly (with a hand across the strings) before the declamation of the phrase "father's revenge" (*chichi no ada*). These words are treated exactly the same as they were in *Gorō Tokimune*. The phrase "every night" (*yogyoto*) is accompanied by a slide down chromatic pitches on the shamisen. The section ends on an *ōsatsuma* cadence pattern.

In the *aikata*, full *hayashi* play patterns that match the rhythm of the shamisen line. The text from "omoi" to "kakarerare" is chanted to *ōsatsuma* patterns.

In the *kudoki*, the *nasake* passage uses the lyrical *tataki* convention (see p. 15).

The next *aikata* could be considered an *odori ji* or *chirashi*. The flute and *tsuzumi* are heard as the topic turns to sword practice (*kendō*). The line "ide ya" is declaimed without accompaniment because in an actual kabuki it is probably performed by the actor.

At "tokishi," the *hayashi* enters at high speed to stir up the scene. The racket (*meidō*) is created in the shamisen line by striking the strings back and forth quickly while blocking the sound with a finger under the strings. The *hayashi* drop out. When the word *tengu* appears again, the shamisen plays another sliding chromatic scale. After Ushiwakamaru's name is called out, the *tsuzumi* join the shamisen in a matched pattern called *hige soru* (beard scratching) which is found in *aragoto* pieces such as *Gorō Tokimune*. The *chiri kara* combination continues through the fight until the singer declaims "kodomo shite" and the shamisen return to the *ōsatsuma* style.

The *chirashi* opens with a typical shamisen convention for that section. This is a line of double stops followed by an ostinato, which continues until the singer enters. Unlike other *chirashi*, the *hayashi* is not used, perhaps in order to leave space for one to hear the virtuoso shamisen interlude. Full orchestration returns at "kuramashi" for the actor strikes a dramatic posture (*mie*) as the curtain closes.

MAEBIKI (*honchōshi* tuning)	Length 16'38"
OKI	
sore	Listen to my story.
tsuki mo Kurama no kage utoku	Under a dark sky
konoha odoshi no sati arashi	deep in the recesses of Mount Kurama,
monosawagashi ya Kibunegawa	where the noisy Kibune River flows, a gusty late-night wind with a desolate sound blows leaves from their branches.
tengu dōshi nomakai no	This enclave of the demon world,
chimata zo	where the *tengu* dwell in great
osoroshiki	numbers, is truly a haunted place.

koko ni Genke no Saidōtaru	Here young Ushiwaka [Genke no
Ushiwakamaru wa chichi no ada	Saidōtaru] comes every night to pray
Heike o hitotachi uramin to	to the deity Tamoten for revenge
yogyoto mōzuru iwakado ni	against the Heike slayers of his father.
Tamonten kinin no tsukare	Tired from fervent prayer, he dozes
iwakado ni shibashi madoromu	for a while seated cross-legged on a
hiza makura	rock with his head in his hand.

AIKATA

omoi idaseba ware imada	Memories come rushing back to him.
sansai no toki narishi ga	I was not even three when my mother,
haha Tokiwa ga futokoro ni	Tokiwa, holding me close to her
kakaerare	breast, escaped to the village of
Fushima no sato nite	Fushima. Thanks to the mercy of
Munekiyo ga	Munekiyo, my life was spared. Later it
nasake ni yorite inochi tasukari	was decided that I should become a
shukake o seyo to tōzan no	monk, so I was brought to this
(ai)	mountain and given into the care of
Tōkōbō e azukerareshi o	Tōkōbō.
kazoete mireba	If you count back,
hito mukashi (ai)	this was all well in the past.
jūyo nen no seisō furedo	For more than ten years have the stars
osanago kokoro ni	crossed the sky and has the frost
	fallen,
wasurezu shite ima	but despite my age
mano atari ni mitaru yume	even now, as if before my very eye, I
sore ni tsuketemo	see it all in a dream of
chichi no ada.	revenge for my father.

AIKATA

kendō shugyō nasu to iedomo	I practice the way of the sword, but
ware ikkō no nama byōchō	still I am a complete novice. Perhaps
negaeba kami no	the gods will hear my prayers and
megumi nite	bestow their blessing.
homō toguru jisetsu o matan	I will wait till the time is ripe to attain
	my goal.
ide ya takuma no shugyō o	But meanwhile I will strive to sharpen
nasan (ai)	my military skills.
kidachi ottori migamae nasu (ai)	He draws his sword and strikes a
tokishi mo niwaka ni	defensive posture.

kaze okori

tengu tsubute no barabara to

meidō nashite susamajishi (*ai*)

Suddenly a wind blows up
and leaves fall with a hideous racket
like the hail of pebbles thrown by the
tengu.

haruka no sugi no

kozue yori (*ai*) mata mo ya

ayashi no shōtengu (*ai*) kidachi

uchifuri (*ai*) tachimukaeba (*ai*)

shi ya kozakashi to

Ushiwakamaru (*ai*) tsukeiru

kidachi o

harainoke (*ai*) jōdan gedan (*ai*)

How frightful; from the branches of a
cedar swoop many ferocious
dwarf *tengu*, flailing their swords.
As he stands facing them, he
adroitly wards off blows with sword
high, then low, with movements swift
and sure.
Wondering who will win, hidden
in the

sassoku no hataraki (*ai*)

shōbu ika ni to kirigakure

ushiro ni ukagō Sōjōbō (*ai*)

masari otoranu ryōnin ga

kidachi no oto wa kodama shite

mezamashiku mo mata

isamashishi

mist, (Sojōbō), watches
(Ushiwakamaru) from behind.

Both sides have superior fighters.
The sound of their swords echoes.
Brilliant and bold is the fighting.

AIKATA

CHIRASHI

sashimo no tengu mo

ashirai kane

But even such warriors as the *tengu*
are no match [for Ushiwaka],

AIKATA

ato o kuramashi usenikeri

so into the darkness they disappear.

DANGIRE

ato o kuramashi usenikeri

Into the darkness they disappear.

Kuruwa Tanzen, 1857

"The Brothel Bathhouse"

Composer: Kineya Katsusaburō II
Text: Unknown
Recording: NHK 3-42-2
Notation: Bunka 3316 and vol. 19

The colorful, sensual text of this composition reflects its origin. It was a spring concert review for the Hanayagi dance guild. This annual event still occurs in the major geisha houses of Tokyo and Kyoto. An alternate title for the piece is *Kuruwa no hanayagi no tategami* (The Willow Leaf Hairdos of the Pleasure Quarters). The music of this review was expanded in 1915 by Kineya Katsusaburō IV. It remains a challenge for professional musicians and dancers and provides an insight into brothel life at the height of the Edo period.

Text. An *utsushie* was a nineteenth-century magic lantern that used an oil lamp for light. It projected glass slides with hand painted images by Hishikawa Moronobu (d. 1694) who created many "floating world" (*ukiyoe*) prints and scrolls of the Yoshiwara. Because of this setting, the text of *Kuruwa Tanzen* is filled with double meanings. They are only noted occasionally so as not to distract from the musical goals of these comments. Brightly colored figurines of Yoshiwara residents and kabuki characters were (and still are) popular souvenir dolls. The three mentioned after the *michiyuki* are the topic of an earlier *tokiwazu* genre piece, "Three Dolls" (*Mitsu ningyō*), and the footman (*yakko*) is found in the *nagauta* piece *Tomoyakko* (see p. 74). Tanzen was a bathhouse near which much Edo social life took place. The fashion of the day became that of the bathhouse and its clients. Six gangs (*roppō*) of ruffians hung about in flashy clothes. The Yoshiya and Shiratsuka were two of them, and, as the text shows, they made trouble. The word *roppō* is declaimed (*serifu*). It refers not only to the gangs but also to a special male exit in kabuki. The term *nejikiri* is declaimed. It could refer to the servant's habit of wearing a short coat and tucking his kimono up behind (see *Tomoyakko*). It also could mean to twist one's body or grab the sword of someone else. It is a common fight scene in prints of Edo period streets. The "date style" is that of the bathhouse, which became the fashion of the area.

In the history of the Yoshiwara, the word *shōji* refers to the official Shōji Jinzaemon. In the bedding display, the mythical mountain of Hōrai is mentioned because it was said to be filled with beauty and pleasure. See the piece *Hōrai* (p. 84) for details. Some performers think that *hozonkakerutaru* is an imitation of the sound of a nightingale as well as an invitation to the brothel.

The *kudoki* song text is in the *kouta* style of ambiguity. The word *sanya* is the old name of the place, later called Asakusa, where the Yoshiwara was built. Even more abstract is the claim that "deep grass" (*kusa fukakeredo*) is a play on *kuse* (grass) because Asakusa means "shallow grass." Note that the courtesan who looks back at her costume is a *hayanagi*. That could be a play on the word *hanayagi*, which is the guild name of the dancers. The conjunction of Altair and Vega occurs on the seventh day of the seventh lunar month. According to the legend, a magpie spreads his wings across the Milky Way to make a bridge for the lovers. Many special items are sold during the summer *obon* festival. Placing pine and bamboo decorations before the door is still common at New Year's.

The last line contains the words *hana* and *yanagi*. These combine with the Chinese reading of *kotobunki* (*jū*) to honor Hanayagi Jūsuke, who underwrote and directed the first performance.

Music. The *maebiki* is fast and bright and uses a series of double stops that remind one of geisha party music. The *tsuzumi* in kabuki style join the shamisen for the *michiyuki*. This is clearly not the moment to evoke courtly or noh drama atmospheres. When the images of samurai appear (at "yoshiya otoko"), the *taiko* and noh flute join the *tsuzumi* in noh patterns to put some class into the music. The *tsuzumi* drop out at the interlude, and the *taiko* and flute change to *wataribyōshi*–based kabuki patterns. When the samurai and his servant (*yakko*) appear, the shamisen play a double-stop passage to add "weight" to the figures strutting on stage. The music changes to kabuki-style *tsuzumi* for the words are those of the servant, who is arranging the tryst. The "leave it to me" is *serifu* in the style of a footman rather than a samurai. The *taiko* and flute return only for the common geisha expression *shongae*. The section ends with a compliment to the beauty (flowers) of the Yoshiwara women.

The orchestration for the history of Edo brothels uses shamisen and *tsuzumi* in simple kabuki style. At the mention of "nakanochō," the *taiko* and flute *wataribyōshi* music returns, for this is the most famous street in the center of the Yoshiwara with its cherry trees and men sneaking past wearing hats to hide their identity. The next *aikata* contains *tsuzumi* and shamisen patterns that no doubt matched the dance movements. A brief ostinato shamisen precedes a *serifu* rendition of the voice of the geisha. The use of such ostinato is a common signal of geisha music as is the double-stop version of figure 13A. This occurs before "sasakigen" and a mention of a geisha singing popular "embankment music" in the short song genre (*kouta no dotebushi*). The embankment around the Yoshiwara helped control one's movements (and prevented escape).

The lyrical *kudoki* begins with a standard slow shamisen ostinato (think of the first three notes of fig. 13A as a dotted eighth and a sixteenth followed by a quarter note). The passage occurs between two lines of text. It precedes the next line, "tama," and moves to figure 13A at "mo oroka," followed by a geisha *serifu* rendition of *degozaru*. The entire *kudoki* opening is a good example of a *nagauta* imitation of *kouta*. Another *serifu* version of a geisha speaking is found at "ware ja yo." The *ru* of *mikaeru* is sung in a long melisma because a *sugatami* is a full-length mirror in which the woman can see herself. The play on the name of the dance guild (*hayanagi/hanayagi*) was mentioned earlier.

We see more views of the dancer's costume and a picture screen that seems to be placed before the bed. The text then moves to the Japanese myth of the star maid and the shepherd constellation (*tanabata*), whose characters meet only once a year.

A solo *taiko* and flute playing the *wataribyōshi* leads to a *taiko ji* with standard use of *taiko* and bamboo flute. The first pattern is *bungo sagari ha* (see p. 18). The *tsuzumi* enter at "shirogasane," and the tempo increases as we approach the lion dance interlude and all the dancing it must accompany.

The next event is based on *kiyari* songs, a fireman's tradition. The *taiko* and flute return at "makura," playing *wataribyōshi* at half speed. This first part of the song is in the folk style with *hayashi kotoba* responses by other singers. The second part involves pulling on ropes to hold up the ladder. It could also refer to the girl putting her clothes back on and tightening her obi. The tempo increases as the New Year's festival begins with *tuzumi* accompaniment. After the festival is announced (at "matsuri no"), the *taiko* and flute are added. The *chirashi* orchestration uses the noh flute with the *taiko* and *tsuzumi* and leads to a traditional *dangire*. No doubt the music supported equally interesting dance.

MAEBIKI (*niagari* tuning)	Length 25'37"
OKI	
wazaogi no mukashi o ima ni	Performers will now show us scenes
utsushie ya	from the past.
oyabanu fude ni hishikawa no	With peerless brushstrokes, Hishikawa
kankatsu detachi sato gayoi	depicted pleasure quarters patrons
sugata irodoru tanzen wa	in their dashing attire; today those
kyō o hare naru hatsu butai	colorful figures make a gala first appearance onstage.

MICHIYUKI AIKATA

yoshiya otoko to na ni takaki	There's a samurai, manly, Yoshiya
Fuji no shiratsuka mabayuku	style, sharp as one of the Shiratsuka,
mo (*ai*)	famous for their gleaming bright swords, bright as Fuji's snow.
murasaki niō tsukubane no,	He's wearing Tsukuba's purple tones in
koshimaki baori roppō ni	his hip-length coat. Waving hands,

AIKATA

futte furikomu yakko	he comes with his servant, swaggering like a ruffian.
kono sono sake nara nejikiri,	If there's sake, there'll surely be a row.
iro jōgo, koi no	"I'll do the matchmaking—
torimochi shite koi makasero	Leave it to me!
shongae	What more can I say?"
hana ni mo masaru	The flowers are outdone by date-style
date na fūzoku, (*ai*)	fashions themselves.
somo ya kuruwa no hajimari wa	Next is the origin of the pleasure quarters: long ago, in the fourth year of
tōtsu Genna no yotsu no toshi	Genna, a certain official opened the
shōji nanigashi Negimachi e (*ai*)	five blocks around Negimachi. Since then, brothels have increased in
itsutsu no chimata hirakite yori	number and inside the Great Gate the occupants of three thousand
ageya no kazu mo omon ni,	establishments displayed their charms
sanzen ro no iro kurabe	
mazu hatsu haru no kazari yagu (*ai*)	First, in early spring there's the bedding display—
Hōraisan to ūmagure	hints of Mount Hōrai and evenings yet to
chimoto no sakura	come,
nakanochō	Nakanochō
kazasu ōgi no	with its thousand cherry trees and
mesekigasa	deep rush hats decorated with fans to shield the eyes.

AIKATA

ozonkaketaru (*ai*)	"Come on now," coax the voices.
hototogisu (*ai*)	The nightingales cry a sweet sound.

otomogaeri no
sasakigen utau kouta no

dotebushi ni

Together drunken customers make
their way home, singing short,
popular
music.

KUDOKI
kakaru sanya no kusa
fukakeredo
(*ai*)
kimi ga sumika to omoeba
yoshi ya (*ai*)
tama no utena mo oroka de
gozaru yoso no miru me mo
itowanu ware ja yo owarai
yaru na na no tatsu ni
sugata mikaeru hayanagi no
musunde toita kumo no obi
kakeshi byōbu no suzumegata
hiyoku makura no akatsuki ni
kasasagi watasu ama no gawa
hoshi machiai no tsujiura jaya
ni
tanabatasan no korobine mo
kinuginu hayaki kusa no ichi

"Though the grass be deep in a valley
like this, if I think of it as your place,
it's all right with me; were it even a
palace, it wouldn't matter at all.
The one who doesn't care what people
think—that's me! Just don't laugh
when you hear what they say."

Imagine the Hayanagi geisha
who turns to give a backward glance,
her flowing sash tied and then untied
hat, the sparrow's spread-wing pattern
on the screen she sets in place.
Teahouses celebrate the Tanabata
rendezvous. Lovers share pillows
when the Milky Way is bridged by the
magpie's widespread wings and
departs at dawn.

HAYASHI AIKATA
AIKATA
ODORI JI (TAIKO JI)
nokiba o teasu hana dōrō
sono hassaku no shirogasane
yuki no sugao ni
hachimaki shanto
tsuki no Niwaka no kioijishi

(*wataribyōshi*)

Flowered lanterns that light up the
eaves. Layered white kimonos for the
eighth month's first day, headbands
framing faces white as snow,
moon viewing and Niwaka with its
boisterous lion.

AIKATA
yaa shimero yare
shimete neta yo wa
makura ga jamayo
kawai kawai no (ai) aizuchi no

"Hey tighten up there . . .
Pillows just get in the way when doing
what I paid for.
Sweet, sweet, the murmur of small

139

oto	talk.
yoi, yoi yoi ya na, ei ei	Good, good,
ei ya na-a	isn't it good, isn't it good.
yare kore kore wate ga soreta ka	Do this—this, did that hand slip?
	It's just because you're such a love
itoshikerya koso	I smacked that little butt, good.
yogoto ni tsumado tataita	
yoi yoi yoi ya na	Ain't it good,
yoi to na (*ai*)	hey it's good
	(*kiyari* music)
yea shimero yara, yoi sa yoi	Hey, tighten up—that's good, good—
sa kore wa no se, sokko de	tighten it there
shimero nakazuna. (*ai*)	on the center rope
yoku saki sorō hanamomiji	Flowers and red leaves in full color, the
akiba matsuri no (*ai*) fuyu no	Akiba shrine festival—winter has come.
kite	In entranceways, branches of pine
kado ni matsutake toshi no	and bamboo announce a year's
seki (*ai*)	turning.
ōtsugomori no daikagura (*ai*)	New Year's Eve. There are street
kitsune de ukase (*ai*)	dances and buoyant, lilting rhythms set
ukase ukase ukare ukaruru	
uki byōshi	in motion by the badger.
omoshiroya	How wonderful.

CHIRASHI

ge ni zensei wa yami no	Thronged with visitors, flourishing
yo mo	even on the darkest night—
Yoshiwara bakari	there's truly nowhere but Yoshiwara
tsuki to hana	for flowers and moon!
yanagi no kuruwa kotobukite	Celebrating that willow world, all make their way

AIKATA
DANGIRE

medetaku ageya e irinikeru	happily into their brothels.

.᠎⌣ ᠎

Renjishi, 1861
"The Lion Pair"

Composer: Kineya Katsusaburō II
Text: Kawatake Kisuro (Mokuami)
Recording: Columbia 70113, NHK 1-12-2
Notation: Bunka 3327; Kineya 88; Yoshizumi, vol. 4

BOOK CD: 2–2

Performers: singers, Nishigaki Yūzō, Miyata Tesuo, Miagawa Ken; shamisen, Kikuoka Hiroaki, Ajimi Tōru, Kineya Yasaburō; *hayashi*, Mochizuke Takio, Mochizuki Sakichi, Mochizuki Chōsaku, Tosha Rosetsu; flute, Fukuhara Hyakunosuke

There are many lion dances in the *nagauta* repertory based on either folk traditions (see *Niwakajishi*, p. 93) or the noh drama (see *Shakkyō*, p. 60) about a lion on a stone bridge (Malm 1986, 54). There are eighteenth-century kabuki *Renjishi* pieces. The 1861 kabuki version accompanied the actual dance of a father and son. The finale is famous for its head-twirling action with long manes. An 1872 version by Kineya Shōjirō is a concert piece with more references to the original noh drama. In 1898, it included noh drama musicians in one performance.

Both pieces remain popular in *nagauta* concerts. The following description of the music concerns only the 1861 *Renjishi* as it is heard on the book CD.

Text. The theme of blooming peonies throughout the piece is derived from a famous Chinese flower. After the *michiyuki*, the valley description is mostly from the original noh drama *Shakkyō*. The words *kokū o* refer to a *shakuhachi* piece, *Kokū*, which is supposed to have been imported from China. The noh text is quoted again in the *chirashi* section. Toraden is a known court music (*bugaku*). *Taikin rikin* refers to lion's heads with and without jewels inserted.

Music. The opening singing and declamations (*serifu*) are accompanied by *ōzatsuma* patterns (see p. 16). Although there are not two lions in the original noh drama (*Shakkyō*), the *tsuzumi* and noh flute are heard to support the formal mood. During the first *aikata*, the shamisen and drums play a brief *kodama* pattern, a kabuki convention for echoes in the mountains, since the mountainous setting soon appears in the text.

In the major dance of the younger lion, the scratch of the claws is heard in the shamisen line for the word *tsume*. The *tsuzumi* change to kabuki-style drumming. The lyricism of the *kudoki* is supported by the bamboo flute that follows the shamisen line. The instrumental interlude after *"yonen naku"* uses a second shamisen line (*uwajōshi*) and a *ko tsuzumi*, which follows the rhythm of the melody closely.

The conventions for the beginning of the *taiko ji* are typical: change of tuning, entrance of the *taiko* drum, and the sound of flute, in this case a noh flute. The flute plays "ghost music" in preparation for the appearance of the supernatural lion.

The most dramatic prelude for this famous dance is the rare *hayashi* music called *ranjo* and *raijo*. Details on this section may be found in Malm 1968, 74. In both the noh and kabuki versions, the interlude functions not only to place the listener in a supernatural mood but also to provide time for major changes in the set (peony plants at each corner and a dance platform center stage) and costume changes with long lion manes that soon will be flung about to the accompaniment of fast shamisen and *hayashi* music. The *chirashi* is typical with full orchestration and the text pouring out at one syllable per beat. The *dangire* finale ends a truly dramatic dance piece.

Oⱪɪ (*honchōshi* tuning)	Length 25'11"
sore botan wa hyakka no ō	As the peony is the king of a
nishite	hundred flowers,
shishi wa hyakujū no	so is the lion the chief of a
chō to ka ya	hundred beasts.
tōri ni masaru botan ka no	The peony is superior to the
ima o sakari ni sakimichite	peach and plum when it is
kohyō ni otoranu renjishi no	blooming at its height. The two
tawamure asobu ishi no hashi	lions are not inferior to tiger or
	panther as they romp playfully on the stone bridge.
Mɪcʜɪʏᴜᴋɪ	
kore zo monju no ōwashimasu	Listen. Now. The venerable Saint Monju dwelled . . .
Aɪᴋᴀᴛᴀ	
sono na mo takaki seiryōzan	on renowned Mount Qingliang.
mine o aogeba senjō no	From the cloud-covered peak far
minagiru taki wa (*ai*)	above, swollen water ascends
kumo yori ochi	through the clouds looking
tani o nozomeba chihiro no	at the base of a deep valley.

soko / The flow resounds with the wind
nagare ni hibiku matsu no kaze / in the pines.
miwatasu hashi wa sekiyō no / Gazing across the bridge
ugo ni eizuru niji ni nitte / resembles dusk after the rain
kokū o wataru ga gotoku nari / when a rainbow appears just like crossing the emptiness.

kakaru kenso no santō yori / From a large rock on a precipitous ledge

gōoku tamesu oyajishi no / a proud lion kicks into the
megumi mo fukaki taniai e / depths of the ravine
keotosu kojishi wa (ai) / his young cub.
koro koro koro / tumble, tumble, tumble
otsuru to mieshi ga / The cub seems to fall headlong.
mi o hirugaeshi / He turns around
tsume o ketate te kakenoboru o / and scrabbles with his claws
mata tsukiotoshi tsukiotosu / only to be shoved again.

AIKATA
takeki kokoro no arajishi mo / The valiant heart of a fierce lion,

KUDOKI (niagari tuning)
botan no hana ni mai asobu (ai) / dancing playfully among the peony flowers.

kochō ni kokoro yawa aragite / Butterflies calm his heart,
hana ni araware ha ni kakure / appearing on a flower, hiding
(ai) / behind a leaf.
oitsu owaretsu yonen naku / Chasing, being chased, totally absorbed.

AIKATA
kaze ni chiriyuku hanabira no / The petals scatter in the wind,
hirari hirahira tsubasa o shitai / fluttering, longing for wings.

AIKATA
tomo ni kurū zo / The lions and the flowers
omoshiroki / together. How enjoyable.

TAIKO JI (honchōshi tuning)
AIKATA
orikara shōchaku kinku go no / Just then the whole ensemble
taenaru shirabe mai no sode / grandly begins with the dance.

GODAN NO AIKATA

CHIRASHI

shishi toraden no bugaku	The season for the lion and
migin	Toraden music and dance.
botan no hanabusa	Bunches of peony flowers fill
nioi michimichi	the air with their scent.
taikin rikin no shishigashira	The lion's head shakes with great
ute ya hayase ya	strength.
botanbō botanbō	Peony perfume, peony perfume.
kōkin no zui arawarete	The stamens of golden yellow
hana ni tawamure	coming forth.
eda ni fushi marobi	Lions frolicking in
ge ni mo uenaki	the flowers, crouching and
shishi ō no ikioi	rolling in the twigs.
nabikanu kusaki mo	The strength of the lion king is
naki toki nare ya	truly unsurpassed. Never will plants and trees fail to part before him.
banzei senshū to mai osame	For myriad harvests and a thousand autumns, he perfects his dance.
banzei senshū to mai osame	For myriad harvests and a thousand autumns, he perfects his dance.

(raijo ranjo)

DANGIRE

shishi no za ni koso naorikere	The lion seats himself on his throne.

144

Shiki no Yamamba, 1862

"Four Seasons of the Old Mountain Woman"

Composer: Kineya Rokuzaemon XI
Text: Unknown
Recordings: Columbia COCF-9793, COCF-7011
Notation: Bunka 3328; Kineya 35; Yoshizumi 1955, vol. 4

Text. The legend of an old woman's spirit who wanders through the mountains is found in Japanese folktales. The earliest surviving *Yamamba* (or *Yamauba*) noh drama is from the fifteenth century (*Japanese Noh Drama*, 1960, vol. 2). There were several *bunraku* and kabuki versions in the eighteenth and nineteenth centuries, as well as concert pieces in other shamisen genres. They came to be classified under the general category *yamauba mono*. A detailed study of this *nagauta* piece in English is found in Malm 1978, so only a few comments will be made here, especially as they relate to conventions in other pieces in this anthology. One is that the piece was not first performed in a theater but rather in the Edo city mansion of the daimyo from Nambu. It is interesting to note the influence of the patron who commissioned it. There are local Edo and southern area (*namba*) scenes to console the residents, who had to spend half of their lives in the capital rather than at home. The addition of the four seasons to the title further supports the opportunities to entertain an audience of what could be called hostages.

Like other concert pieces, *Yamamba* was later used for dance accompaniment, but these comments deal only with the concert version.

Music. Oki. If offstage *geza* musicians are available, the piece is preceded by the deep sound of the *ōdaiko* drum, a conventional way of setting a kabuki scene it in the mountains. The *ōzatusma* pattern *sanju* begins the piece in the dramatic spirit of the story. The first words are accompanied by a standard *ōzatsuma jo* pattern (see fig 11A). The menacing location in the mountains is reinforced by the shamisen line, which plays a radical series of phrases using the "danger" pitches such as B-flat and F-sharp.

In the *michiyuki*, the sudden change of scene from a mountain hag to a beautiful geisha in Kyoto in spring includes the *wataribyōshi taiko* and flute pattern and then a shamisen ostinato, which both evoke the gay quarters and flower viewing. The summer coolness is supported by the sound of just a voice and shamisen. The *kudoki* begins with a standard *tataki* pattern but in a fresh pitch area (F-sharp).

The music from "samisen" to "naikai na" is shown in Malm 1978 to illustrate possible musical responses to the scene. At "onaji omoi," the "cries of sympathetic insects" become active with *tsuzumi chiri kara* patterns in a livelier tempo. The sound (*utsu*) of wooden blocks beaten to launder clothes is a conventional reference in classical poetry. It combines here with insect sounds to produce a long *aikata* shamisen duet. The *niagari* section may have been added to the piece by one of the women of the estate. The shamisen responds to the rising plovers (*chidori tatsu*) by chirping with pizzicatos blocked by a finger under the string. When the scene changes to one of clam diggers, the music uses the *yo* pentatonic scale mimic the sound of peasants at work. The crow (*karasu*) laughs (*watau koe*) with a repeated "aho" at the folly of men. After "nori o," the shamisen creates the rhythms of workers collecting seaweed.

The *odori ji* begins the winter quiet scene with a slow shamisen ostinato common to geisha songs (see p. 16). The *sansagari* tuning contributes to that same style. After "gomoru," the bamboo flute and noh-style *hayashi* enter, adding further traditional elements of an *odori ji*. In the short interlude that follows, the shamisen play at the very top, "icy" range of their sound in rhythm with the *tsuzumi*. The noh flute enters with slow, "cold" sounds as snow-laden roofs appear. The *tsuzumi* follow the slow rhythm of the melody except for one quick set of "ponpon" strokes when the first snowflakes flutter down. As the snowfall increases, the *tsuzumi* use *chiri kara* patterns to support the accelerating shamisen melody. The "chiri chiri" is declaimed (*serifu*), and the "patto" is followed by a special shamisen effect in which the sound is stopped with the left hand. The short, high-speed *aikata* is kabuki style all the way. Before "ara," one hears *tsuzumi* strike one beat followed by a long "yo." This is the standard signal for passages derived from a noh drama (see *Musume Dōjōji*, p. 22). In this case, it is one line from the original play, *Yamamba*. It is sung in noh style. The *tsuzumi* play noh drama patterns in the next interlude. When the text returns at "dokkoi," a totally different kabuki style appropriate for battle scenes is used and the drums return to *chiri kara* patterns. The noh flute is added to the next *aikata*. The full *hayashi* performs three strong beats and a long full ensemble interlude starts the *chirashi*. Tempo increases as the words return. After "shimete," there is a fast *hayashi* drum roll, which leads to a dramatic *dangire*.

MAEBIKI (*honchōshi* tuning)	Length 27'15"
OKI	
ochikochi no tstuski mo shiranu	Dwarfed in the vastness of nature,
yamazumai ware mo mukashi wa	a solitary mountain dwelling. I, too,
nagare no mi semaki iori ni	once floated aimlessly but now
miwataseba	gaze from this humble hut and reminisce.

146

MICHIYUKI

haru wa kotosara yaegasumi
sono
Yaegiri no tsutome no mi
yanagi sakura o kokimazete
miyako zo haru no nishiki kite
teren tekuda ni kyaku a matsu
natsu wa suzushi no kaya no uchi
hiyoku no goza ni tsuki no kage

The eightfold haze of Yaegiri
rises from the earth, enhancing
the beauty of Yaegiri the courtesan
who decorates herself with willow
and cherry blossoms, and,
garbed thus in the brocade of a Kyoto
spring, awaits her customers. In the
cool of a summer eve, she joins a lover
on straw mats inside a moon-
bathed mosquito net.

AIKATA

KUDOKI

aki wa sansagara en saki no
samisen hiite shinkibushi (*ai*)
kami no midare o kanzashi de
kakiage nagara tatamizan
nemuru kamuro muri ni bakari
hon ni tsurai ja nai kai na (*ai*)
onaji omoi ni naku mushi no
matsumushi (*ai*) suzumushi kutsū
mushi (*ai*) umaoimushi no yaruse
naku

In autumn, she sits on the
veranda, playing shamisen and
singing sad love songs. While fixing
she lets drop a hairpin to
divine this evening's luck and
regrets her futile waiting. She
always scolds the sleeping page
girl. The insects of fall cry in
sympathy over the helplessness of
it all.

AIKATA

izure no sato ni koromo utsu

In the distance, the hollow sound of a
fulling block.

AIKATA

yoku mo awaeta mono kai na (*ai*)
(*niagari* tuning)
furisake mireba Sode ga Ura (*ai*)
oki ni shiraho ya chidori tatsu (*ai*)
shijimi toru naru aru samasae mo
(*ai*) are tō asa ni niyo jirushi
(*ai*)
matsu hō kuie nogarekite
maseta karasu yo no naka

How well these night sounds mix.

Out on the Bay of Sleeves, plovers
rise amid white sails.

Buoys mark a safe passage across
the shallows, and close by clam
diggers digging.
A smart-aleck crow stops to rest on

ahō ahō to warau koe (*ai*)
tatetaru shibi ni tsuku nori o (*ai*)
toridori meguru ama obune
ukie ni Awa Kazusa

a pine mooring post and cackles at
the folly of men.
The scene of fishermen collecting
seaweed in their boats is like a
painting of Awa no Kazusa.

ODORI JI (*sansagari* tuning)
fuyu wa tanima ni fuyu gomoru
mada uguisu no kata koto mo
ume no tsubomi no hanayaka ni
(*ai*) yuki o itadaku kuzuya no
nokiba
ada no matsukaze fuki-ochite
chiri ya chiri ya chiri, chiri,chiri
chiri patto chiri wa

The warbler winters deep in the
valley and has yet to emerge with
its first song of spring, but already
the plum trees are budding.
Across the snow-laden eaves of
thatched roofs, the fickle wind
blows and sends snowflakes
fluttering: chiri chiri ya chiri chiri,
chiri chiri,

AIKATA
kochō ni nitaru keshiki kana
ara omoshiro no yama meguri

like butterflies
Oh, how beautiful is this mountain
journey.

AIKATA
dokkoi yaranu to torite no waka-ki
konata wa oiki no chikara waza

Attackers swarm about like young
saplings, but this old tree is tough and
strong.

AIKATA
CHIRASHI
AIKATA
naka yori futto nejikiru taiboku
kakeri kakerite taniai no
tan no irori ni anzen to

With an extra burst of inner
strength, the old woman uproots a
tree and flails her assailants. Then she
returns to her hut deep in the
mountains and there sits in peace

DANGIRE
iku toshi o okurikeri

to pass the countless months and
years.

Twentieth-Century Compositions

1903 Haru Aki
1904 Shima no Senzai
1911 Kanda Matsuri
1967 Ame no Shiki

Haru Aki, 1903

"Spring and Autumn"

Composer: Kineya Kangorō V
Text: Uncertain
Recording: NHK 1-2-4
Notation: Bunka 3360; Kineya 39; Yoshizumi, vol. 1

The author of the text is uncertain, although it has been ascribed to a Buddhist priest named Nyoren. It is one of the more successful "modern" concert compositions and is designed to show off the skills of both the shamisen players and the singers. It was meant to be performed without *hayashi*. Later drums were sometimes added, particularly when the piece was used as dance accompaniment.

The sections dealing with each season contain several instrumental interludes, sometimes with descriptive titles such as those found on rolled scroll pictures (*makimono*). For example, the opening *maebiki* is entitled "A Scroll of Cherry Blossoms in the Wind" (sakurahana no maki kaze no kokyu).

The *michiyuki* uses two shamisen lines. It is noteworthy that most of such duets in post-1900 compositions demonstrate an aharmonic, horizontal orientation. This creates tonal clashes to Western listeners, who expect two sounds to coalesce as they would in a vertical harmonic orientation.

The playing of the birds (at "chidori") is portrayed by a long vocal melisma. The next interlude is set in an unusual tuning (*ichisagari*) in which the lowest string is a pitch lower, thus creating a totally new tonality. The shamisen line remains very active while the text describes the gusts of wind. Upstrokes of the plectrum, pizzicatos, and banjolike hammer-on identify this musical style as something different and exciting. The shamisen music of the "wind" in the *aikata* reinforces this image of new music. The return to *honchōshi* tuning produces music with more traditional sounds, but its style has some changes in tempo to keep it interesting. The butterfly music is another shamisen duet with one instrument playing an octave higher (*uwajōshi*). The cadence in the finale is a fast tremolo like those usually associated with mandolins. Another tuning (*niagari*) begins a section marked "Maple leaves in the rain" (momiji ni wa ame no kyoku). Its text and tempo are like a *kudoki*, but what is unique about it is that it does *not* begin with a clear *tataki* pattern. There is plenty of lyrical melodic tension, such as pauses on upper leading tones, but it all seems different and refreshing. After "oridasua," some of the new, "modern" sounds are (1) a double octave with one string plucked and (2) the other played upstroke, (3) a slow hammer-on, (4) slides with the fingernail between two pitches, and (5) three quick pizzicatos. Any shamisen fan would be thrilled at the unique combination. At "hito no kokoro," a *tataki* pattern is finally played. At "hatate no," the tempo matches the text by accelerating. Another tuning (*sansagari*) prepares listeners for rain music, the next *aikata*. It begins with quick dripping sounds followed by double-string shamisen lines. From the *chirashi* section on, things are more traditional, first with a standard short ostinato and then with many syllables and notes per line. However, the last *aikata* is an unusual, fast, virtuoso shamisen duet. The *dangire* is traditional. The composition is a fine combination of the old and the new.

MAEBIKI (*honchōshi* tuning)   Length 15'10"

OKI

yayoi nakaba no sora uraraka	The skies in the middle of the
ni	third month are clear and
nobe mo yamaji mo	fine. The fields and mountain
tokimekite	paths prosper.
ge ni nodakanaru haru no iro	The Goddess of Spring wears

MICHIYUKI (AIKATA)

sao hime ga	a mist that shrouds the
kasumi kaketaru	cherry trees like a light veil.
usuginu wa	Even the skies seem
sora sae hana ni eigokoro	drunk with the luxuriance of
tsukinu nagame ni wake	flowers.
yukeba	In this scene of inexhaustible
kono ma ni asobu (*ai*)	delights, birds in great
momo chidori	numbers play among the
haru no kouta ya utauran	branches, singing the song of
	spring.

AIKATA (*ichisagari* tuning)

orishimo satto fuku	Suddenly the wind gusts,
kaze ni	rustling the treetops, which
mizunaki sora e	seem like waves in a waterless
tatsu nami no	sky.
mata fuki ororsu	Now sweeping down, the wind
yuki no niwa	scatter flowers like snowflakes on the garden.

AIKATA *(kaze no kyoku)*
(*honchōshi* tuning)

	"Music of the wind"
cho mo tawamurete	Butterflies dance and flutter,

151

hira,hira, hira
tomo ni ukaretsu

making merry with the
floating currents of the wind.

AIKATA
tachimaeru tegoto ni
kazasu hana no eda
akanu iro naru
haru no tasogare

All find for themselves a
garnishing spray of blossoms
as evening approaches.

AIKATA (*niagari* tuning)
sonō no kaki ni ka o tomuru
kiku no hazuyu mo itsushika
ni
itsushi ga ni
onozukara naru aki no iro

The garden fence holds a
scent.
Suddenly the dew on
chrysanthemum leaves
naturally becomes the color of
autumn,

tezome no ito no tatsudahime
oridasu nishiki kusagusa ni
hito no kokoro no nabiku
made
miyuru sugata no (*ai*)
yasashisa mo
hatate no kumo nohayaku (*ai*)
(*sansagari* tuning)
shigure furunari sara sara sara
AIKATA (ame no kyoku)
nurete iro masu momijiba no

hand-dyed threads of the
Goddess of Autumn. The
brocade she weaves is so
varied that it
sways a person's heart.
The elegance of it appears
quickly.

A brief shower, drip, drip, drip.
"Rain music"
Wet the colors of the maple leaves are
more vivid.

CHIRASHI
kazuwa yashio ka kokonoe

jūnihitoe no kurenai to
kazoe, kazoete
ikushio ka ame ni fuzei mo
ito fukaki

Numbering the layered eight or nine
imperial dyes or
the maiden's crimson twelve.
Count as many as you can.
In the rain the scene is moving.

AIKATA
DANGIRE
aki no nagori o nagamu
naramashi

Gazing at the traces of
autumn.

Shima no Senzai, 1904

"Isle of Paradise"

Composer: Kineya Kangorō
Text: Ōtsuki Joden
Recordings: NHK 1-2-18; Columbia COCF 70124, 70114
Notation: Bunka 3358; Kineya 42

This piece was written in honor of the name-taking ceremony of the drummer Mochitsuki Bokusei III when he acquired the rank of Mochitsuki Tazaemon VII. Shima no Senzai is said to have been the name of one of the first twelfth-century female entertainers called *shirabyōshi* (white rhythms). Costumed in the white (*shira*) male clothing worn in a Shinto shrine and sometimes carrying a sword, they played rhythm (*byōshi*) on the *ko tsuzumi* drum and sang *imayō,* a popular genre (see Malm 2000, 55). The *shirabyōshi* also wore courtly *eboshi* hats. The same costume and drum are seen in the Shinto dance, *Okina* (see p. 87). The *nagauta* composition reflects its origins by using only a singer, shamisen, and one *ko tsuzumi.*

Text. All but the first two lines of the text are supposed to have been sung in honor of the benevolence of the emperor.

Recall that *nagauta* is basically a lyrical not a narrative music. As a modern congratulatory concert piece set in an ancient period, this text presents a series of unrelated images of *shirabyōshi* plus exotic water scenes. The opening text uses special names for a cranes and tortoise that relate them to the Chinese mythical Hōrai mountain. Both that mountain and the crane/tortoise image are common congratulatory topics (see *Tsuru Kame,* p. 118; and *Hōrai,* p. 84). The image of the sun passing over the sea leads to a pivot word, *yomogi ga shima* (sagebrush island). It turns into *Shima no Senzai,* the title of the piece. In the second line of the supposed *imayō* song, the *ko* of *kofuku* is the character for a drum. The patting of a belly may evoke an image of the fat, happy god Hotei, who rides on the treasure boat (see *Takarabune,* p. 55).

The *kudoki* section is swimming in water references. A legend says that the Buddha took water from the White Heron pond after explaining the meaning of the Hannya Sutra. *Saitenjiku* is one word for India in old Chinese and Japanese. The Chinese emperor's favorite lake (Konmeichi) actually exists in Xian, China. A late Han dynasty legend places Emperor Kōbutei as an imperial sage noted for his fishing on the river.

The next section of the text features Japanese watery scenes that no doubt are known to art connoisseurs, and the last line returns to the congratulatory spirit. With this fluid text in mind, we should glide down the sonic stream of the actual music.

Music. In the *maebiki*, rubato tempos dominate a shamisen and drum introduction.

In the *oki*, the singer chants the first two lines of text, which evoke the mood of noh drama even though the text is not derived from a noh play. It is right to evoke the era of a *shirabyōshi* and her drum since we have no sonic record of how it sounded. A solo drum interlude occurs when the name "Shima no Senzai" is heard. The word *imayō* is sung solo to prepare the listener for the imitation of *imayō* music that follows. At "kawaran," a curious congratulatory song proceeds with full ensemble in a steady beat until a rubato cadence occurs. Normally in *nagauta* form, a vocal introduction is followed by an instrumental interlude to prepare for the actor's entrance (*michiyuki*), but there is no actor for this concert piece. The music for these two lines may serve the sonic needs of an experienced listener for some "entrance" music.

The final lines of the *imayō* song are performed by only the singer and a drum to provide an "authentic" sound. The waves (at "yomo no *shikinami*") rush back and forth to a rolling pattern on the drum. Actual noh drama patterns are used in a drum solo, perhaps because with the return of the singer the final line is marked *utaigakari* (noh singing style).

A change of tuning and reduction of texture to only voice and shamisen imply a *kudoki* section, as does the conventional *tataki* pattern at "yuku sue hisashiki" (see p. 15). Unusual shamisen styles such as finger slide, plectrum backstroke, and left-hand pizzicatos give the 1908 composition a "modern" sound.

Another change in tuning, full orchestration, and a faster tempo are all characteristic of an *odori ji* section. The rhythm of the shamisen melody and the *tsuzumi* are the same. Western-style call-and-response is heard between the two instrumental parts during an exceptionally long interlude (*aikata*) after "wakamizuwa."

Form follows function, and the function of this piece is to honor the drummer. Formally, perhaps this interlude fills the need for a more active traditional *chirashi* section.

The *dangire* ending is noteworthy in its use of new versions of the *dangire* melodic conventions so common in a majority of *nagauta* compositions. The entire piece is a pleasant mixture of old and new ideas.

MAEBIKI (*sansagari* tuning)	Length 13'38"
OKI	
tanchō ryokumō no iro sugata	Scarlet cranes and emerald tortoises,

asahi utsurō wadatsu umi | the sun passing over the vast sea,
yomogi ga Shima no Senzai ga | Shima no Senzai
utau mukashi no imayō mo | sings an ancient *imayō* song.
kawaranu miyo no ontakara | "The treasured people of our blessed
kofuku no koegoe uchiyosuru | and unchanging age pat their well-filled bellies and raise their voices in joy.

yomo no shikinami tatsu ka | Waves from all directions rush in and
kaeru ka kaeru ka tatsu ka | out, out and in. I throw my dancing
kaeru tamoto ya tate eboshi | sleeves and tilt my *eboshi* cap."

AIKATA *(honchōshi* tuning)
KUDOKI
mizu no sugurete oboyuru wa *(ai)* | Places known for water are White Heron

saitenjiku no hakurōchi *(ai)* | pond in Western India and Xi Yu's
shinshō kyoyū ni sumiwa taru *(ai)* | favorite, the crystal clear Hun Ming Lake,
 | where the blue waves stretch forever.

konmeichi no mizu no iro
yuku sue hisashiku sumu tokaya *(ai)*
kenjin no tsuri o tareshi wa *(ai)* | A wise man used to fish in the waters of

genryōrai no kawa no mizu | the Yen Linglai River.

ODORI JI *(niagari* tuning)
tsukikage nagare moru naru | The moon's reflection flows along the
yamada no kakei no mizu tokaya | eddies in the culverts of the mountain fields. They close

ashi no shitaha o tozuru wa | off the leaves of reeds.
Mishima irie no kōrimizu | The ice spreads over Mishima inlet.
harutatsu sora no wakamizu wa | Fresh water taken on the first morning of spring.

AIKATA
DANGIRE
kumu tomo kumu tomo | Drawing water, drawing water
tsuki mo seji tsuki moseji | inexhaustibly.

.‿ ⌣·

Kanda Matsuri, 1911
"The Kanda Festival"

Composers: Kineya Rokushiō III and Yoshizumi Kosaburō IV
Text: Kodo Tokuchi
Recording: NHK 2-3-1
Notation: Bunka 343; Yoshizumi, vol. 8

In 1839, a dance piece called *Kanda Matsuri* appears in the *kiyomoto* genre of shamisen music. The *nagauta* composition was written in honor of the one-hundredth concert of the Kenseikai school of *nagauta*, whose primary goal was to create new concert, rather than dance accompaniment, compositions. It was the second part of a set of texts called Hohoyogusa (Grasses of a Hundred Nights). This piece was studied in detail in Malm 1986 and so will be discussed only briefly here.

History. Kanda and Sannō were the two major festivals in Edo. They are less grand in modern Tokyo. The Kanda Festival featured a procession of dignitaries, floats, and music or dance ensembles. Like the Kyoto Gion Festival or the Pasadena Rose Bowl Parade, crowds lined up along the route of the procession to enjoy the pageant.

Words and Music. Descriptions of the preparations for and beginning of the festival are provided by program sellers and souvenir hawkers. The Kettle of Fortune (Bunbuku Chagama) is a pottery model of a magic badger in the shape of a teakettle. He is said to never cease pouring good luck for you.

At the *michiyuki*, the *hayashi* plays behind the shamisen line one of the basic Shinto festival pieces called *Shoden*. This is an interesting expansion of the traditional combinations of drum pattern and shamisen music into two kinds of music at the same time. The mnemonics of the large processional drum sound (ton ton kakka don) are played by the *hayashi* dummerrs as well. For variety, the *tsuzumi* then enter briefly in *chiri kara* style as floats go by. Next the flute and *taiko* with thin sticks play the beginning pattern of another famous festival piece, *Yatai*. It continues in the fast virtuoso *aikata* that follows. At "Sumiyoshi," the percussion changes to *tsuzumi chiri kara* and the kabuki *taiko* pattern *bungo sagari ha*. Note that the two major guilds of the Kenseikai, Yoshizumi and Kineya, are in the procession. The pattern *wataribyōshi* is also mentioned and then played by the *taiko* and flute alone as a prelude to the *kudoki* section, which is performed by singer and shamisen alone. The love and drinking scenes seem out of place until one realizes that the best views of the parade are from the second-floor verandas of the geisha houses. The *odori ji* section adds the *taiko* and flute-playing *wataribyōshi* at half speed. At "onaji omoi," the tempo increases slightly and the orchestration changes to *tsuzumi chiri kara* patterns until the young lady starts to leave. The music then returns to shamisen and voice alone and the girl's sad words are like a separate song. The tempo picks up as drinking begins. The flute and drum return, too, as the lover rushes back to the festival. The *aitaka* that follows is based on the fastest festival piece, *Shichome*. The *tsuzumi* are added to increase the excitement. Playing *chiri kara* at such a speed is a real challenge.

The singer then calls out *kiyari* music of the firemen. Their acrobatics, done on high ladders held up in space by other firemen's ropes, is a spectacular event at festival time. It is not a surprise that the fast *chirashi* section uses full orchestration and there is a standard *dangire* finale. This exciting concert composition is not frequently performed or recorded, perhaps because it is not danced, uses a highly trained (and expensive) ensemble, and 'belongs" to one guild.

MAEBIKI (*honchōshi* tuning)	Length 17'26"
Kanda Matsuri o matsuri no	Waiting for the Kanda Matsuri
mikoshi ni iketa myōtobana	in the early evening with the
taga tezuabi ka shiragiku to	sacred wine are placed a pair of
kigiku no tsuyu mo atarashiku	flowers.
kazuru meika no kin byōbu	Who has arranged them? The white chrysanthemum and the yellow one, too, freshly bedecked with dew, are like a master artist's gold folding screen.
yukikai shigeki tsuji tsuji ni	Coming and going are crowds of
kasane-kotoba mo kiki nareta	people at every corner. The
gosairei omatsuri banzuke	repeated phrases one hears
yatsuya tōri ni kawaru	have become familiar sounds.
bunbuku chagama	Programs for the grand festival
nanatsu no kane wa itsu tsuita	On eighty-eighth street the Magic Kettle
yara	of Fortune. Who knows when the seven bells rang?
MICHIYUKI	(piece "Shoden")
honobono to shirami watarite	Faintly, the dim light of
tōtenkō	morning sweeps across the

157

ichibandori wa taihei no
miyo o iōte koke musu kanko

niban no hoko wa Barekijin
masaru medetaki
shōzobu eboshi
don don kakka don kakka
(*ai*)
tsuzuku sanban shiki toshite

okina no dashi wa kanda maru
goban juban tsugi tsugi ni

AI NO TE
machi nenban no tsuke matsuri
Sumiyaoshi odori dai kagure
yatai-bayashi wa Yoshizumi to
Kineya ga mochi no kikugasane

Shomō shomō ni tekomai no
tateshu ga ō no koe ni tsure
wataribyōshi o uchi agete

AIKATA
KUDOKI
mukashi yori koi to iu ji wa
taga kakisomete mayoi no tane o
makinuran ahinobu no wa
kaze mo fuki soro ame mo furi
niku ya togamuru sato no inu

ODORI JI
Magaki ni yotte hoto hoto to

reddening eastern sky
as the first cockcrow sounds its omen
for a peaceful reign with a moss-
covered drum.

The second float is the
Protective God of Horses.
What exquisite ceremonial robes and
courtly headgear! Boom, rat-a-tat!
Boom, rat-a-tat.
The third one follows according to
schedule. It is the float of the
elders called Kanda Maru. The
fifth one! The tenth one! On and on
they come.

(piece "Yatai")
The special music and dances of
town after town, the Sumiyoshi
dance, shrine festival music,
yatai-bayashi. Yoshizumi and Kineya
are wearing white costumes with
dark red linings.
Play it!
The performers respond to the
requests of the bystanders watching
the festival dances by striking up
the processional beat to the shouts
of approval from the onlookers.

AI NO TE
wataribyōshi played

From the first time, long ago,
when someone first wrote the
word called *love*, it has been
sowing the seeds of temptation
and doubt. In the dark of night the
winds blow, the rains fall, and spite
is inflamed by spies in the brothel.

They meet by the fence and

tatakeba kiku ni okimaru	because they hit it off so well they stay too long in the chrysanthemums.
tsuyu wa parai to mina chirinuredo	And, although the dew is scattered in large drops, they
onaji omoi ni machi wabishi	wait impatiently with the same desires.
hime wa toboso ni tate idete	The young lady starts to go
iza konata e to tommonaeri	toward the gate, and, saying "Come on, this way," they leave together.
yo kaze ni omni mo hienuran	In the evening wind my body
kokoro bakari ni habere domo	will not grow cold even though I am all alone with only my heart beside me.
warawa ga mōke no kiku no sake	I offer a toast with ceremonial
kikoshimese ya to sakazuki no	chrysanthemum wine, and raising the wine cup I say, "Have a drink!"
kazu kasanareba uchi tokete	As the number of cups piles up
ai to ai to no aioi renri	inhibitions are cast off and love
yoso no miru me mo uratamashi	with love is intertwined in mutual love. The eyes of others are filled with envy.

AIKATA
Ato no shomō wa eshaku naku	(piece "Shichome") Wanting to do something else, he
suban no dashi ni oware owarete	leaves without a bow and rushes off, chasing after the numerous festival floats.

AIKATA
ōnyaryōi	(*kiyari* music) Yo-heave-ho!
kogan hana sake	The golden flowers bloom for a
yukate na miyo	prosperous reign.
ni sore	Look out!
shimeryo yare nakazuma	Tie up the middle rope!
enyaryōi	Yo-heave-ho!

CHIRASHI
date mo kenka mo Edo no hana	For wooing as well as quarreling
sono hanagasa no saki sorō	the flowers of Edo are blooming
sakura no baba e dodo to	on that flower-adorned hat.
yosekuru hito no name ma yori	The light of the setting sun shines brightly on the people approaching

the Cherry Grounds with festive
pomp and excitement.

DANGIRE
hikari mabayuku hi no kage   The shadows of night fall.

Ame no Shiki, 1967

"Seasons of Rain"

Composer: Yamada Shōtarō
Text: Ikeda Katsusaburō
Notation: Kineya

BOOK CD: 2–3

Performers: singers, Nishigaki Yūzō, Miyata Tetsuo, Minagawa Ken; shamisen, Kikuoka Hiroka, Ajimi Tōru Kineya; *Kisaburō* flute, Fukuhara Hyakunosuke; *tsuzumi*, Mochizuki Takio, Mochizuki Takiuemon Mochizuki Sakichi, *taiko*, Tōsha Rosetsu.

Yamada Shōtarō was the first professor of shamisen at the Tokyo National University of Fine Arts. He was also the founder, in 1956, of the Toonkai, a *nagauta* guild of university graduates who kept their family names rather than paying for a guild name. The singers and shamisen players on the book CD are his former students. The life and works of Yamada Shōtarō, including this piece, are discussed in Malm 1998. This essay will help listeners follow the piece as it is performed on the book CD.

Text. This piece was Yamada's last concert composition. The text leads one through all the interesting bridges of Tokyo as a year goes by. It is a dying man's last view of some of his fondest places. The text is exceptionally straightforward. It describes scenes without double meanings or innuendos. We move through a spring shower to a unique market scene in which we savor all the foods and fruits of old Edo, as well as the sounds of the street hawkers, which can still be heard today. (The author's favorite such market is near Ueno Station).

The brief "get out of the way" seems to evoke the samurai fights often seen in old pictures of Edo streets. The words then turn to a major topic in the rest of the piece, bridges. All distances in the Edo period were measured in relation to the Nihonbashi so that bridge is the best place to start. After the shrine scenes and summer festival music, the text becomes poetic with a mix of water symbols, meditations on life's transience, and memories, perhaps recollections especially meaningful to the old man who composed the piece.

The *taiko ji* names all the major bridges and returns to the Nihonbashi area as an autumn rain falls. The Gotō family was part of the new, rich, merchant class that became powerful in the modern era. A museum that holds its art collection can still be found in the area. The Kisarazu boats travel between Chiba and Edo and are heading back to Chiba as the scene closes. "The Bridge of Eight Views" is famous for its view of Mount Fuji. With the final words "winter rain," the composition has taken us through the four seasons and an aged master's views of old Edo.

Music. The composition has been placed in the traditional formal units of *nagauta,* though only the term *maebiki* is found in the music notation. However, these terms can help us see how this modern piece has skillfully combined the conventions of the previous two hundred years with concepts of the twentieth century. The quiet *maebiki* and lyric *oki* set the spring dawn mood of the opening scene. The *michiyuki* launches into a faster tempo with the *taiko* and flute *wataribyōshi* pattern colored by the *kane* hand gong. One can picture a walk into the city with a stimulating drink for the road. As we arrive at Edo, the bustle of the crowd is pictured with double strokes on the shamisen plus *taiko* and bamboo flute patterns. The spring setting (at "haru de") is backed by the sound of a rattling cymbal. This is a conventional stage signal for flower-viewing events. The drum, flute, and hand gong return as the market is described. The tempo and instrumentation change when the grated pepper salesman's call is heard. Note that this *serifu* is not that of the kabuki but rather a direct imitation of the vendor's call. It has no *ōzatsuma* pattern accompaniment. We are in a different environment. The background use of clicking on a small, wooden, fish mouth gong (a *mokugyō*) is combined with the *kane* sound. Both sounds are what one might have heard accompanying such a vendor. The *taiko* is briefly heard between sales pitches accompanied by a shamisen ostinato. The challenge is for the singer to be a convincing vendor. Having sung it, the author can attest that it is not easy. The solo shamisen interlude that follows uses double strokes and finger slides in a novel way. The *tsuzumi* appear in fast *chiri kara* style to a slow, short, shamisen solo and a cadence as the sound of the Nihonbashi bell is evoked (though not heard).

The new tuning and scene bring us to two of the most famous shrines in Edo. The orchestration uses a *daibyōshi* drum and *suzu* bell tree as they are specific shrine ceremonial accessories. The structure of their rhythm pattern seems to use the magic 3, 5, and 7 numbers of Shinto (see Malm 1999, 119). The *kagurabue* Shinto flute is also imitated. A small pair of cymbals used in some Shinto dances and the drum appear at "Edo." After "summer festival" (*natsu matsuri*), the shamisen, *daibyōshi,* and flute launch into a fast, complicated version of the *kagura* piece *Nimba*. After the gods parade by (at "uchikoete"), the drummer changes to a *matsuri bayashi* drum with light sticks and the flautist to a festival bamboo flute (*takebue*). The sudden shower evokes a challenging virtuoso shamisen interlude. The transience of life (at "haka") is marked to be in *kudoki* style, and the shamisen does play the lyrical *tataki* pattern. The waterway and channel markers place us in a fishermen's area, so the melody converts to the "folk" sound of the *yo* scale (see p. 3), but it returns to another *in* scale *tataki* pattern at "nurete."A modulation to a new tonal center makes for a smooth transition into a new tuning (*sansagari*) and another shamisen interlude.

The *taiko ji* uses the traditional opening: three strokes of the *taiko* under a B–E–B sound on the shamisen and the flute playing the melody. This is followed by the *tsuzumi chiri kara* patterns. Once the text gets back to Nihonbashi the *taiko* is added and the full *hayashi* remains until the autumn rain is mentioned (at "orishimo") The fast shamisen interlude slows down as the boats fade from sight. The next interlude title (*tsukuda*) refers to the music on the taxi boats that ferried customers to the brothels across the Sumida River from the Yoshiwara area. The musical convention is double stops (see p. 16), and the *aikata* begins that way. The two shamisen lines' bright interchanges show the instrument at its best. Unlike traditional instrumentation the *chirashi* uses shamisen only. The text leads us to winter and a unique *dangire* finale. A single singer and shamisen perform the last words. A flute is sometimes added to evoke the cold winter mood. One can imagine an old, satisfied man walking off into the sunset of his life. His farewell musical gesture is beautiful.

MAEBIKI (*honchōshi* tuning)   Length 18'38"

OKI

oto mo naku furutomo mienu

harusame no

ei o sumuru toki no kyō (*ai*)

Without a sound, without
      appearing to

fall, the spring rains offer the

intoxication of festivities.

MICHIYUKI

ge ni tori ga naku

azumaji no

na ni ō-Edo no

nigiwai o (*ai*)

koko ni tsukushite honchō ya (*ai*)

haru de oboro de goennichi

nasubi no nae ya uri no nae

dekodeko oden miso oden

toppiki to no ji no tongarashi

commeya ga utau kuni zukushi

Ah, the birds that cry on the eastern

road.

We travel to Edo, known for its

bustling streets.

Anything you want is in Honchō.

Hazy spring. The festival days!

Eggplant and cucumber seedlings.

Bubbling hotchpotch, miso stew,

grated spicy pepper,

and the candy man's song has flavors
      of every province.

Bizen no meisan suimitsu tō	Bizen's famous sweet peachs,
Kishu ja Arita no mikan-iri	tangerines from Arita in Kishu.
Tsugaru no meibutsu ringo-iri.	Tsugaru's famous apples,
Taiwan nadai no banana-iri (*ai*)	bananas from Taiwan.
Shinshū no meisan goma to	Ground mint and sesame fresh from
hakka no suriwase	Shinshu.
Osaka meibutsu Ichioka-shinden	The pride of Osaka, Ichioka-shinden's
tane made makka na suika-iri	watermelons. Red right down to the
(*ai*)	seeds.
Edo wa Yanaka no shōga-iri	Ginger from Yanaka in Edo. Apricots
Hitachi ja Nishiyama anzu-iri	from Nishiyama in Hitachi and, last
mo hit	but not least, a special bargain.
omake ni	
Kōshū neesan shibori	Squeezed by a young girl in Koshu.
agetaru budō-iri	Just for you, the best grapes ever
hoi maketoke	tasted. Hey, make it cheap!
soe toke	Bargain it down.
omakeda omakeda	For you a special deal.

AIKATA
sore soko noita	Out of the way there.
nagagatana (*ai*)	A long sword is drawn.
kane mo kemuru ga Nihonbashi	The bell sound at Nihonbashi.

KUDOKI (*niagari* tuning)
AIKATA
Sannō ya Kanda myōjin	The gods of Sannō and Kanda shrines
nanboku no Edo o shizume no	quiet the streets of Edo. North and
natsu matsuri	south they emerge for the summer
	festivals.

AIKATA (*kagura hayashi*)	(music for the dance *Nimba*)
kami no miyuki no uchikoete	The procession of the gods moves on.

AIKATA
niwaka ni suguru yūdachi no	In a sudden shower at dusk . . .

AIKATA
mizu ni wa o kaku aya ni sae	the river water draws ring patterns,

KUDOKI
hakanaki hito ni ōkawa no
sono funeguchi no mojirushi *(ai)*
nurete fukamu ka
iro to ka no yoshiashi sore mo
mukashigōto
(ai) *(sansagari* tuning)

transient as human life.
In the boat waterway, channel marker
colors seem to deepen in the rain and
a sweet wet smell reminds us of days
long past.

TAIKO JI
Tokiwabashi, Edobashi,
Kajibashi, Gōfukubashi
furuki tsutae no
Nihonbashi *(ai)*
tosan dōsan yukikai no
hito no yo utsusu mizu no se ni
kamei mo takaki kawagishi wa
gotō gotō no mukai dachi
orishimo sosogu
aki no ame ni

Tokiwa bridge, Edo bridge,
Kaji bridge, Gofuku bridge,
and, standing since ancient times, the
bridge at Nihonbashi.
People hustle, bustle past. The river
rapids reflect their world.
On opposite banks, the proud old
houses of the Gotō family face each
other.
As autumn rains fall . . .

AIKATA
Kisarazubune no miegakure
sore mo yatsumi no
hashi no kei

the boats bound for Kisarazu slowly
fade from sight. This, too, is a scene
from the Bridge of Eight Views.

AIKATA *(tsukuda no aikata)*
CHIRASHI
kyō mo isogu ka hayadachi no
tabibito shigeki hashigeta ni
kikudani samuki *(ai)*

In a hurry again today? Travelers are
up early. Even footfalls on the
bridge boards chill the bones.

DANGIRE
fuyu no ame

Cold as winter rain.

Japanese Texts

Aki no Irogusa

秋の色種

弘化二年

十代目　杵屋六左衛門　作曲

本調子ヘ秋くさの、吾妻の野辺の葱草　合　しのぶ昔や古へぶりに　合　住みつく里は夏苧ひく、麻布の山の谷の戸に　合　朝夕むかふ月雪の　合　春告鳥の　合　あとわけて　合ヘなまめく萩が花ずりの、衣かりがね　合　声を帆に　合　上げておろして玉すだれ　合　はしゐの軒の庭まがき　合　うけら紫葛尾花　合　共寝の夜半に荻の葉の　合　風は吹くとも露をだに、するゑじと契る女郎花　合　その暁の手枕に、松虫の音ぞ　虫の合方ヘ　たのしき　合ヘ　変態繽紛たり、神なり又神なり、新声婉転す　二上り合ヘ　夢は巫山の雲の曲　合　雲の曙雨の夜に、うつすや袖の蘭奢待　合　とめつ　合　うつしつ睦言も、いつかしゞまのかねてより、言葉の真砂敷島の、道のゆくての友車、くるとあくとに通ふらん　合ヘ　峰の松風岩超す浪に　合　清掻く琴のつましらべ　琴の合方・三下りヘ　うつし心に花の春　合　月の秋風ほとゝぎす　合　雪に消えせぬ　合　たのしみは、尽きせじつきぬ千代八千代　合ヘ　常磐堅磐の松の色　合　いく十かへりの花にうたはん

Ame no Shiki

雨の四季

昭和四十二年九月

池田弥三郎　作詞

山田抄太郎　作曲

本調子へ　音もなく　合　降るとも見えぬ春雨の　合　酔を勧むる時の興　合　実に、とりがなく、東路の　合　名に大江戸の賑いを　合　こゝに盡して本町や　合へ　春で朧で御縁日　合　なすびの苗や　合　瓜の苗　合　でこでこおでん、味噌おでん　合　とっぴきとの字のとんがらし　合　飴屋がうたう、国づくし　合へ　備前の名産水蜜桃、紀州じゃ有田のみかん入り、津軽の名物りんご入り、台湾名代のバナナ入り　合　信州の名産胡麻と薄荷のすり合せ、大阪名物市岡新田種子まで真赤な西瓜入り　合　江戸は谷中の生姜入り、常陸じゃ西山杏入り、も一つおまけに甲州姐さん、絞り上げたる葡萄入り、ほいまけとけ、そえとけ、おまけだおまけだ　合　それ、そこのいた長刀　合　鐘もけむるか　合　日本橋、へ　山王や、神田明神、南北の江戸を鎮めの　合　夏祭り、神楽囃子合方『神の御幸の、うち越えて』　合へ　にわかに過ぐる夕立の　合　水に輪をかく紋にさえ　合　はかなき人に大川の　合　その舟口のみをじるし　合　濡れて深むか色と香の、葭葦それもむかしごと　合へ　常盤橋、江戸橋、鍛冶橋　合　呉服橋　合　古き伝えの二本橋　合　『とさん、どうさん、往き交いの、人の世うつす水の瀬に、家名も高き川岸は　合　後藤、後藤の対い建ち』へ　折しも注ぐ、秋の雨に　合　木更津船の、見えがくれ、それも八つ見の橋の景　合方へ　今日も急ぐか早立ちの、旅人しげき橋桁に、聞くだに寒き、冬の雨。

Azuma Hakkei

吾妻八景
文政十二年
杵屋六三郎　作曲

前弾キ・本調子〳〵　実に豊かなる日の本の、橋の袂の初霞、江戸紫の曙
染めや　合　水上白き雪の富士、雲の袖なる花の波　合〳〵　目許美し御
所桜、御殿山なす人群の、かをりに酔ひし園の蝶、花のかざしを垣間見に、
青簾の小舟、謡ふ小唄の声高輪に　佃ノ合方・二上り〳〵　遥か彼方のほ
と〴す、初音かけたか羽衣の、松は天女の戯れを、三保にたとへて駿河
の名ある、台の余勢の弥高く、見下す岸の筏守、日を背負うたる阿弥陀笠、
法のかたへの宮戸川、流れ渡りに色々の、花の錦の浅草や、御寺をよそに
浮れ男は、何地へそれし矢大神、紋日に当る辻占の、松葉かんざし二筋
の、道のいしぶみ露踏み分けて、含む矢立の墨田川、目につく秋の七草に、
拍子通はす紙砧　砧ノ合方・三下り〳〵　忍ぶ文字摺乱る〳〵雁の玉章に
合　便りを聞かん封じ目を、きりの渡に棹さす舟も、いつ越えたやら衣紋
坂、見世清掻に引き寄せられて　合　つい居続けの朝の雪、積り積りて情
の深み、恋の関所も忍ぶが岡の、蓮によれる糸竹の、調べゆかしき浮島の、
潟なすもとに籠りせば　楽合方〳〵　楽の音共に東叡よりも、風が降らす
る花紅葉、手に手合せて貴賎の誓ひ、弁財天の御影もる池のほとりの尊く
も、巡りてや見ん八ツの名所

Fuji Musume

藤娘

文政九年九月

藤井源八　作詞

四世杵屋六三郎　作曲

三下りへ　津の国の　合　浪花の春は夢なれや、はや二十年の月花を、眺めし筆の色どりも　合　書き尽されぬ数々に、山も錦のをりを得て、故郷へ飾る袖袂　鼓唄へ　若紫に十返りの、花を顕す松の藤浪へ　人目せき笠塗笠しやんと、振りかたげたる一枝は　合　紫深き水道の水に、染めて嬉しき由縁の色の　合　いとしとかいて藤の花、エゝ　合　しよんがいな、裾もほら／＼しどけなく　合へ　鏡山人のしがより此身のしがを　合　かへりみるめの汐なき海に、娘姿の恥かしやへ　男心の憎いのは、外の女子に神かけて、あはづと三井のかねごとも へ　堅い誓ひの石山に、身は空蝉のから崎や、待夜をよそに比良の雪へ　解けて逢瀬のあた妬ましい、ようもの瀬田にわしや乗せられてへ　文も堅田のかた便り、心矢橋のへ　かこちごとへ　松を植ゑよなら有馬の里へ、植ゑさんせ、何時までも　合　変らぬ契かいどり褄で、よれつもつれつまだ寝が足らぬ、宵寝枕のまだ寝が足らぬ、藤に巻かれて寝とござる、アゝ何としやうかどしやうかいな、わしが小枕お手枕へ　空も霞の夕照に、名残を惜しむ帰る雁がね

Funazoroi

安政三年
二世　杵屋勝三郎　作曲
船揃
(風流船揃)

本調子へ　抑船の始まりはへ　唐土皇帝に仕へし、貨狄といへる臣下あり　合　秋吹く風に庭の池へ、散り浮く柳の一と葉の上に、蜘蛛の乗りてさゝがにの、絲引きはえし姿より、匠み出だせし船とかやへ　見渡せば、海原遠く真帆片帆　合　行きかふ船の数々は、霞の浦に見え隠れ、白波寄する磯近く、千鳥鷗の浮き姿　合　網曳く船や釣舟の、皆漕ぎ連れて行き通ふ、眺め長閑き春景色、面白やへ　筑波根の、峯より落つる水筋も、積もり／＼て秩父より、清く流るゝ隅田川、月よ花よと漕ぎ出だす　合　屋形屋根船　合　猪牙荷足、御厩隅田の渡し舟、遙か向ふをへ　竹屋と呼ぶ声に、山谷の堀を乗り出だす、恋の関屋の里近く、花見の船の向島、軒を列べし屋根船の、簾の内の爪弾はへ　もしや夫かと人知れず、気をもみ裏を吹き返し、追手の風に　三下りへ　上汐に、佃々と急いで押せば　合　又上手から二挺三味線弾き連れて、様はさんやの三日月様よ、宵にちらりと見たばかり、しょんがいな　合　負けず劣らぬ　合　行き合の、船の横から三筋の絲に　合　二挺鼓を打つやうつゝの浪の船へ　自体我等は都の産れ、色にそやされこんな形にならられた、見事な酒は多けれど、聞いてびっくり、丸三杯飲んだ盃、つい／＼／＼ついのついへ　面舵取舵声々に、乗りしお客の気も浮かれ、リウチエイハマカイ、払って一拳押へましよ、拳うちやめて踊るやら　合　扇鳴らして唄ふやら、しどもなやへ　賑はふ隅田の川面は、是ぞ真の江戸の花、栄ふる御代こそ目出たけれ

Gorō Tokimune

五郎時致
天保十二年
十代目杵屋六左衛門　作

本調子へ　さる程に　合　曾我の五郎時致は倶不戴天の父の仇討たん
すものと撓みなき矢猛心も春雨にぬれて廓の化粧坂名うてと聞し少将の
　出合方へ　あめの降る夜も雪の日も通ひ／＼て大磯や　合へ　さとの
諸分のほだされ易く誰に一筆鴈の伝てへ　野暮な口舌を返す書へ　粋な
手管につい乗せられてへ　浮気な酒によひの月　合　晴てよかろか晴れ
ぬがよいか　合　とかく霞むが春の癖へ　いでオゝ夫よ我も又　合　何
時か晴さん父の仇十八年の天津風今吹返す念力に遁さじ遣らじと勇猛
血気その有様は牡丹花に翼ひらめく胡蝶の如く　合　勇ましくも又健気
なり　二下りへ　藪の鶯気まゝに啼いてうらやましさの庭の梅　合　あれ
そよ／＼と春風が浮名立たせに吹き送る　合　堤の菫鷺草はつゆの情
に　合　濡た同士色と恋との実競べ実浮た仲の町よしやよしへ　孝勇無
双の勲しは現人神と末の世も恐れ崇て今年又花のお江戸の浅草に開帳
あるぞ賑しき

174

Haru Aki

明治三十六年
五世 杵屋勘五郎 作曲
春秋

＜桜花の巻は風の曲＞
前弾・本調子へ　弥生半ばの空麗らかに、野辺も山路も時めきて、実にのどかなる春の色　合方へ　佐保姫が、霞かけたる薄衣は、空さへ花に酔ひ心、尽きぬ眺めに分け行けば、木の間に遊ぶ百千鳥、春の小唄や唄ふらん　三下り・風の合方へ　折しもさっと吹く風に、水なき空へ立つ波の、また吹き下ろす雪の庭　本調子・蝶の合方へ　蝶も戯れてひらひらひら、ともに浮かれつ　合方　立ち舞へる、手ごとにかざす花の枝、あかぬ色なる春のたそがれ＜紅葉の巻は雨の曲＞
二上りへ　園生の垣に香をとむる、菊の葉露もいつしかに、自らなる秋の色、手染めの糸の立田姫、織り出す錦くさぐさに、人の心のなびくまで、見ゆる姿の優しさも、旗手の雲のいと早く、三下りへ　一時雨降るなりさらさらさらさら　雨の合方へ　濡れて色増す紅葉ばの、数は八汐か九重の、十二単衣の紅と、数へ数へて幾汐か、雨に風情もいと深き　合方　秋の名残を眺むならまし

Hōrai

天保年間
四世 杵屋六三郎 作曲
蓬莱

二上り・前弾へ　うらゝかな、日の色そみて木の間にも　合　葉毎の花の綾錦、重ねし縫の伊達模様　合　着つゝ馴れにし山姫は、人の眺めの迷ひ草、結びかねたる空解けは、いっそ浮気なそよ風や　合へ　うらみて煙る塩竈は、胸に焚く火の消えかぬる、ヱ、何とせう　合　仇し仇浪寄せては返す岩枕、浮名はぱっと立つ鳥の、塒を慕ふ恋の山　本調子合方へ萩の白露、起き伏し辛き　合　色と香の　合　茂りてふかき床のうち、今朝の別れに袖濡らす、しょんがえ　合へ　招く芒はいたづら者よ　合　女郎花、あぢな気になる花の色、さめぬ桔梗の可愛ゆらし、しょんがえへ　うつゝなや　合へ　眺め尽きせぬ殿づくり、実に蓬莱を見上ぐれば、高き調べの松が枝に、琴弾くやうな鶴の足どり

Kairaishi

文化十二年
四世　杵屋三郎助　作曲
傀儡師
（外記節傀儡師）

前弾・本調子へ　浮世の業や西の海、汐の蛭子の里広く、国々修行の傀
儡師、連れに離れて雪の下　合　椿にならぶ青柳の雫も軽き春雨に、楽
屋を冠り通るにぞへ　堀構へなる窓の内、呼びかけられて床しくも、立ち止
まれば麗しき、女中の声にて傀儡師、一曲舞はせと望まれし、詞の下より
取あへず、声悪しけれど箱皷、拍子とりどり人形を、あまた出だして夫々と、
唄ひけるこそをかしけれ　二下りへ　小倉の野辺の一本薄、何時か穂に
出て尾花とならば、露が嫉まん恋草の、積り積りて足曳の、山猫の尾のな
がながと、独りかも寝ん淋しさに　本調子へ　夕べ迎へし花嫁様は、鎌も
よく切れ千草も靡く、心よさそなかみ様ぢゃ　合　おらが女房を誉めるぢ
ゃないが、物もよく縫い機も織り候　合　綾や錦や金襴緞子、折々事の睦
言にへ　三人持ちし子宝の、総領息子は鷹揚にて、父の前でも懐手、物を
云うても返事せず、二番息子は脊高く、三番息子は悪戯にて、悪さ盛の六
つ七つ、中でいとしき乳の余り　合　肩に打乗せて都の名所廻れ廻れ風
車　合　張子羯鼓や振鼓、手に持って遊べさ　三下りへ　花が見たくば
吉野へ御座れ、今は吉野の花盛、よいさよいさ花盛、花笠着つれしゃなし
ゃなと　本調子へ　このはしたは吸筒を、袂に巻きてから玉や、つい明ら
けき天津空、桜曇に今日の日も、桜曇りに今日の日も呉羽綾羽のとりどり
に、　へ呉羽綾羽のとりどりの貢物、供ふる御代こそ目出度けれと、箱の内
にぞおさめける

Kanda Matsuri

神田祭

明治四十四年

幸堂得知　作歌

杵屋六四郎・吉住小三郎　作曲

前弾・本調子へ　神田祭を待つ宵の、神酒所に活けた女夫花、誰が手す
さびか白菊と、黄菊の露も新しく、飾る名家の金屏風、行き交い繁き辻々
に重ね言葉も聞き馴れた、御祭礼お祭り番付、八つ八通りに変わる文福
茶釜、七つの鐘はいつ撞いたやら　二上りへ　ほのぼのと、白みわたりて
東天紅、一番鶏は泰平の、御代を祝うて苔むす諫鼓へ　二番の鉾は馬櫪
神、まさるめでたき装束烏帽子、ドンドンカッカ、ドンカッカへ　続く三番
式として、翁の山車は神田丸、五番十番次々に　合方　町年番の附祭へ
　住吉踊り太神楽、屋台囃子は住吉と、杵屋が持ちの菊襲へ　所望々々
に手古舞の、達衆が応の声に連れ、渡り拍子を打ち上げて　合方　本調
子へ　昔より、恋という字は誰が書き初めて、迷いの種を蒔きぬらん、忍ぶ
夜は、風も吹き候雨も降り候、憎や咎むる里の犬へ　籬に寄ってほとほと
と、叩けば菊に置きあまるへ　露はばらりと皆散りぬれど、同じ思いに待ち
わびし、姫は枢に立ち出でて、いざこなたへと供えりへ　夜風に御身も冷
えぬらん、心ばかりに侍れども、妾が設けの菊の酒、きこし召せやと杯のへ
　数重なればうち解けて、愛と愛との相生連理へ　よその見る目も羨ま
しへ　あとの所望は会釈なく、数番の山車に、追われ追われて　二上り・
合方へ　オンヤーリョイへ　黄金花咲く豊かな御代にソレ、締めろやれ中
綱へ　エンヤーリョイ　伊達も喧嘩も江戸の花、その花笠の咲き揃う、
桜の馬場へ堂々と、寄せ来る人の波間より、光りまばゆく昇る日の影

Kanjinchō

勧進帳
天保十一年
杵屋六翁　作曲

謡ヒガヽリ次第ヘ　旅の衣は篠懸の、旅の衣は篠懸の、露けき袖やしをる
らん　外記ガヽリ・本調子ヘ　時しも頃は如月の　合　きさらぎの十日の
夜ヘ　月の都を立ち出でて　寄ヒノ合方ヘ　これやこの、往くもかへるも
別れては、知るも知らぬも逢坂の、山かくす　合　霞ぞ春はゆかしける
合　波路はるかに行く舟の、海津の浦に着きにけりヘ　いざ通らん旅衣、
関のこなたに立ちかヽる　合ノットヘ　夫山伏といつば、役の優婆塞の行
義を受け、即身即仏の本体を、此処にて打ちとめ給はんこと、明王の照覧
はかりがたう、熊野権現の御罰当らんこと、立どころに於て疑ひあるべから
ず、唵阿毘羅吽欠と、珠数さらさらとおし揉んだりヘ　元より勧進帳のあら
ばこそ、笈の内より往来の、巻物一巻取出だし、勧進帳と名付けつヽ、高ら
かにこそ読み上げけれヘ　（天も響けと読み上げたりヘ　感心してぞ見え
にけるヘ）土卒がはこぶ広台に、白綾袴一とかさね、加賀絹あまた取揃へ、
御前へこそは直しけれヘ　こは嬉しやと山伏も、しづしづ立って歩まれけ
りヘ　すはや我君あやしむるは、一期の浮沈こヽなりと、おのおの後へ立
ちかへるヘ　金剛杖をおつ取って、さんさんに打擲すヘ　通れとこそは罵
りぬヘ　かたがたは何故に、かほど賤しき強力に、太刀かたなを抜きたま
ふは、目垂れ顔のふるまひ、臆病のいたりかと、皆山伏は、打刀抜きかけて
　外記ガヽリ　勇みかヽれる有様は、いかなる天魔鬼神も恐れつべうぞ見
えにけるヘ　土卒を引連れ関守は、門の内へぞ入りにける　合ヘ　つひ
に泣かぬ弁慶も、一期の涙ぞ殊勝なる　一中ガヽリヘ　判官御手を取り
たまひ　合ヘ　釣にそひし袖枕、かた敷く隙も波の上　合　或時は舟に
浮かび、風波に身をまかせ、又或時は山脊の、馬蹄も見えぬ雪の中に、海

179

少しあり夕浪の、立ち来る音や須磨明石　合　とかく三とせの程もなくな
く痛はしやと、萎れかかりし鬼あざみ、霜に露置く斗りなり　一中ガヽリヘ
　互ひに袖を引き連れて、いざさせたまへの折柄に　説教ブシ・二上りヘ
　実にげに是も心得たり、人の情の盃を、受けて心をとゞむとかやヘ　今
は昔の語り草ヘ　あら恥かしの我心、一度見えし女さヘヘ　迷ひの道の
関越えて、今又こゝに越えかねる　半太夫ガヽリヘ　人目の関のやるせな
やヘ　あア悟られぬこそ浮世なれ　本調子ヘ　面白や山水に、おもしろや
山水に、盃を浮かべては、流に引かるゝ曲水の、手先づさへぎる袖ふれて、
いざや舞を舞はうよ　合舞ヘ　元より弁慶は三塔の遊僧、舞延年の時の
和歌　合舞ヘ　是なる山水の、落ちて巌に響くこそ、鳴るは滝の水、鳴る
は滝の水　合舞ヘ　鳴るは滝の水、日は照るとも、絶えずとうたり、疾く疾
く立てや手束弓の、心ゆるすな関守の人々、いとま申してさらばよとて、笈を
おっとり肩に打ちかけ　合ヘ　虎の尾を履み毒蛇の口を、遁れたるこゝち
して、陸奥の国へぞ下りける

Kokaji

小鍛冶
文政四年
杵屋勝五郎　作曲

本調子へ　稲荷山三つの燈し火明かに、心を磨く鍛冶の道、小狐丸と末の代に、残す其名ぞ著るき　セリ合方へ　夫唐土に　合　伝へ聞く、竜泉太阿はいざ知らず　合　我日の本のかな工、天国天の座神息が、国家鎮護の剣にも、優りはするとも劣らじと、神の力の合槌を、打つや　合　丁々　合　しつていころり　合　余所に聞くさへ勇ましき　合方へ　打つと云ふ、夫は夜寒の麻衣　合　をちの砧も音添へて、打てやうつゝの宇津の山　合　鄙も都も秋更けて、降るや時雨の初紅葉　合　焦がるゝ色を金床に　合　火加減湯加減秘密の大事、焼刃渡しは陰陽和合、露にも濡れて薄もみぢ、染めて色増す金色は、霜夜の月と澄みまさる、手柄の程ぞ類ひなき、清光凛々　合　うるはしき、若手の業物切れ物と　合　四方に其名は響きけり

Kuramayama

安政三年

二世 杵屋勝三郎 作曲

鞍馬山

本調子へ　夫　合　月も鞍馬の影うとく、木葉おどしの小夜あらし　合
物さわがしや貴船川　合　天狗倒しのおびたゞしく魔界のちまたぞ恐ろし
き　合方へ　爰に源家の正統たる、牛若丸は父の仇、平家を一太刀恨み
んと、夜毎詣づる多門天、祈念の疲れ岩角に、暫しまどろむ　合　肱まく
ら　セリ合方へ　思ひ出せば、我いまだ三歳の時なりしが、母常磐が懐に
抱へられ、伏見の里にて宗清が　合　情によりて命助かり、出家をせよと
当山の　合　東光坊に預けられしも、算へて見れば一と昔　合　十余年
の星霜経れど、稚心に忘れずして、今まのあたり見たる夢、それにつけても
父の仇　合　剣道修行なすと雖も、我一向の生兵法　合　願へば神の
恵にて、本望遂ぐる時節を待たんへ　イデや琢磨の修行をなさん　合へ
　木太刀おつとり合身がまへなす　合　時しも俄に風起り、天狗礫のば
らばらと、鳴動なしてすさみじゝ　合へ　遥の杉の梢より　合　又もや怪
しの小天狗　合　木太刀うち振り　合　立向へば　合へ　シヤ小賢し
と牛若丸　合　つけ入る木太刀を払ひのけ　合　上段　合　下段　合
　早速の働き　合　勝負いかにと霧隠れ　合　後に窺ふ僧正坊、優り劣
らぬ　合　両人が　合　木太刀の音は谺して、目覚ましくもまた　合
勇ましゝ　合へ　さしもの天狗もあしらひかね　合　跡を晦まし失せにけ
り、跡を　合　くらまし　合　失せにけり

Kuruwa Tanzen

安政四年
二世 杵屋勝三郎 作曲
廓丹前
（廓花柳立髪）

へ　俳優の昔を今に写画や、及ばぬ筆に菱川の、寛濶出立廓通ひ、姿彩る丹前は、今日を曠なる初舞台　二上りへ　よしや男と名に高き、富士の白柄まばゆくも　合　紫匂ふ筑波根の、腰巻羽織六法に　合　振つてふり込む　合　やつこのこのこの、酒ならねぢきり　合　いろ上戸、恋の取持してこいまかせろ、しょんがえ、花にも優る伊達な風俗へ　抑や廓の始まりは、遠つ元和の四ツの年、庄司何某弥宣町へ、五ツの街開きてより、揚屋の数も大門に、三千楼の色競べへ　先づ初春の飾夜具　合　蓬莱山と夕間ぐれ、千本の桜仲の町、翳す扇の目せき笠　コイヨネイと一と声をへ　ほぞんかけたる　合　時鳥　合　お供帰りの酒機嫌、謡ふ小唄の土手節にへ　かゝる山谷の草深けれど　合　君が住家と思へばよしや　合　玉の台もおろかでござる　合　余所の見る目もいとはぬ我ぢやよ、お笑ひやるな名の立つに、姿見かへる葉柳のへ　結んで解いた雲の帯、掛けし屏風の雀形、比翼枕の暁に、鵲渡す天の川、星待合の辻うら茶屋に、七夕さんのころび寝も、きぬぎぬ早き草の市へ　軒端を照らす花燈籠、其八朔の白襲ね、雪の素顔に鉢巻しやんと、月に仁和賀の勢ひ獅子へ　やアしめろやれ、〆て寝た夜は枕が邪魔よ、ヤア可愛可愛の相槌の音　ヨイヨイイヤナア　エイエイヨエイヤナア　やれこれこれは手がそれたか、いとしけりやこそ、おいどをちつくりたゝいた　ヨイヨイヨイヤナ　よいとな　合　やア〆ろやれ、よいサよいサよいこれはのサ、そつこでしめろ中綱へ　よく咲揃ふ花紅葉　合　秋葉祭の冬の来て、門に松竹年の関、大晦日の大神楽、狐で浮かせ、うかれ浮るゝ浮拍子へ　実に全盛は闇の夜も、吉原ばかり月と花、柳の廓寿きて、目出度揚屋へ入りにける

183

Matsu no Midori

松の緑

安政年間

初代杵屋六翁　作曲

前弾キ・本調子へ　今年より千たび迎ふる春毎に　合　なほも深めに、松のみどりか禿の名ある、二葉の色に太夫の風の吹き通ふ　合　松の位の外八文字　合　華美を見せたる蹴出し褄、よう似た松の根上りも、一つ囲ひの籬にもるゝ　合　廓は根曳の別世界　合　世々の誠と裏表、くらべごしなる筒井づゝ、振分髪もいつしかに、老となるまで末広を、開き初めたる名こそ祝せめ

Musume Dōjōji

娘道成寺
寶暦三年
杵屋彌三郎　作曲

謡ヒ〳　花の外には松ばかり、花の外には松ばかり、暮れそめて鐘や響く
らん　三下り〳　鐘に恨みは数々ござる、初夜の鐘を撞く時は、諸行無
常と響くなり、後夜の鐘を撞く時は、是生滅法と響くなり、晨鐘の響は生滅
々己、入相は寂滅為楽と響くなり、聞いて響く人もなし、我も五障の雲晴れ
て、真如の月を眺め明かさん　二上り・合〳　言はず語らぬ我が心、乱れ
し髪の乱るゝも、つれないは唯移り気な、どうでも男は悪性もの　合〳
桜々と謡はれて、言うて袂のわけ二つ、勤めさへ唯浮々と、どうでも女子は
悪性もの〳　都育ちは蓮葉なものぢやえ　合毬唄〳　恋の分里、武士も
道具も伏編笠で、張と意気地の吉原　合　花の都は歌でやはらぐ敷島
原に、勤めする身は誰と伏見の墨染　合　煩悩菩提の撞木町より、難波
四筋に通ひ木辻に、禿だちから室の早咲、それがほんに、色ぢや一イ二ウ
三イ四ウ、夜露雪の日、下の関路も、共に此身を馴染重ねて、仲は丸山、た
だ円かれと、思ひ染めたが縁ぢやえ　三下り・合〳　梅とさんさん桜は、
何れ兄やら弟やら　合　わきて言はれぬな、花の色え　合〳　菖蒲杜若
は、何れ姉やら妹やら　合　わきて言はれぬな、花の色え　合〳　西も東
も、みんな見にきた花の顔、さよえ　合　見れば恋ぞ増すえ、さよえ　合
　可愛ゆらしさの花娘　合〳　恋の手習つい見習ひて、誰れに見せよと
て、紅鉄漿つけよぞ、みんな主への心中立て、おう嬉し嬉し　合　末はかう
ぢやにな、さうなる迄は、とんと言はずに済まそぞえと、誓紙さへ偽りか、嘘
か誠か、どうもならぬほど逢ひに来た、ふつつり悋気せまいぞと、たしなん
で見ても情なや、女子には何がなる　合　殿御殿御の気が知れぬ、気が
知れぬ、悪性な悪性な気が知れぬ、恨み恨みてかこち泣き、露を含みし桜

花、さはらば落ちん風情なり　羯鼓ノ山尽し合方へ　面白の四季の眺め
や、三国一の富士の山、雪かと見れば、花の吹雪か吉野山、散り来るちりく
る嵐山　合　朝日山々を見渡せば、歌の中山石山の　合　末の松山い
つか大江山、いく野の　合　道の遠けれど、恋路に通ふ浅間山、一と夜の
情有馬山　合　いなせの言の葉　合　あすか木曾山待乳山、我三上山
祈り北山稲荷　合　山、縁を結びし妹脊山、二人が中の黄金山、花咲くえ
いこの、このこの姥捨山、峯の松風音羽山、入相の鐘を筑波山、東叡山の
　合　月のかほばせ三笠山　合(去る程にさるほどに、寺々の鐘、月落ち
鶏鳴いて霜雪天に、満潮程なく此山寺の、江村の漁火、愁ひに対して人々
眠れば、好き隙ぞと、立舞ふ様にねらひ寄つて、撞かんとせしが、思へば此
の鐘恨めしやとて、竜頭に手をかけ飛ぶよと見えしが、引きかづいでぞ失
せにける)へ　[concert text ends here] 只頼め、氏神様が可愛がらしやんす
合　出雲の神様と約束あれば、つい新枕、廓に恋すれば浮世ぢやえ　合
　深い仲ぢやと言ひ立てゝ、こちやこちやこちやよい首尾で、憎てらしい程
いとしらしへ　花に心を深見草へ　園に色よく　合　咲初めて、紅をさす
が、品よくなりよく、あゝ姿優しやしほらしや、さつささうぢやいな、そうぢやい
な　合　皐月五月雨、早乙女早乙女川植唄、早乙女早乙女田植唄、裾や
袂を濡らした、さつさ　合へ　花の姿の乱れ髪、思へば思へば恨めしやとて
て、竜頭に手を掛け飛ぶよと見えしが、引きかづいでぞ失せにけるへ　謡
ふも舞ふも法の声、えエ何でもせいせい　合　春は花見の幕ぞゆかしき、
夏は家形の船ゆかし、よいよいよいよいよい、ありやりや、こりやりや、よいと
な　合　秋は武蔵の月ぞゆかしき、冬は雪見の亭ゆかし、よいよいよいよ
いよい、ありやりや、こりやりや、よいとな　合　浮きに浮かれて、第一中有
に迷うた、懺悔々々、六根罪障、南無不動明王、えエ何でもせい、えエ何で
もせい　合　動くか動かぬか、曩謨三曼陀縛日羅南、こりや動かぬぞ、真
言秘密で責かけ責かけ、珠数の有たけやつさらさら、旋伱摩訶嚕遮那、何
のこつちやえ、娑婆多耶吽多羅、何のこつちやえと祈りけるへ　謹請東方
靑龍清浄、謹請西方白體白龍、一大三千大千世界の恒沙の龍王、哀愍頻
の砌なれば、何國に恨みの有るべきぞと、祈り禱られ飛び上がり、御法の
聲に禁色の、花を降らせし其の姿、実にも妙なる奇特かや

Niwakajishi

天保五年
四世 杵屋六三郎 作曲
俄獅子

鼓唄・二上りヘ　花と見つ、五町驚かぬ人もなし、なれも迷ふやさまざまに　合　四季折々の戯れは、紋日物日のかけ言葉　合　蝶や胡蝶の禿俄の　合　浮れ獅子　合　見返れば、花の屋台に見えつ隠れつ色々の、姿やさしき仲の町　合ヘ　心づくしのナ其玉章も、いつか渡さん神の中、心一とつに思ひ草、よしや世の中　合ヘ　狂ひ乱るゝ女獅子男獅子の、あなたへひらり此方へひらり、ひらひらひら　合　忍ぶの峰か襲ね夜具、枕の岩間滝つ瀬の、酒に乱れて足もたまらず　合　他処の見る目も白浪や　合方キヤリヘ　ヤア秋の最中の、月は竹村、更けて逢ふのが間夫の客、ヨイヨイヘ　辻占みごと繰返し、何故この様に忘られぬ、恥ずかしいほど愚痴になるヘ　と云ふちやア無理酒に、何でもこっちの待人、恋のナ、恋の山屋が豆腐に鎹、しまりのないので、ぬらくらふわつく嘘ばかり、ヨイヨイヨイヤナヘ　宵から待たせて又行かうとは、エゝあんまりなと膝立直しヘ　締ろやれ、たんだ打てや打て、打つは太鼓が取持顔か、拗ねて裏向く水道尻に　合　お神楽蕎麦なら少し延びたと囃されて、ちんちん鴨の床の内、たんたん狸の空寝入、狐つた跡のゆかりの色に、打つて変つた中直り、あれはさ、これはさ、よい声かけや、ヨイヤナ、しどもなや　合三下りヘ　人目忍ぶは裏茶屋に、為になるのを振捨てゝ、深く沈みし恋の淵、心がらなる身の憂さは、いとそ辛いぢやない　合　かいな、逢はぬ昔が懐かしやヘ　獅子に添ひてや戯れ遊ぶ、浮きたつ色の群りて、夕日花さく廓景色、目前と貴賎うつゝなりヘ　暫く待たせ給へや、宵の約束今行く程に夜も更けじ　クルヒ・合方ヘ　獅子團亂旋の舞楽もかくや、勇む末社の花に戯れ酒に臥し、大金散らす君達の、打てや大門全盛の、高金の奇特あらはれて、靡かぬ草木もなき時なれや、千秋万歳万々歳と　合　豊に祝す獅子頭

87

Oimatsu

文政三年
四世 杵屋六三郎 作曲
老松

謡ガヽリ・本調子次第ヘ　実に治まれる四方の国、実に治まれる四方の国、関の戸さゝで通はんヘ　是は老木の神松の、千代に八千代にさゞれ石の、巌となりて苔のむすまで　合　松の葉色も時めきて　合　十返り深き縁のうち、眠れる夢のはや覚めて　合　色香にふけし花も過ぎ、月に嘯き身はつながるゝ　合　糸竹の、縁にひかれて、うつらうつらと長生の、泉を汲める心地せりヘ　先づ社壇の方を見てあれば、北に峨々たる青山に、彩る雲のたなびきて、風にひらり、ひらめきわたる此方には　合　翠帳紅閨の粧ひ、昔を忘れず、右に古寺の旧蹟あり　合　晨鐘夕梵の響き、絶ゆることなき眺めさへ、赤間硯の筆ずさみ、こゝに司を　合　しるしけり　二上りヘ　松といふ、文字はかはれど待つ言の葉の　合　其かひありて積む年に　合　寿祝ふ常磐木の、調べぞつづく高砂の、名あるほとりに住吉の、松の老木も若きをかたる、恥かしさ、唯変らじと深緑、嬉しき代々に相生の、幾世の思ひ限り知られず、喜びもことわりぞかし、何時までもヘ　清きいさめの神かぐら、舞楽を備ふる此家に、声も満ちたつ、有難や　神楽舞合方・三下りヘ　松の太夫のうちかけは、蔦の模様に藤色の、いとし可愛も、みんなみんな男は偽りぢやもの　合　拗ねて見せても其儘よそへ、或夜ひそかにつきあひの、雲の籬のかけ言葉　合　エヽ憎らしい木隠れに、晴れて逢ふ日を松の色ヘ　ゆたかに遊ぶ鶴亀の、齢を授くる此君の、行末守れと我神託の、告を知らする松の風　松風合方ヘ　富貴自在の繁栄も、久しき宿こそ目出度けれ

Okina Sanbasō

翁三番叟

杵屋六左衛門　作曲

前弾・本調子・翁地へ　とうどうたらり、たらりら、たらりあがり、ららりどう へ　ちりやたらりたらりら、あらりあがり、ららりどうへ　所千代までおわ しませへ　われらも千秋さむらおうへ　鶴と亀との齢にてへ　さいわい心 にまかせたりへ　鳴るは滝の水、鳴るは滝の水、鳴るは滝の水、日は照ると もへ　絶えずとうたり、ありうどうどうへ　君の千歳を経んことは、天津乙 女の羽衣よ、鳴るは滝の水、日は照るともへ　絶えずとうたり、ありうどうあ りうどう　合の手へ　総角やとんどやへ　尋ばかりやとんどやへ　坐して いたれどもへ　参ろうれんげりや、とんどやへ　千早振る、神のひこさの昔 より、久しかれとぞ祝いへ　そよや、れいちや、とんどやへ　およそ千年の 鶴は、万歳楽と謡うたり、また万代の池の亀は、甲に三極をいただいたりへ 　滝の水麗々と落ちて、夜の月あざやかにい浮かんだり、渚の砂さくさくと して、朝の日の色を朗すへ　天下泰平国土安穏の、今日の御祈祷なりへ 　在原や、なじょの翁ともへ　あれはなじゃの翁とも、そよやいずくの翁と もへ　そよや　舞の合方へ　千秋万歳の喜びの舞なれば、一さし舞お うへ　万歳楽へ　万歳楽へ　万歳楽

　三番叟・揉み出しへ　おおさえおさえ、喜びありや、我がこの所よりほか へはやらじとぞ思う　本調子・素舞の合方へ　あらめでたや、物に心得た る、あどの太夫殿に、そと見参申そうへ　ちょうど参って候へ　誰がお立ち にて候ぞへ　あどと仰せ候ほどに、御身あどのために罷り立って候、今日 の三番叟、千秋万歳と舞うておりそえ、色の黒い尉殿へ　この色の黒い尉 が、今日の三番叟、千秋万歳所繁盛と、舞い納めうずることは、なにより以 て安うそう、まずあどの太夫殿は、もとの座敷へ、おもおもとお直りそえへ 某座敷へ直ろうずることは、尉殿の舞よりいと安うそう、御舞い無うては直

り候まじへ　ああらようがましやへ　さらば鈴を参らしょう　鈴の段へこれのんなんな、池の汀に宝御船が着くとんの　合方へ　艫舳にはんな、恵比須大黒、中は毘沙門吉祥天女　合方・二上りへ　四海波風静けき君が、御代はかしこき天照神の、影も曇らず怨敵退散、五穀成就民豊か、八百万代も国や栄えん

Renjishi (Katsusaburō)

勝三郎連獅子
文久元年
二代目杵屋勝三郎　作曲

本調子へ　夫牡丹は百花の王にして、獅子は百獣の長とかや、桃李にまさ
る牡丹花の、今を盛りに咲き満ちて、虎豹に劣らぬ連獅子の、戯れ遊ぶ石
の橋へ　是ぞ文珠の在します　合　其名も高き清涼山へ　峰を仰げば
千丈の、漲る滝は　合　雲より落ち、谷を望めば　合　千尋の底　合
流れに響く松の風、見渡す橋は夕陽の、雨後に映ずる虹に似て、虚空を渡
るが如くなりへ　かゝる嶮岨の山頭より、強臆ためす親獅子の、恵みも深き
谷間へ、蹴落す子獅子は　合　転々々、落つると　合　見えしが、身を飜
し、爪を蹴たてゝ　合　駈登るを　合　又突き落し突き落す　合　猛き
心の荒獅子も　二上りへ　牡丹の花に舞ひあそぶ　合　胡蝶に心やは
らぎて、花に顕はれ葉に隠れ　合　追ひつ　合　追はれつ余念なく　合
　風に散り行く　合　花びらの　合　ひらりひらひら　合　翼を慕ひ
合　共に狂ふぞ面白き　本調子へ　折から笙笛琴箜篌の妙なる調べ舞
ひの袖　獅子舞・五段合方へ　獅子団乱旋の舞楽のみぎん、獅子団乱旋
の舞楽のみぎん、牡丹の花ぶさ香ひ満ちみち、大巾利巾の獅子頭、打てや
囃せや牡丹芳、牡丹芳、黄金の蘂あらはれて、花に戯れ枝に臥しまろび、
実にも上なき獅子王の勢ひ、靡かぬ草木もなき時なれや、万歳千秋と舞ひ
納め、万歳千秋と舞ひをさめ、獅子の座にこそなほりけれ

Sagi Musume

鷺娘
寶暦十二年
富士田吉治　作曲

鼓唄三下りへ　妄執の雲晴れやらぬ朧夜の、恋に迷ひしわが心へ　忍山、口舌の種の恋風が　合へ　吹けども傘に雪もつて、積もる思ひは泡雪の、消えて果敢なき恋路とや　合へ　思ひ重なる胸の闇　合　せめて哀れと夕暮に、ちらちら雪に濡鷺の、しょんぼりと可愛らし　合へ　迷ふ心の細流れ、ちょろちょろ水の一筋に怨みの外は白鷺の、水に馴れたる足どりも　合　濡れて雫と消ゆるものへ　われは涙に乾く間も、袖干しあへぬ月影に、忍ぶ其夜の話を捨て〻　合クドキへ　縁を結ぶの神さんに、取り上げられし嬉しさも、余る色香の恥かしや　合方へ　須磨の浦辺で潮汲むよりも、君の心は汲みにくい、さりとは、実に誠と思はんせ　合へ　繻子の袴の襞とるよりも、主の心が取りにくい、さりとは、実に誠と思はんせ　合　しやほんにえ　合へ　白鷺の、羽風に雪の散りて、花の散りしくへ　景色と見れど、あたら眺の雪ぞ散りなん、雪ぞ散りなんへ　憎からぬ　合鼓唄へ　恋に心も移ろひし、花の吹雪の散かゝり、払ふも惜しき袖笠やへ　傘をやへ　傘　合へ　それえそれえ、匂ひ桜の花笠へ　縁と月日を廻りくるくるへ　車がさ、それそれそれさうぢやえへ　それが浮名の端となる　合へ　添ふも添はれず剰へ、邪慳の刃に先立ちて、此世からさへ剣の山　合へ　一じゆのうちに恐ろしや、地獄の有様悉く　合　罪を紏して閻王の、鉄杖正にありありと、等活畜生、衆生地獄、或は叫喚大叫喚、修羅の太鼓は隙もなく　合へ　獄卒四方に群りて、鉄杖振り上げくろがねの　合　牙噛み鳴らしぼつ立てたて　合へ　二六時中がその間、くるり、くるり、追ひ廻りおひまはり、遂に此身はひしひしひし、憐みたまへ我が憂身、語るも涙なりけらし

Shakkyō

石橋
文政三年
十代目杵屋六左衛門　作曲

謡ヒガヽリ詞ヘ　是は大江の定基出家し、寂照法師にて候、我入唐渡天の望候うて波濤を越え、是は早石橋にて候、向ひは文珠の浄土清涼山にて候程に、此あたりに休らひ、橋を渡らばやと思ひ候　本調子ヘ　松風の、花を薪に吹き添へて、雪をも運ぶ山路かな　合方ヘ　樵歌牧笛の声、人間万事様々に、世を渡り行く業ながら、余りに山を遠く来て、雲又後を立ち隔て、入りつる方も白浪の、谷の川音雨とのみ、聞えて松の風もなし、実に過つて半日の客たりしも、今身の上に知られつゝ、妻木脊負うて斧かたげ、岩根烈しき　合　伝ひ、小笹を分けて歩み来る　ワキヘ　如何に其れなる山人、是は石橋にて候か　シテヘ　さん候、是は石橋にて候よ、向ひは文珠の浄土にて、清涼山とぞ申すなり、よくよく御拝み候ヘ　ワキヘ　我身の上を仏慮に任せ、橋を渡らばやと思ひ候　シテヘ　暫く候、そのかみなり名を得給ひし高僧、貴僧と聞えし人も、此処にて月日を送り給ひ、難行苦行捨身の行にてこそ、橋をも渡り給ひしが、獅子は小虫を食まんとても、先づ勢ひをなすとこそ聞け、我が法力のあればとて、容易く思ひ渡らん事、あら危ふしの御事や　ワキヘ　謂れを聞けば有難や、なほなほ此橋の謂れ、詳しく御物語り候へや　シテヘ　語つて聞かせ申すべし　大薩摩ヘ　夫れ　合　天地開闢のこのかたヘ　雨路を降して国土を渡る、是れ即ち天の浮橋とも云へり　合　其外国土世界に於いて、橋の名所様々にして、水波の難を遁れては、万民富めり世を渡るも、則ち橋の徳とかや、然るに此石橋は、巌峨々たる岩石に、己れと架かる橋なれば、石橋とこそ名付けたれ、実に此橋の有様は、其画僅にして、尺よりは狭う、渡せる長さ三丈余り、苔は滑りて足もたまらず　合　谷のそくばく深きこと、数千丈とも覚

193

えたり、遥かに峰を見上ぐれば　合　雲より落つる荒滝に　合　霧朦朧
と闇うして、下は泥犁も白波の、音は嵐に響き合ひて、虚空を渡るが如くな
りへ　橋の景色を見渡せば、雲に聳ゆる粧ひは、譬はば夕陽の雨の後、虹
を成せる其形又、弓を引ける如くにて　合　神変仏力にあらずしては、進
んで人や渡るべき、向ひは文珠の浄土にて、常に笙歌の花降りて、簫笛琴
箜篌、夕日の雲に聞ゆべき、目前の奇特あらたなりへ　暫く待たせ給へや、
影向の時節も今幾程によも過ぎじ　狂ヒノ曲合方へ　獅子団乱旋の舞
楽のみぎん　合　獅子団乱旋の舞楽のみぎん、牡丹の英匂ひ満ちみち、
大巾利巾の獅子頭、打てや囃せや牡丹芳、牡丹芳、黄金の蘂顕はれて、花
に戯れ枝に臥し転び、実にも上なき獅子王の勢ひ、靡かぬ草木もなき時な
れや、万歳千秋と舞納め、万歳千秋と舞納め、獅子の座にこそ直りけれ

194

Shiki no Yamamba

文久二年
十一世 杵屋六左衛門
四季の山姥

本調子・前弾キへ　遠近の、たつきも知らぬ山住居、我も昔は流れの身、狭き庵に見渡せば　合へ　春は殊更八重霞、其八重桐の勤めの身、柳桜をこきまぜて　合　都ぞ春の錦着て、手練手管に客を待つ　合へ　夏は涼しの蚊帳の内、比翼の蓙に月の影　合へ　秋はさながら縁先に、三味線弾いてしんき節　合　髪の乱れを簪で、かき上げながら畳算　合　眠る禿に無理ばかり、ほんに辛いぢやないかいなへ　同じ思ひに啼く虫の　合　松虫　合　鈴虫轡虫　合　馬追虫のやるせなく　合　何れの里に衣擣つ　虫ノ合方へ　よくも合はせたものかいな　二上りへ　振りさけみれば袖が浦　合　沖に白帆や千鳥立つ　合　蜆採るなる様さへも、あれ遠浅に澪標　合　松棒杭へ遁れ来て　合　ませた鴉が世の中を、あはうあはうと笑ふ声　合　立てたる粗朶に附く海苔を　合　とりどり廻る海士小舟、浮絵に見ゆる安房上総　三下りへ　冬は谷間に冬籠る　合　まだ鶯の片言も、梅の荅の花やかに　合　雪を頂く葛屋の軒端　合　仇な松風吹き落ちて、ちりやちりや、ちりちり、ちりちりぱつと、散るは　合　胡蝶に似たる景色かな　謡ヒガヽリへ　あら面白の山めぐり　合へ　どつこい遣らぬととり手の若木、こなたは老木の力業　合方へ　中よりふつと捻ぢ着る大木　合　かけりかけりて谷間の、谷の庵に晏然と、其儘そこに座を占めて　合　幾年月を送りけり

Shima no Senzai

明治三十七年
五世 杵屋勘五郎 作曲
島の千歳

三下りへ　舟頂緑毛の色姿、朝日うつらふ和田津海、蓬が島の千歳が、諷ふ昔の　合　今様も　合　変らぬ御代の御宝、鼓腹の声々うち寄する、四方の敷浪立つか　合　返へるか　合　返へるか立つか　謡ヒガゝリへ　返す袂や立烏帽子、中の舞　本調子・合へ　水のすぐれておぼゆるは、西天竺の白鷺池　合　新せう許曲に澄渡る　合　昆明池の水の色　合　行末久しくすむとかや　合　賢人の釣をたれしは　合　厳陵院の河の水　二上りへ　月影流れもるなる山田の筧の水とかや　合　芦の下葉をとづるは、三島入江の氷水、春立つの空の若水は　合　汲むとも汲むとも尽もせじ、尽もせじ

196

Suehirogari

末廣がり

安政元年三月

十代目杵屋六左衛門　作曲

本調子へ　画く舞台の松竹も、千代をこめたる彩色の、若緑なるシテとア
ド　合へ　罷出でしも恥かしさうに、声張上げて　合　太郎冠者あるか
　合　御前に合念なう早かつた　合　頼うだ人は今日も又、恋の奴の
　合　お使ひか、返事待つ恋　合　忍ぶ恋、晴れて扇も名のみにて　合へ
　ほんに心も白扇、いつか首尾して青骨の、ゆるぐまいとの要の契り　合
　かたく締緒の縁結び、神を頼むの　合　誓ひごと、濡れて色増す花の
雨　合へ　傘をさすなら春日山　合　これも花の宴とて、人が飲みてさす
なら、我も飲みてささうよ　合　花の盃　合　はんな傘　合　実にもさう
よの、やよ実にもさうよの、実にまことへ　四つの海、今ぞ治まる時津風、波
の鼓の声澄みて、謡ふつ舞ふつ君が代は、万々蔵も限りなく、末廣がりこそ
目出度けれ、末廣がりこそ目出度けれ

Takarabune

文政・天保ごろか
四世 杵屋六三郎 作曲
宝船（長き夜）

二上りへ　長き夜の、遠の眠りの皆目覚め、恵方に当たる弁天の、笑顔に
見とれていつまでか、茶屋が床几に根が生え抜きの、毘沙門さんのじゃら
つきを、見かねて布袋がのっさのさ　合方へ　そうはならぬと押し合う中
へ〻　連れ立つ勇みの大黒恵比寿、これはたまらぬ、こりゃどうじゃへ
恋争いは吉原の、派手な大尽福禄寿へ　そもそも廓の全盛は、幇間末社
の大一座、三日は客のきそ初め、こなたに髭の意休と見たるは、心やさしき
寿老人へ　袖に禿が鹿の縫い、これも仕着せの伊達模様へ　皆さざめき
て勇ましく、廓の内に入海は、波乗り船の、音のよきかな

Takasago Tanzen

天明五年
初代 杵屋正次郎 作曲
高砂丹前

謡ヒ次第へ　今を始の旅衣、今を始の旅衣、日も行末ぞ久しき　二上
りへ　高砂や木の下蔭の尉と姥　合　松諸共に我見ても、久しくなり
ぬ　合　住吉の　合　此の浦船に打乗りて、月諸共に出で潮や、是は
目出度き世のためしへ　老木の姿引きかへて、妹脊わりなき女夫松、
葉色は同じ深緑、見れども思ひの尽きせぬは、真なりけり恋衣、実に恋
は曲者　合へ　たとへ万里は隔つとも　合　慕ふ心はそりや云はん
すな、朝な夕なに空吹く風も、落葉衣の袖きまとふ、思ふ殿御はつれな
の身にし、塒に残る仇枕　合　扨も見事になア、振つて振り込む花槍
は、雪かあらぬかちらちらちらと白鳥毛、振れさドツコイ、ふれさドツコ
イ袖は　合　ひらひら　合　台傘立傘恋風に靡かんせ　合　ずんと
伸ばして、しやんと受けたる柳腰　合　しなやりふりやり流し目は、可
愛らしさの色の宿入り　合三下りへ　松の名所はさまざまに、あれ三
保の松羽衣の、松にかけたる尾上の鐘よ　合　逢ひに相生夫婦松
合　中に縁のいとしらしさの姫小松、二かい三蓋五葉の松、いく代重
ねん千代見草、しほらしや　合へ　西の海、青木が原の波間より、現
はれ出でし神松に、降り積む雪の朝かんがた、玉藻刈るなる岸陰の
謡ヒへ　松根に倚つて腰を摩れば、千年の縁手に満てり、指す腕には
悪魔を払ひ、をさむる手には寿福を抱き　合へ　入り来るいりくる花
の顔見せ貴賤の袂、袖を連ねてさつさつの　合　声ぞ楽しむいさぎよや

Tokiwa no Niwa

常磐の庭
嘉永四年
杵屋六左衛門　作曲

前引・本調子へ　抑も厳島の御社は、人皇七十四代の御宇かとよ、再建
ありし宮柱、幾百歳か白波に　合へ　数の燈火輝り渡り、其面影を東な
る　合　眺めはつきじ海原の　合　南は蒼海雲に続き　合　遠山遥に
薄霞　合　千舟百船　合　行き通ふ、春の曙富士の　合　雪、長閑に
匂ふ朝日影　二上り合へ　仇と恋とをうつせ貝、若しやみる布を打ち寄る
波に、粋な酢貝の其お姿を、いつか忘れんわすれがひ　合　顔は恥かし
紅葉貝、撫で子貝の可愛らし　合へ　さし来る汐に漕ぎ出づる　合三下
りへ　ゆかしき船の青簾　合　音締も高き高縄に　合　馴れて鷗の三
つ四つ二たつ　合　六つ睦し竹　合　芝に　合　見えつ隠れつ沖洲の
蘆に、翼涼しき夕まぐれ、身に沁む頃は立秋の　合へ　苫屋の煙り隈取り
て、絵島が崎や明石潟　合　須磨の浦辺で汐汲む海女は、辛気らしいぢ
やないかいな、よいよいよいよいよいやさ、それえ　合へ　此処は御浜の
月を愛で　合　霜を重ねて擣つ砧へ　初冬の、板屋を敲く玉霰　合　音
も寒けき　合　閨の戸を、さゝで慰む友千鳥、散やちりちり　合　ちりちり
ぱつと、夜半のいざり火　合　四つ手　合　網、世渡る業のしなじなは、
言の葉草の及びなき　合・本調子へ　たゞ、此の庭は年毎に、松の緑のお
び茂り、四季折々の風景は　合　弁財天女の御恵み、福寿円満限りなき
　合　舞の秘曲の面白や　三保神楽合方・舞へ　波の鼓に笛竹の、十
二の律を　合　三筋の糸に、調べとゝなふ一節は、春夏秋冬楽の、千代に
万代祝し祝して

Tomoyakko

文政十一年
十世 杵屋六左衛門 作曲
供奴

二上りへ　仕て来いな　合　やつちや仕て来い今夜の御供　合　ちつ
と後れて出かけたが、足の早いに、我が折れ田圃は近道、見はぐるまいぞ
や、合点だ　合　振つて消しやるな台提灯に、御定紋付でつかりと、ふく
れた紺のだいなしは、伊達に着なしたやつこらさ　合　武家の気質や奉
公根性、やれ扱いつかな出しやしよない　合　胼や輝かゝとや臑に、富士
の雪程有るとても、何時限らぬ　合　お使は、かゝさぬ正直　合　正道
者よ、脇よれ　合　頼むぞ　合　脇よれと、急ぎ廓へ　合　一目散、息
を切つてぞ駆け付ける　合へ　おんらが旦那はな、廓一番隠れないかく
れない、丹前好み　合　華奢に召したる　合　腰巻羽織、きりゝとしやん
と、しやんときりゝと、高股立の袴つき、後に下郎がお草履取つて、夫さ、是
さ　合　小気味よいよい六法振が　合へ　浪花師匠の其の風俗に、似
たかへ　似たぞ、似ましたり、扨々なへ　寛濶華麗な出立　合へ　おはも
じながら去る方へ、ほの字とれの字の謎懸けて、解かせたさの三重の帯、
解けて寝た夜はゆるさんせ、アゝまゝよ浮名がどうなろと、人の噂も七十五
日、てんとたまらぬ、小褄とりやつた其姿　合方・本調子へ　見染めみそめ
て　合　目が覚めた　合　醒めた夕べの拳酒に　合　ついついついつ
いさゝれた杯は、りうちえいばまでんす　合　くわいと云うて払つた　合
貼つた肩癖ちりちり身柱、亥の眼灸がくつきりと　合　ねぢ切おいどが真
白で、手ツ首掌しつかと握つた　合　石突、こりやこりやこりやこりや、成
駒やつとこよんやさ　拍子合方・二上りへ　面白や、浮かれ拍手に乗が来
て、ひよつくり旦那に捨てられた、狼狽眼で提灯を、つけたり消したり灯し
たり、揚屋が門を行き過ぎる

Tsuru Kame

鶴亀

嘉永四年

十代目杵屋六左衛門　作曲

本調子ヘ　夫青陽の春になれば　合　四季の節会の事初め　合ヘ　不老門にて日月の、光りを君の　合ヘ　叡覧にて　合ヘ　百官卿相袖を連ぬ　合ヘ　其数一億百余人　合ヘ　拝を進むる、万戸の声、一同に、拝する其音はヘ　天に　合　響きてヘ　夥しヘ　庭の砂は金銀の　合　玉を連ねて敷妙の　合　五百重の錦や瑠璃の扉　合　碑礎の行桁　合　瑪瑙の橋　合　池の汀の鶴亀は、蓬莱山も余所ならず、君の恵みぞ　合　有がたき　詞ヘ　如何に奏聞申すべき事の候　詞ヘ　奏聞とは何事ぞ　詞ヘ　毎年の嘉例の其く、鶴亀を舞はせられ、其後月宮殿にて舞楽を、奏せられうずるにて候　詞ヘ　ともかくもはからひ候ヘ　合ヘ　亀は　合　万年の齢を経　合ヘ　鶴も　合　千代をや重ぬらん　二上りヘ　千代のためしの数々に、何をひかまし姫小松　合　よはひに比ふ舟頂の、鶴も羽袖をたをやかに、千代をかさねて舞遊ぶ　合　みぎりに　合　しげる呉竹の　合　みどりの亀の幾万代も池水にヘ　棲めるも安き君が代を、仰ぎ奏でて鶴と亀ヘ　齢を授け奉れば、君も御感の余りにや、舞楽を奏して舞たまふ　本調子楽の合方ヘ　月宮殿の白衣のたもと　合月宮殿の白衣の袂、色々妙なる花の袖　合方ヘ　秋は時雨の紅葉の羽袖、冬は冴え行く雪の袂を、翻す衣も薄紫の、雲の上人の舞楽の声々に、霓裳羽衣の曲をなせば　合方ヘ　山河草木国土豊に、千代万代と舞たまへば、官人駕輿丁御輿を早め、君の齢も長生殿に、君の齢も長生殿に、還御なるこそ芽出度けれ

Yoshiwara Suzume

明和五年
初世 富士田吉治・初世 杵屋作十郎 作曲
吉原雀

本調子へ　凡そ生けるを放つこと、人皇四十四代の帝、光正天皇の御字
かとよ、養老四年の末の秋、宇佐八幡の託宣にて
、諸国に始まる放生曾へ　浮寝の鳥にあらねども、今も恋しき一人住み、
小夜の枕に片思ひ、可愛心と汲みもせで、何ぢややら憎らしい　二上りへ
　其手で深みへ浜千鳥、通ひ馴れたる土手八丁、口八丁に乗せられて、沖
の鷗の、二挺立　合　三挺立　合　素見ぞめきは椋鳥の、群れつゝ啄木
鳥格子先　合　叩く水鶏の口まめ鳥に、孔雀ぞめきて目白押し、店清掻の
てんてつとん、さつさ押せおせ　大津投節合本調子へ　馴れし廓の袖の
香に　合　見ぬやうで見るやうで、客は扇の垣根より、初心可愛く前渡り、
さア来た又来た障りぢやないか、又おさはりか、お腰の物も合点か　合
それ編笠も其処に置け　合　二階座敷は右か左か、奥座敷で御座りや
す、はや盃持つて来た、とこへ静にお出なさんしたかへ、と云ふ声にぞつと
した、しんぞ貴様は寝ても覚めても忘られぬ、笑止気の毒またかけさんす、
何な、かけるもんだえ　三下りへ　さうした黄菊と白菊の、同じ勤の其中
に　合　外の客衆は捨小舟、流れもあへぬ紅葉ばの　合　目立つ芙蓉
の分け隔て　合　たゞ撫子と神かけて、いつか廓を離れて紫苑、さうした
心の鬼百合と、思へばおもふと気も石竹になるわいなア末は姫百合男郎
花、其楽みも薄紅葉、さりとはつれない胴慾と、垣根にまとふ朝顔の、離れ
難なき風情なり　詞へ　東雲かごとが過ぎし口説の仲直り　鼓唄へ　一
とたきくゆるなかうどの、其継木こそ縁のはし、そつちのしやうが憎い故、隣
座敷の三味線に、合はす悪洒落まさなごと　二上りへ　女郎の誠と玉子
の四角、あれば晦日に月も出る、しょんがいな、玉子のよいほいよいほいよ

203

いほい　玉子の四角、あれば晦日に月が出る、しょんがいな、一とたきは、お客かえへ　君の寝姿窓から見れば、牡丹芍薬百合の花、しょんがいな、芍薬よいほいよいほいよいほい　芍薬牡丹牡丹芍薬百合の花しょんがいな、つけ差は濃茶かえへ　エヽ腹が立つやら　三下りへ　憎いやら、どうしやうかうしやう、憎む鳥鐘　合　暁の明星が、西へちろり東へちろり、ちろりちろりとする時は、内の首尾は不首尾となつて、親父は十面囃は五面、十面五面に睨み付けられ、いなうよ　合　戻らうよと、云うては小腰に取付いて　合　ならぬぞいなしやせぬ、此頃のしなし振、憎くいおさんがあるわいなへ　文のたよりになア　合　今宵ごんすと其噂、いつの紋日も主さんの、野暮な事ぢやが比翼紋、離れぬ仲ぢやとしょんがえ、染まる縁の面白やへ　実に花ならば初桜、月ならば十三夜、いづれ劣らぬ粋同士の、あなたへ云ひ抜けこなたのだて、いづれ丸かれ候かしく

Glossary

ageuta (上げ 歌) a song type in noh
ai or **aikata** (合い　合い方) instrumental interlude
atarigane. See *kane*
atouta (後歌) after song in *kumiuta* form

bachi (撥) a plectrum or drum stick
banzuke (版け) a kabuki performance ad
bungo sagari ha (豊後下がり羽) a *taiko*/flute rhythmic convention
bunkafu (文化譜) shamisen notation system
buyō (舞踊) Japanese classical dancing

Chevé notation, a French numeric music notation
chirashi (散らし) a finale section in shamisen genres
chiri kara (ちりから) a kabuki style of *tsuzumi* drumming

daibyōshi (大拍子) a drum
daishō (大小) an abbreviation for *ō* and *ko tsuzumi* drums
dangire (段伐) final cadence
de, deha, deru (出、出端、出る) entrance music
debayashi (出囃子) music on stage
dotebushi (土手節、土佐節) a shamisen music genre

gagaku (雅楽) court music
gakko (がつこ) a two-headed struck drum
gaku (楽) music depicting courtly scene
geikibushi (外記節) an old shamisen genre
geza (下座) off stage music in kabuki
gidayū (義太夫) a narrative shamisen genre

hanamichi (花道) the entrance ramp to a kabuki stage
handaiyū (半太夫) an early narrative shamisen genre
hauta (端唄) a lyric shamisen genre
hayashi (囃子) generic term for percussion and flute ensembles
hayashigashira (囃子頭) head of percussion section
hayashikotoba (囃子言葉) vocal rhythmic interjections
hengemono (變化物) kabuki dance using costume changes
hige soru or **higehiki** (髭反る) masculine dance gesture and music

honchōshi (本調子) shamisen tuning of fourth and a fifth
hyōshigi (拍子木) wooden clappers used in kabuki

ichisagari (一下がり) shamisen tuning of two perfect fifth
in (陰) a Japanese scale
iroha (いろは) a syllabic ordering system
issei (一声) early song in a noh drama
itchūbushi (一中節) an old shamisen narrative genre

jiuta (地唄) an early shamisen and later *koto* genre
jo (序) a class of *ōzatsuma* patterns. See also *jo ha kyū*
jo ha kyū (序破急) an aesthetic theory of form

kabuki (歌舞伎) in popular traditional Japanese theater
kagurabue (神楽笛) a shinto ritual flute,
kakari (掛り) music in a style, eg. *utagakari*
kakeai (掛合い) a mixture of genre in performance
kakegoe (掛け声) vocal calls in drum patterns
kakekotoba (掛言葉) pivot words in poetry
kakko (鞨鼓) a small two-headed drum
kamigata (上方) in Kyoto style
kamuro (禿) an apprentice geisha
kane (鉦) a small hand gong
kangen (管絃) a shamisen pattern imitating court music
kase (加) a higher bridge for the shamisen finger board
kashira (頭) a drum cadence pattern
katarimono (語り物) narrative music
katashagiri (片シヤガリ) opening curtain music
kakekotoba (掛け言葉) pivot words in poems
katōbushi (河東節) a genre of shamisen music
kenseikai (研清会) a *nagauta* shamisen group
ki. See *hyōshigi*
kin (金) a Buddhist gong
kinuta (絹歌) The sound of beating clothes on wooden blocks: often referred to in poetry
kiri (切り) an ending section in noh
kiyari (木遣り) firemens' song genre
kiyomoto (清元) a genre of shamisen music
kizami (刻み) a *taiko* drum pattern
ko tsuzumi (小鼓) a shoulder-held drum hit with the hand
kōken (後見) a stage assistant in dance
koto (琴) a thirteen-stringed Japanese zither
kouta (小唄) a genre of short songs
kuchijamisen (口三味線) a shamisen mnemonics

kudoki (口説き) a lyrical section
kumiuta (組歌) a form of alternate songs and interludes
kuri (繰り) a high pitch, a formal section in noh
kuse (曲) a dance section in noh
kyōgen (狂元) a comic interludes in noh drama performances
kyōgen gakko (狂元) a *taiko*/flute conventional pattern
kyū. See *jo ha kyū*

maebiki (前引き) an opening instrumental interlude
maeuta (前歌) first song in *kumiuta* form
mai (舞) term for dance or dance section
makigai (巻き外) music in front of the curtain
makimae (巻き前) music before the curtain opens
matsuri bayashi (際囃子) festival music
michiyuki (道行) stage entrance and its music
mie (見得) actor's dramatic pose
mitsuji (三つ地) a drum pattern in noh and kabuki
mokugyō (木魚) Buddhist percussion block
mondō (問 筒) a dialogue section in noh drama

nagashi (流し) a cadencing shamisen pattern
nagauta (長唄) a lyric shamisen genre
nakauta (中歌) the middle song in *kumiuta* form
naniwabushi (浪花節) a shamisen genre from Osaka area
niagari (二上) a shamisen tuning of a fifth and a fourth
noh (能) a major Japanese drama genre
nōkan (能管) a noh drama flute

ōdaiko (大太鼓) a large drum
odori ji (踊り地) a section of kabuki dance form
ogiebushi (荻江節) an early shamisen genre
oki (置き) the opening section of a piece
ondo (音頭) a type of folk dance
onnagata (女方) a female impersonator
orugōru (オルゴオル) a set of small bells
ozashiki (御座しき長唄) concert *nagauta*
ōzatuma (大薩摩) a shamisen narrative genre and its patterns

raijo (来序) a dance section in noh
ritsu (律) a basic Japanese scale
roppō (六方) a kabuki dance style and its rough origin

sageuta (下歌) a song type in noh and other genre
samisen (三弦) a Kyoto dialect pronunciation of shamisen

sandame (三駄目) a noh drama conventional combination of drum patterns used in *chirashi* sections of *nagauta*.

sanjū (三獣) opening music in *gidayū*. A shamisen pattern

sansagari (三下がり) a shamisen tuning of two fourths

sarashi (曝し　さらあし) a style of dance and its music

sekkyōbushi (説教節) a musical narrative style

serifu (台詞) words declaimed rather than sung

shakuhachi (尺八) a Japanese end blown flute

shamisen (三弦) a three-stringed plucked lute

shiagari (し上がり) music after curtain closes

shinobue (篠笛) a bamboo flute: see *takebue*

shite (シテ) principal actor in noh

sugagaki (すがぎ) a pattern depicting geisha scenes

suzu (鈴) bell tree instrument

taiko (太鼓) stick drum

taiko ji (太鼓地) a section in kabuki dance form

takebue (竹笛) a bamboo flute

tataki (たたき) a lyrical shamisen pattern

tegoto (手事) instrumental sections

tengu (天ぐ) a goblin

tokiwazu (常我磐) a shamisen narrative genre

tomimoto (富本) an old shamisen genre

toonkai (東音会) a nagauta guild

tsukechō (付帳) lead sheets for music

tsukuda (津田) a shamisen music representing brothel areas

tsunagi (繋ぎ) a transition section in shamisen genres

tsuzumi (鼓) generic term for hour-glass drums

tsuzumi uta (鼓 唄) a song with *tsuzumi* accompaniment

uchi (打ち) to strike a drum

uta (歌) a song section in *kumiuta* form

utamono (歌物) a lyrical style of music

uwajōshi (上調子) a second shamisen obbligato part

waki (わき) supporting actor in noh drama

wataribyōshi (渡拍子) a *taiko* and flute pattern

yakko (奴) a male servant

yo (陽) Japanese scale

yokobue (横笛) a bamboo flute

Bibliography

Asakawa Gyokuto. 1955. *Nagauta hikikata, utaikata*. Tokyo: Daidokan.

———. 1956. *Hōgaku buyō jiten*. Tokyo: Fuzambō.

———. 1980. *Nagauta meikyoku yōsetsu*. Tokyo: Hōgakusha Atsumi Seitarō.

Brandon, James. 1992. *Five Classic Plays*. Honolulu: University of Hawai'i Press.

Brandon, James, and Samuel L. Leiter. 2002. *Kabuki Plays on Stage*. 4 vols. Honolulu: University of Hawai'i Press.

Hirano Kenji. 1983. "An Investigation into the Old Shamisen Notations." In *Shamisen kofu no kenkyū*. Tokyo. Toshiba EMI LPs and booklet THX-9O212-17.

Japanese Noh Drama, 3 vols. 1959–60. Tokyo: Nippon gakujitsu shinkōkai.

Kineya Eizō, 1932. *Nagauta no utaikata*. Tokyo: Sōgen-sha.

Kominz, Lawrence. *Avatars of Vengeance*. Ann Arbor: Center for Japanese Studies, 1995 University of Michigan.

Leiter, Samuel. 1979, 1984. Kabuki Encyclopedia. Tokyo: Heibonsha.

Malm, William P. 1959a. *Japanese Music and Musical Instruments*. Tokyo: Tuttle.

———. 1960. "A Short History of Japanese Nagauta Music." *Journal of the American Oriental Society* 80.2:124–131

———. 1963. *Nagauta: The Heart of Kabuki Music*. Tokyo: Tuttle.

———. 1978. "Music in the Kabuki Theater." In *Studies in Kabuki*. By James Brandon, William P. Malm, and Donald Shively. Honolulu: University of Hawai'i Press.

———. 1978. "The Four Seasons of the Old Mountain Woman." *Journal of the American Musicological Society* 31.1: 83–117.

———. 1984. "The Toon-kai: A Study of Socio/Musical Relations in a Shamisen Tradition." In *Proceedings of the Thirty-first International Congress of Human Sciences in Asia and North Africa*. Tokyo: Toho Gakkai.

———. 1986. *Six Hidden Views of Japanese Music*. Berkeley: University of California Press.

———. 1990. "Japanese Nagauta Notation and Performance Realities." *Musicology Australia* 11–12:87–105.

———. 1994. "The Rise of Concert Music in Nineteenth-Century Japan." In Studies in Anthropology and History, vol. 12. In *Recovering the Orient*, Andrew Gerstle editor. Reading, U.K.: Harwood.

———. 1996. *Nagauta: The Heart of Japanese Music*. Norman: University of Oklahoma School of Music Video.

———. 1996. Music Cultures of the Pacific, the Near East, and Asia 3rd edition. Upper Saddle River, NJ; Prentice Hall.

————. 1998. "Yamada Shōtarō: Japan's First Shamisen Professor," in Asian Music, vol. 39-1, pp. 35–73.

————. 2000. *Traditional Japanese Music and Musical_Instruments*. Tokyo: Kodansha.

Richie, Donald, and Miyoko Watanabe, trans. *Six Kabuki Plays*. Tokyo: Hokuseido, 1963.

Scott, A. C., trans. 1953. *Kanjinchō*. Tokyo: Hokuseido.

MUSIC NOTATION COLLECTIONS

Kineya Yanotsuke. Nagauta kenkyū keikobon, Aoyagi Shigezō ed. 127 pieces. Tokyo: Yamada Oseidō.

Kineya Mishiki *Shamisen Bunkafu, Nagauta*. Kineya Yashichi, ed. 1925–58. Tokyo: Hōgaku-sha.

Kineya Sakichi *Kineya Sakichihon* vol. 3 Tokyo: nagauta sakichikai.

Mochizuki Tanzaemon *Nagauta Hayashi Tetsuke* Tokyo: MochizukiFuhon Seikyūkai, 6 vols.

Yoshizumi Kosaburō. *Nagauta shin-keikobon*, Kineya Sakichi, ed. 8 vols. Tokyo: Hōgaku-sha.

About the Author

William P. Malm is professor emeritus of ethnomusicology and retired director of the Stearns Collection of Musical Instruments and the Japanese Music Study Group at The University of Michigan. Among his publications are *Nagauta: The Heart of Kabuki Music* (1963); *Music Cultures of the Pacific, the Near East, and Asia* (1966); *Six Hidden Views of Japanese Music* (1986); *Theater as Music: The Bunraku Play "Mt. Imo and Mt. Se: An Exemplary Tale of Womanly Virtue"* (1990, with C. Andrew Gerstle and Kiyoshi Inobe), and *Traditional Japanese Music and Musical Instruments* (2001, a revised edition of his classic 1959 work *Japanese Music and Musical Instruments*). As a teacher at Michigan he received the Henry Russell, Alumni Merit, and Legislature awards, and in 1993 he was given the Koizumi Fumio Prize in Ethnomusicology.